The Trinity of Love
A Theology of the Christian God

NEW THEOLOGY SERIES
General Editor: Peter C. Phan
*
Editorial Consultants:
Monika Hellwig
Robert Imbelli
Robert Schreiter
*
Volume 4: The Trinity of Love

The Trinity of Love
A Theology of the Christian God

by
Anthony Kelly, CSSR

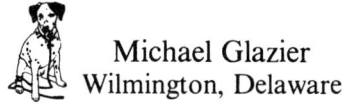
Michael Glazier
Wilmington, Delaware

About the Author

Anthony Kelly, an Australian Redemptorist, completed his doctoral studies in Rome (Anselmianum, 1966) and post-doctoral work in Toronto and Paris. He is Past-President of the Yarra Theological Union, Melbourne, Australia (1980-85), and Past-President of the Melbourne College Divinity (1984-85). He has written over a hundred articles in Australian and international journals (The Thomist, Theological Studies, Compass Theological Review, Outlook, the Australian Catholic Record). The most recent of his seven books is *The Range of Faith. Basic Questions for a Living Theology* (St. Paul Publications: Homebush, NSW, 1986).

First published in 1989 by Michael Glazier, Inc., 1935 West Fourth Street, Wilmington, Delaware 19805.
Copyright © 1989 by Michael Glazier, Inc. All rights reserved.
No part of this publication may be reproduced or transmitted in any form or by any means, electronic or mechanical, including photocopy, recording, or any information storage and retrieval system, without permission in writing from the publisher: Michael Glazier, 1935 West Fourth Street, Wilmington, Delaware, 19805.

Library of Congress Cataloging-in-Publication Data

Kelly, Anthony, 1938-
   The trinity of love.
   (New theology texts)
   Bibliography: p.
   Includes index.
   1. Trinity. I. Title. II. Series.
BT111.2.K45 1989   231'.044   88-82458
ISBN 0-89453-743-1
New Theology Texts ISBN: 0-89453-776-8
Cover Design by Pat Harris
Typography by Phyllis Boyd LeVane, Laura Burke
Printed in the United States of America by Edwards Brothers

Contents

Editor's Preface	ix
Preface	xi
1. Perspectives	1
1. The Starting Point: The People of God	3
2. The Trinitarian Form of the Eucharist	6
3. The Trinity and the Contemporary Paradigm of Reality	8
4. The "Turning Point" and the Trinity	11
5. Preconceptions	13
6. The Role of Questions	16
7. The Functions of Trinitarian Meaning	18
8. Techniques of Theological Reflection	19
9. Risks, Demands, Advantages	24
2. The Scriptural Foundations	28
1. The Trinitarian Meaning of Scripture	28
2. The Rhetoric of Trinitarian Expression	30
3. The Trinitarian Narrative	39
4. Trinitarian Symbolism	45
5. Trinitarian Experience	47
3. Mystery and Definition	59
1. The Doctrinal Mode	59
2. The Problematic Character of Trinitarian Faith	61
3. Faith Seeking Its Appropriate Expression	64
4. The Apologetic Phase	65
5. The Dogmatic Phase	69
6. Theological Development	83

4. Connections 89

1. A Systematic Understanding 90
2. The Image of God 92
3. The Trinity and Creation 94
4. The Trinity and Revelation 99
5. The Trinity and Grace 103
6. The Trinity and the Paschal Mystery 107
7. The Trinity and the Church 113

5. Analogies 115

1. "Analogical Imagination" 115
2. Theological Terms 117
3. The Psychological Analogy 119
4. Aquinas' Trinitarian Theology 120
5. Divine Be-ing 121
6. Divine Processions 123
7. Twelve Questions 126
8. Evaluation 135

6. Transpositions 139

1. An Experiential Foundation 139
2. From Doctrine to the Phenomenon of
   Christian Experience 141
3. The Johannine Experience 142
4. 'God is Love' 145
5. From Divine "Be-ing" to "Being-in-Love" 147
6. The Psychological Analogy and Self-Transcendence 149
7. Self-Transcendence and Religious Experience 152
8. The Features of Religious Experience 155
9. Correlating Divine and Human "Being in Love" 157
10. The Trinity as Divine "Being in Love" 159
11. The Psychological Analogy of Love Applied 159
12. "Being in Love" as Gift 163
13. God's Love Communicated in Global Experience 165
14. The Trinity 'En-Worlded' and the World 'Trinified' 168
15. Trinitarian Meaning 169

7. Applications 174

1. The Trinity and the Dimensions of Experience 174

2. Experience and Christian Mystery 176
   3. The Mystery of Love 177
   4. The Community in Love 180
   5. The Language of "Three Persons" 184
   6. The Trinity and Process 189
   7. The Divine Compassions 195

8. Models 203
   1. The Therapeutic Significance of Trinitarian Faith 203
   2. The Trinity and Psychological Development 209
   3. The Political Meaning of the Trinity 215

9. Trinity and World Religions 228
   1. The Trinity and Religious Dialogue 228
   2. The Trinity as Orientation to Mission 232
   3. The Trinitarian Model of Inter-Faith Dialogue 234
   4. Different Spiritualities in East and West 236
   5. The Resources of Tradition 243
   6. Different Phenomenologies of Self in East and West 245

10. Conclusion 249
    1. The Trinity and the Feminine 250
    2. The Filioque 256
    3. Love's Excess 259

Questions for Discussion 261
Bibliography 264
Index of Names 271

Editor's Preface

This series entitled *New Theology Series,* composed of eight volumes, is an attempt to answer the need felt by professors and students alike for scholarly yet readable books dealing with certain Catholic beliefs traditionally associated with dogmatic theology. The volumes treat of fundamental theology (revelation, the nature and method of theology, the credibility of the Christian faith), trinitarian theology, christology, ecclesiology, anthropology, and eschatology.

There has been, of course, no lack of books, published singly or in series, both in this continent and elsewhere, which are concerned with these central truths of Christianity. Nevertheless, there is room, we believe, for yet another series of texts on systematic theology, not because these offer entirely novel insights into the aforementioned teachings, but because it is incumbent upon Christians of every age to reflect upon their faith in light of their cultural and religious experiences and to articulate their understanding in terms accessible to their contemporaries.

Theology is traditionally described as faith in search of understanding, *fides quaerens intellectum.* The faith to which the contributors to this series are committed is the Christian faith as lived and taught by the (Roman) Catholic Church. It is, however, a faith that is ecumenically sensitive, open to ways of living and thinking practiced by other Christian communities and other religions. The understanding which the series seeks to foster goes beyond an accumulation of information, however interesting, on the Christian past to retrieve and renew, by means of the analogical imagination, the Christian Tradition embodied in its various classics. In this way, it is hoped, one can understand afresh both the meaning and the truth of the Christian beliefs and their multiple interconnections. Lastly, the contributors are convinced that theology is a never-ending quest for insights into faith, a *cogitatio fidei.* Its ultimate purpose is not to provide definite and definitive answers to every conceivable problem posed by faith, but to gain an understanding, which will always be imperfect and fragmentary, of its subject, God the incomprehensible Mystery. Thus, theology remains an essentially unfinished business, to be taken up over and again in light of and in confrontation with the challenges found in every age. And our age is no exception, when, to cite only two examples, massive poverty and injustice structured into the present economic order, and the unprecedented meeting of religious faiths in new contexts of dialogue, have impelled theologians to reconceptualize the Christian faith in radical terms.

Contrary to some recent series of textbooks, *New Theology Series* does not intend to advocate and advance a uniform or even unified viewpoint. Contributors are left free to present their own understanding and approach to the subject matter assigned to them. They are only requested to treat their themes in an integrating manner by situating them in the context of Tradition (highlighting their biblical, patristic, medieval, and modern developments), by expounding their theological meaning and function in light of current pronouncements of the Magisterium, by exploring their implications for Christian living, and by indicating possible different contemporary conceptualizations of these doctrines. The goal is to achieve some measure of comprehensiveness and balance by taking into account all the important issues of the subject matter under discussion and at the same time exhibit some thematic unity by means of a consistent method and a unifying perspective.

The eight volumes are intended primarily as resource books, "launching and landing bases," for upper-division theology courses in Catholic colleges and seminaries, but it is hoped that they will be useful also to people—priests, permanent deacons, religious, and educated laity, inside and outside of the Roman Catholic communion—interested in understanding the Christian faith in contemporary cultural and ecclesial contexts. We hope that these volumes will make a contribution, however modest, to the intellectual and spiritual life of the Christian Church as it prepares to enter its third millennium.

Peter C. Phan
The Catholic University of America

Preface

In that mood of slightly melancholic modesty that comes over authors on the completion of a work in an area already explored by many great minds, I find myself stalked by the question, what have I really got to offer here? Surely there were better things to do during a precious sabbatical year in North America, thousands of miles from home, than to write up my 'Trinity Book' which had been slowly taking shape in Melbourne in recent years. In the event, a gracious providence allowed for, and imposed, many other involvements and responsibilities in that time. Still, through it all, it was the theological issue that occupied me most, as it had done for so many years. So this book. But it is one book among many recent works that treat of the Trinity, many of them far more learned than anything I can offer. So why *this* book exactly?

I think there are two ways of answering that question. The first is that the Trinity is the heart and centre of all Christian theology, and it is surely a healthy theology which permits plenty of approaches and allows for yet another angle in the ongoing conversation about the infinite, the inexhaustible and the limitlessly loving. Such an expansive statement evidently presupposes a conviction that trinitarian theology is meant to be creative and meaningful in the deepest sense. I have always felt that something was deeply wrong when it has usually been regarded not only as ineffable but unspeakably, well, ... boring, if that is not too strong a word. Certainly, it has caused something of a mental block in both student and teacher and preacher (the dreaded Trinity Sunday homily!). If the beauty of the fabled Helen shone in that face that launched a thousand ships, the mystery of the Trinity in past ages provoked a thousand books and certainly dozens of exciting controversies. But then things went quiet for many centuries, and the creativity of theology, up to the recent past, consisted in meticulously re-issuing the doctrines that had been defined and the positions that had been reached literally over a thousand years ago. But with each reissue, the original investment of faith tended to be diminished, and the stock appeared less attractive: the original excitement was replaced by a slightly puzzling form of higher mathematics about three and one, just as the intellectual adventure of that faith found itself contained in a cleverly designed philosophical and doctrinal maze.... This appears to have been the case until comparatively recent times, when suddenly the dead wood sprouted and blossomed and bore good fruit in writings of Barth and Rahner, Macquarrie and Muehlen, Lonergan and Juengel, Kasper and Hill, Moltmann and Lafont to name but a few.

Nonetheless, my congratulatory remarks about theology in general does not provide the reason for this book; indeed, it might be used as an argument against "one more book". Still, in this new context, I think there is a job to be done, and with it a chance for another kind of creativity. My contribution seems to be more in the domain of making connections in the new context, more an exercise in the "analogical imagination" (David Tracy) than in fresh research or even startling new hypotheses; for I have been little concerned to "drive out the paraclete or crucify the Father" (Hippolytus of Rome). Still, trinitarian faith continues to inspire and certainly to challenge. So I have tried in the ten chapters of this book to stress how the Love of God and Trinity come together in the one mystery and explain one another. In the progression of chapters, I searched in "Perspectives" for a starting point, and found it in the life of the church and the contemporary (quest) for a whole new vision of reality, as culturally and historically, we experience a massive "turning point" (Capra). In the explicitly scriptural chapter, I try to show how this is witnessed to in a variety of ways,—in the rhetoric, the narrative, the symbols, the key experiences that formed the scriptural expression. Even in the chapter on doctrine it seems to me that the key issue was that of making the scriptural story of the limitless Love of God most telling; the very term *homousion* was in the end merely a way of keeping the original Love-Story intact. With the specifically theological chapters, I indicate in "Connections" how the mystery of the Trinity is a kind of hologram made up of all the mysteries of faith, and in "Analogies" how this focal meaning has been classically explored. Chapter six, "Transpositions" is, as the names implies, a rather prolonged effort to found the meaning of trinitarian faith in the experience of our personal and global becoming, especially in the experience of love. If "God is Love" it seems to me that we have most chance of penetrating in some small measure the mystery that has found us in terms of the love that we have found to be the fundamental energy of our being. All this is so intense that another chapter was needed, "Applications", to tease out the meaning of trinitarian Love further into the classic and modern questions of divine persons, community, and compassion. Then "Models" took these fundamental insights further into the psychological and social significance of trinitarian faith. If it is true, ultimately true, that God is Love by being Trinity, it makes a difference to how we develop as persons and how we belong together. Then in "Extensions" we explored the meaning of this Trinity, not as an eccentric piece of Christian lore exclusive of other faiths, but as the deep structure of our Christian communication with such other faiths. The "Conclusions" extends my reflections into topics the feminist or ecumenical reader might have thought I was timidly avoiding.

This is not a controversial book in the sense of refuting other opinions, except for chapter 7 where I take issue, regrettably in a too summary manner, with some recent approaches. I know there is a lot more discussion needed, but I kept myself pretty much to developing my own position and avoiding technicalities. My basic thesis is that God is confessed as Trinity because God has been revealed as Love, and that the more we allow the notion of love to interpret the Trinity and the Trinity to interpret the meaning of love, the more radically healthy Christian theology will be. I realize that when theologians talk of love this is often taken as a sign of a certain softheadedness. But as far as I can see, Love is "the way it is",—ultimately, originally, and most transformatively, now. Rereading these pages, I can understand how some might find them too 'romantic' or mystical. That's the risk I am prepared to take. Even theologians must be prepared to appear a little foolish; after all, I remind myself, there are biblical precedents.... The mystery will remain to heal and transform even though any expression will doubtless be defective and needing correction in many ways.

I must now make some acknowledgement of the gracious friends that made this work possible. In the first place, I must thank Fr. Kevin O'Shea, CSSR, for not only his years as my theological mentor, but in his present capacity as Provincial of the Australian Province of Redemptorists. Still, it is one thing to get a sabbatical and another to enjoy it in pleasant circumstances; so here I must thank Fr. Des Scanlan, CSSR, Provincial of the Toronto Province of Redemptorists and the community of Gerard House. Because of such hospitality, I had access to the resources of the Toronto School of Theology, and was able to accept the position of Visiting Scholar at St. Michael's College University through the kind offices of Michael Fahey, SJ. Professor Michael Vertin offered most valuable suggestions for one of the more problematical chapters, whilst Gene Laverdiere, SSS, helped me with his notable scriptural expertise in some sections. The Lonergan Centre was a great reference point for me here in Toronto, and I thank Fr. Fred Crowe, SJ for such intellectual hospitality. The deep theological wisdom of Walter Principe, CSB, has always been both a resource and an inspiration to me, especially in friendly exchanges of this past year. Finally among all the people that encouraged me in this project, especially when through extraneous circumstances its completion was in jeopardy, Mary Ann Brandt and Marsha Skain are deserving of very special recognition. Without such people, theology is paper-thin. In such company, trinitarian Love is a vitalizing reality.

Anthony Kelly, CSSR

1

Perspectives

At the outset of a prolonged reflection on the mystery of the Trinity, there are many options . . . and just as many possibilities of getting off on the wrong foot. The Trinity has been such an object of intense speculation and doctrinal definition, that even the term, "Trinity" causes in many something of a mental block. For such, the Trinity is already inextricably linked to abstruse philosophical analyses or highly formal dogmatic pronouncements. Who needs more of that? So, one must ask, is there some way of conducting a theological exploration in this area in a more engaging manner? Is there some way of escaping from a theology that is experienced as, in fact, deeply alienating in regard to the real living concerns of faith? How can we start reflecting on this apparently central mystery of faith without meeting it merely as a problem, thus to anticipate endless further complexities ending with the original problems merely developed to a higher degree of insolubility? In short, do flies need to capture more fly paper?

An image most suggestive of the right starting point for any theology of the Trinity is the great 15th-century icon of Andrei Roublev, *Philoxenia*[1]. It contrasts with so many artistic depictions of the Trinity, with their patriarchal stress, triangular scheme and their limited movement of descent and ascent. Roublev depicts the

---

[1] For a reproduction of this icon and commentary see Victor Lasareff, *Russian Icons from the 12th to the 14th Century* (Milan: Collins, Unesco Art Books (1962) pp. 17-24.

three divine visitors in a youthful, rather androgynous form; they are related to one another in an attitude of mutual deference and yielding. The whole thing breathes loving communion, for the fundamental movement of this representation of the Trinity is circular. It suggests the divine communion as an open circle, enfolding the believer and creation into itself. The foreground is an open space: it invites the beholder to come from the outside into the realm of ultimate love, to be a participant in trinitarian life. Roublev thus evokes a sense of the Trinity as approachable 'from within', in a kind of 'inside knowledge', made possible through participating in the trinitarian love sustaining and transforming the world. This marvelous icon slowly brought home to me that all our trinitarian doctrines and theologies are really complex ways of keeping faith concentrated in its most intense statement: 'God is Love' (I Jn 4:8). God is God by self-giving; and the communion that God is, is an open circle enfolding all and everyone into it.

At no stage does thinking about the Trinity mean starting from complex problems. For me the starting point was focused in an icon, just as it was condensed into the three-word statement. The artist behind the icon, the inspired writer behind the statement, witness to what is also most obvious: from the beginning, and at every stage of theological reflection, faith begins not from inherited problems, but from the given presence of the Love[2] that gives "life to the full" (Jn 10:10), as it animates, unsettles, heals and expands everything we routinely call "real life".

---

[2]At the risk of causing irritation, I have decided to use the upper case 'L' when referring to God's Love, e.g., God is Love. There are several reasons for this. First, it has 'iconic' value in my effort to emphasize that the trinitarian formulation is a way of invoking and understanding the divine reality as Love. Secondly, because in later chapters I have to use the longer phrase, 'being-in-love' in a quasi-technical sense, it is sometimes less cumbersome, when referring to God, to use the single word, 'Love'. Thirdly, it serves as a reminder that the symbolic names, Father, Son, and Spirit, are relative to the disclosure of the ultimate Love. Thus the way is open to a less sexist-sounding language in which both male and female symbols can have their place. Though, in the present work, I have kept pretty much to traditional trinitarian language and its English equivalents, e.g., The Father gives his Son/Spirit, the 'L' indicates my concern for the development of a more adequate language. Having tried numerous experiments ending in unprintable complexities, I now await in patience that transformation of language which only poets, mystics, and theologians deeply attuned to contemporary feminist consciousness can bring about.

1. The Starting Point: The People of God

More concretely, this means beginning with a recollection of the Church existing only because of the presence and movement of the mystery we have been taught to name, "God, Father, Son, Holy Spirit". More expressly still, this divine presence, this divine movement with which we are involved as Christians is articulated in the seemingly spontaneous invocations and blessings found in the pages of the New Testament. At the end of Paul's second letter to the Corinthians we find a good example: "The grace of our Lord Jesus Christ, the Love of God, and the fellowship of the Holy Spirit be with you " (2 Cor 13:14).

Paul's farewell greeting to the Corinthians suggests a starting point for a theology of the Trinity. It points to the church's experience as the People of God,—this community of historical people who have an identity in 'God', in God as Love, as revealed Word, as limitless Gift. This blessing, and many like it, is extensively used in modern liturgies. As such, it illumines essential dimensions of the church's worship. More fundamentally, it brings to light the character of church as the People of God,—a "people made one by the unity of the Father, Son and Holy Spirit."[3]

The church is a community. Its members 'co-exist' in the mystery of God. The loving initiative of the Father calls it into being. Its form and meaning derive from living union with Christ, crucified and risen. Its structure is animated by the Holy Spirit, the principle of its life and growth.

To confess the Trinity means to affirm that the divine life is a communion. It is this communal life of self-giving Love that holds the church together. Jesus prays for those who will believe in him through the ages:

> ". . . that they may all be one; even as thou, Father, art in me, and I in thee, that they may also be in us . . . that they may be one as we are one, I in them and thou in me, that they may become perfectly one." (Jn 17:20-24)

---

[3] *De Oratione Dominica* 23, *PL* 4, 553.

Vatican II [4] elaborates the existential significance of this prayer for the church:

> ... the Lord Jesus, when praying to the Father, 'that they may all be one ... even as we are one' has opened up new horizons closed to human reason by implying that there is a certain parallel between the union existing among the divine persons, and the union existing among the children of God in truth and love ... the human (person) can only fully discover his true self in a sincere giving of himself.[5]

This trinitarian 'Love-Life' not only inspires a new form of community in the church. It is the impetus to an ever larger belonging. As the ever-open circle of Love, it energizes the church's mission to the world:

> The church on earth is of its very nature missionary since, according to the plan of the Father, it has its origin in the mission of the Son and of the Holy Spirit.[6]

The 'Love-life' of the Trinity is the energy, form and motive of the life of the church: the energy, as that which empowers the church to move outward and forward; the form as incarnate in the crucified Christ; the motive, in the goal of final communion, when 'God will be everything to everyone.' (1 Cor 15:28)

The mystery of the Trinity is thus the reality in which the identity of the church is centered. The People of God find their corporate selfhood in "the grace of our Lord Jesus Christ, the Love of God, and the fellowship of the Holy Spirit." For the Trinity exercises a centripetal attraction. By inhaling the Holy 'Breath', the church is drawn more deeply to the mysterious Origin out of which the Spirit comes, to be centered in Christ, in whom "all things hold together." (Col 1:17)

But the Trinity is also a centrifugal impulse in the church's life: it is an impetus to mission, to the ever-wider domain of God. This will be attained only when all lives and all the aspirations of human history

---

[4]For a fuller treatment of Vatican II's presentation of the Trinity, see Bertrand de Margerie, *La Trinite chretienne dans l'histoire* (Paris: Beauchesne, 1975).

[5]*Gaudium et Spes*, #23.

[6]*Ad Gentes*, #1.

are enfolded and transformed in ultimate Love.

From both these points of view, the Trinity wholesomely unsettles any secure self-possession of the People of God. For this self-possession must continually prove itself as a self-transcendence into the fulness of trinitarian meaning and love. When the Trinity is truly adored as the centre and circumference of Christian community, it means that a continuing conversion is provoked, from our present ecclesial disunity to a more redemptive approximation to the unity of the divine three: "... that they may be one, even as we are one" (Jn 17:11). The Trinity is the inspiration, the form and the goal of our passing from a dismembered self-justification into authentic corporate identity 'in God'.

The Trinity provokes the self-transcendence of the church also in its mission. If it is to live authentically from the Father's mission of the Son and Spirit, the People of God must realize its identity in a self-transcending outreach to others. Its life must be an open circle, never closed in on itself: this means a life of overture to all history and cultures, to the 'all nations' of the Gospel command: "Go, therefore, make disciples of all nations, baptizing them in the name of the Father, and of the Son, and of the Holy Spirit." (Mt 28:19) Thus,the words of the Risen Jesus express the logic of the trinitarian mystery, as it is revealed in him and lived by the baptized community.

By locating the beginning of this reflection on the Trinity within the life of the church, we achieve one advantage. Trinitarian theology will look less like a complex, alienating *reductio ad absurdum*. It is not a precious indulgence in a form of supercelestial mathematics, nor a needless complication for an already sufficiently complicated Christian life. Rather, it appears for what it is: an *introductio in mysterium,* an in-depth reflection on the life and praxis of the church. It is bringing out what is already there, expressing the determining factor in ecclesial identity. The Trinity is more than the lapidary collections of doctrines about it. It is a matter once more, of not reducing the bull to the bouillon cube. There are essential doctrines, to be interpreted and cherished, but they must serve the articulation of that 'Love-Life' of which the church is the living sacrament.[7]

---

[7] See the thorough study, V. Mondello, *La Chiesa del Dio Trino* (Naples, 1978), and the entry, 'The Church' in Michael O'Carroll's *Trinitas, A Theological Encyclopedia of the Holy Trinity* (Wilmington, Del.: Michael Glazier, 1986).

2. The Trinitarian Form of the Eucharist

The eucharist is the "summit and source" of ecclesial life. It enacts the mystery of the Trinity intimately and vividly involved in the religious imagination and community-forming *praxis* of the church. In a fundamental way, the eucharist is a trinitarian sacrament. Now, there are three movements in this central sacrament of the Church: *eucharistia,*—the sacrifice of praise and thanksgiving offered to the Father; *anamnesis,*—the sacramental 'calling to mind' of Christ Jesus; and *epiclesis*—the invocation of the creativity of the Spirit. This triple movement modulates the manner in which the People of God experience the trinitarian life enfolding them. The mystery of the Trinity does not intrude into Christian sacramental awareness. It pertains rather to what is lived and breathed, eaten and imbibed in the eucharistic liturgy: in the words of the great doxology, "Through him, with him, in him, in the unity of the Holy Spirit, all glory and honour is yours, Almighty Father, forever and ever."

The *lex orandi* here notably expresses the *lex credendi*. A word, then, on each of these three movements in the sacrament of the eucharist, unfolding as it does "in the name of the Father, and of the Son, and of the Holy Spirit."

Addressed to God the Father, the origin and goal of all, the eucharist is eminently what its name signifies, thanksgiving for the grace that has been given in Christ and praise for incalculable goodness and wisdom so revealed: "Father, you are holy indeed, and all creation rightly gives you praise ... so that from East to West, a perfect offering may be made to the glory of your name." (Eucharistic Prayer III)

Such thanks and praise is offered to God in the light of all the gifts of creation and grace. It is participation in the song of the whole universe, the "holy, holy, holy" of all the angels and saints. God's essential glory has been made manifest in Christ. To live now means to be released to a life of radical joy, "abounding in thanksgiving" (Col 2:7), in a universe so penetrated and comprehended by the Original Love that "nothing in all creation" can diminish or oppose it (Rom 8:39).

This act of thanksgiving occurs both at the command of Jesus, "do this in memory of me", and in the context of "calling to mind" the whole mystery of the life, death, resurrection of the Son. In his whole existence, he is from and for the Father. His eucharistic command arises from the essential law of his being. Thus to celebrate the eucharist in continuity with what Jesus did, said and suffered is to remember his whole existence of surrender and consecration to the Father that determined the life of Jesus with his identity as Son. In hearing the command of the Son to honour the Father, the followers of Jesus 're-member' the whole meaning of the mystery of Christ: "Father, calling to mind the death your Son endured, ... his glorious resurrection and ascension into heaven, and ready to greet him when he comes again, we offer in thanksgiving this holy and living sacrifice." (Eucharistic Prayer II)

This "calling to mind" reaches back to the Gospels' account of the life of Jesus, and out into the historical context of the church in the contemporary world. *Anamnesis* does not mean that the followers of Jesus reduce the life of Jesus to a purely spiritual or cultic mode of existence. The practical adoration of the Father, the God in whose name Jesus had insisted that the sabbath was made for man, not man for the sabbath (Mk 2:27), entailed Jesus' solidarity with the poor and the suffering. Consequently, "my body given up for you", and "my blood poured out for you" were not merely poetic or mystical expressions. Rather, such an expressiveness in word and gesture summed up the commitment of the life he freely lived, and the death that resulted from that choice. For to serve the cause of the real God, to be truly Son of such a Father, necessarily meant that he was the agent of compassionate and liberating Love. The Kingdom of his Father had room for all those to whom the world offered no hope. His relationship to this Father meant his involvement with the least and the lost.

This eucharistic self-giving expresses the character of the historical existence of the Son and the manner in which he is now glorified. His risen existence is entirely relational. Present to the church in the Spirit, he nourishes all who receive him with the reality of what he is, as the way, the truth and the life. In following such a way, in affirming such a truth, in living such a life the Christian community expands in the Love that Jesus embodies.

But all this is brought about through the ceaseless creativity of the Spirit. If the liturgy of praise and thanksgiving offered to the Father is unthinkable without "calling to mind" the mystery of Christ the

Son, it is impossible without the activity of the Spirit. The liturgy invokes the power of the Spirit so that Jesus will be "the real presence", in the real world of the Christian community. Such a world is symbolized in "the fruits of the earth and the work of human hands",—the bread and wine of our embodied, social, historical existence. On these the Spirit is invoked: " . . . we ask you to make them holy that they may become the body and blood of Our Lord Jesus Christ." The church prays to the Spirit to transform these elements of the human world into their ultimate reality: that they may become both "the bread of life" and our "spiritual drink". Then the Spirit is invoked in the wider context of the community of believers, that they may be transformed by what has become present among them: "Grant that we who are nourished by his body and blood may be filled with his Holy Spirit, and become one Body, one Spirit in Christ."

Thus transformed by the Spirit into the Body of the Son to the glory of the Father, the Christian community is renewed in its authentically trinitarian life.

What is done "in the name of the Father, and of the Son, and of the Holy Spirit" is expressed in the forms of *eucharistia, anamnesis,* and *epiclesis*. Through Jesus Christ, with him in his service of the world, in him in his self-giving for the sake of the Kingdom, in the unity of the Christ-forming Spirit, all glory and honour is offered to the Father. Trinitarian Love thus achieves its purpose in progressively enfolding dismembered creation into its eternal life.[8]

3. The Trinity and the Contemporary Paradigm of Reality

It is not only a matter of expressing trinitarian meaning in terms of the identity of the church. If the Trinitarian mystery is true, it is very true; and its meaning must necessarily cohere with all our most inspired and intelligent versions of what ultimate truth really is. To this degree, trinitarian theology is best expressed in a dialogical situation, when the church is truly seeking to become the "church in

---

[8]See C. Vaggagini, *Theological Dimensions of the Liturgy* (Collegeville, Minnesota, 1976) pgs. 192-240.

the modern world", when it is speaking with and for the whole contemporary world. The church in today's world participates in an experience of reality as it is articulated in contemporary science and sought after in contemporary movements. In the reflections that follow I will note that the typical modern version of the real is holistic, processive, and marked by a manifold, complex relationality. The unexpected thing is that even the most traditional trinitarian theology may well expect to be greeted as a long lost relative by those who are aware of the shift in the way reality is being experienced and expressed. Why is this so?

As contemporary science pursues its path, the former classical mechanistic model is breaking down. This classical model can be best suggested by a closed circle, perhaps most of all in the physical form of a clock. It implied a vision of the world as essentially fixed, essentially complete and unchanging as a clock-face, with its dynamics as predictable as clockwork, its parts mathematically computed and definitively designed. In principle, reality had been mastered by science. The physical sciences possessed incontrovertible truth, and a demonstrably successful technology proved its own case.

What has begun to emerge is quite another sense of reality. Scientists, thinkers, artists, mystics and social activists have realized that the old imperialistic technological view of what was real sold short the full scope of both human and cosmic truth. Today, science imagines reality in a far more open, expanding, participative manner. There is no 'complete circle' of science containing the real. In contrast, we apprehend an increasingly mysterious manifold. As the limits of past knowledge are surpassed, we touch on further limits to the knowledge we come to. The universe increasingly resists any one-dimensional systematization. Reality appears as unbounded, emerging, relational and incredibly complex. Far from appearing as a machine whose parts can be separately disassembled and analysed, the whole of reality looks more like a restless living organism pregnant with possibilities of novel emergences and further developments. It is more like a huge event of inter-relationship and interaction, involving the human participant, and to an ever greater extent affected by human consciousness. This contrasts with the previous scientific myth of comprehending and controlling it as a fixed material entity, somehow watched and analysed by the all-knowing scientific mind, which remained oddly external to the whole thing.[9]

In an obvious sense this type of scientific imagination is more hospitable to a trinitarian conception of ultimate reality than the former dominant world-view. For this had little patience with any theology, let alone any theology needlessly complicated with trinitarian references to processions, relationships, or unity in distinction. But the emerging contemporary imaginative sense of the universe might be expected to find some of these traditional trinitarian positions quite intriguing. When a more holistic science realizes that for centuries theology has regarded the ultimate as a realm of interpersonal life, manifesting itself in a markedly processive way in the two trinitarian processions, with the divine reality concretely one through a manifold of relationships potentially inclusive of all conscious entities, such a traditional version of ultimate reality cannot be dismissed as an irrelevant model. For it is strikingly hospitable to contemporary apprehensions of the nature of the real when the accent is placed on the processive and the relational, when its search is characterized by an exploration into the original 'field' in which all the discovered complexity finds its dynamic unity.

In traditional trinitarian terms, we are presented with the ultimate origin, form and goal of the universe communicating itself progressively to creation. Reality reaches its final consistency and coherence inasmuch as the ultimate reality, God, enfolds all that is into its own field of relationships: reality emerges from the Divine Originating Ground in the Word, to return to it, through the Spirit, on a new level of coherence and being. Any deistic conception of the divine that presides over the world in an anonymous, extrinsic manner sits oddly with this intensely processive and relational understanding, instanced in both contemporary science and traditional trinitarian theology.

I am not implying that the world-view of past theology was itself especially hospitable to the trinitarian mystery. Indeed, in many ways, the medieval world-view, with its implications of fixed hierarchical order did not have much room for the singularity of the Trinity, with its essential implications of procession, relationship and

---

[9]An excellent coverage of these points can be found in Harold K. Schilling's *The New Consciousness in Science and Religion* (Philadelphia: United Church Press) pgs. 43-45.

unity in distinction. Theological theory had so imbibed classical Greek metaphysics that the vitality and communal nature of the trinitarian mystery could not find a full philosophical welcome in such a scheme. The data of faith were, of course, accepted; but it was rather awkwardly integrated into the prevailing metaphysics and physics of that time.[10]

4. The "Turning Point" and the Trinity

In contrast to the detached, mono-dimensional mechanistic view of reality, the contemporary sense of reality is well described in terms of a "turning point".[11] A vast change is occurring in our experience of reality and in our understanding of it, as we attend to the data drawn from such diverse areas as physics, biology, psychology, sociology, economics, and ecological studies. Be they related to such sciences as cause or effect, key cultural movements of our time, such as the collapse of patriarchy, women's liberation, global communication and concern, the ecological crisis and so forth, are powerful indicators of this change in perception. Decades ago, Karl Jaspers described the present era as a "new axial period" in human history. The new holistic and ecological emphasis surprisingly resonates with a mystical experience of reality as it has been analogously shared in all ages and traditions.[12]

This sense of a new paradigm of reality has not gone unacknowledged in authoritative Christian expression. To give but one example from Vatican II, ". . . the human race has passed from a rather static concept of reality to a more dynamic, evolutionary one. In consequence, there has arisen a new series of problems . . . calling for new efforts at analysis and synthesis."[13]

Unsettlement there surely is, but there is, too, the joy of recognition. The tradition of a trinitarian manner of conceiving of ultimate

---

[10]This is well documented in N. Max Wildiers, *The Theologian and his Universe. Theology and Cosmology from the Middle Ages to the Present* (New York: Seabury,1982).

[11]See the impressive general study, Fritjof Capra, *The Turning Point. Science, Society and the Rising Culture* (London: Flamingo Fontana, 1984).

[12]Capra, *The Turning Point,* e.g., pgs. 323ff.

[13]Vatican II, *Gaudium et Spes* #5.

reality with an emphasis on the relational, the processive, the communal, unity in distinction can find many points of convergence with the new paradigm of reality as it has been described.[14] It would be a very timid theology that does not try to make the most of this opportunity.

Admittedly, we are a long way from suggesting that the trinitarian conception of God and the new paradigm of reality are identical. For the moment, we are merely aligning the trinitarian paradigm to the context of the "turning point". But a new paradigm is being called for. It will mean a new basic comprehensive pattern of reality. It will necessitate a fundamental change in our thoughts, perceptions, and values, as shifts occurring in the sciences interact with the vast cultural transformations that are taking place. Three thousand years of patriarchal culture are coming to an end. The crisis in the availability of fossil fuels induces a new ecological awareness in our existence. The industrial revolution has brought us to see the need of global values other than those reducible to unlimited material progress. The older scientific 'methods' functioned by denying so much human experience and aspiration. It is not uncommon for modern analysts to resort, somewhat esoterically, to oriental notions of reality such as the ancient Chinese notion of the *Tao,* with its fluctuating polarities of *yin* and *yang*.[15]

For in this new paradigm, the universe can no longer be coherently appreciated as a huge, machine-like entity, made up of a multitude of separate objects, examined by objective scientists and, perhaps, presided over by a dispassionate deity. The aspiration embodied in the new view is a sense of an indivisible universe, a 'whole' existing in a network of dynamic inter-relationships which essentially includes the phenomenon of human consciousness, the action of the human participant, the role of the human observer. Admittedly, there is as yet no well-established conceptuality that can accommodate such a paradigm: the holographic metaphor is suggestive of what contemporary physics is putting forward in Geoffrey Chew's "bootstrap theory" and David Bohm's notions of "implicate order".[16]

---

[14]Capra, pg. xviii.

[15]Cf. Capra, *Op.cit.,* pgs. 17-20; 458.

[16]For various applications of this metaphor drawn from new techniques of lensless photography, see Capra, *Op.cit.,* pgs. 87ff; 323ff.

In trying to express the main features of the emerging 'postmodern' culture, Capra does suggest some theological options which, to him, seem to accord with the new paradigm he is commending. The notion of God would need to be expressed in terms of an overall "Systems Theory", so that the notion of God could be associated with the self-organization and self-transcendence of the cosmos as we are coming to know it. For him, such a notion of God fits well with the mystical traditions of both East and West. He singles out Teilhard de Chardin's notion of God as the ground and goal of evolution as deserving special consideration. If this were liberated from its patriarchal connotations, it "may well come closest to the modern views of science."[17]

Such, then, is some indication of the new paradigm emerging at the "turning point" of so many disciplines and cultural movements. Now, there are many points of possible contact between this new paradigm and trinitarian theology. Obviously, both accent relationality and co-inherence as fundamental features of reality. Both accent the dynamism of being and the self-transcendence structured into the movement of the universe. Both accent existence as personal and the communion of consciousness in which that existence is fulfilled. Both, in their respective ways, accent a 'Systems' approach to reality, even to ultimate reality, in which the 'whole' is considered before the 'parts'. The question for us is, how much, in a new age of human awareness, the trinitarian conception of God, so little exploited in the past, can contribute to, and learn from, the shaping of the new paradigm of reality?

Up to this point, we have been positioning our trinitarian reflection in the experience of the church and in the experience of the world, above all in its present sense of the global "turning point".

5. Preconceptions

There is always the danger in the early stages of any study that we get trapped in a less than serviceable preconception of what we

---

[17]*Op.cit.* pgs. 33ff. Capra is, of course, no specialist in Judaeo-Christian tradition which, in his judgment, "adheres to the image of a male god, personification of supreme reason and source of ultimate power who rules the world from above by imposing his divine law upon it ... " (pg. 24).

intend to explore. A bad map makes for an unhappy journey. In the present case, the main danger lies in possessing a collage of dogmatic concepts, detached from the historical context from which they emerged. Whilst such distortions might appear as the starting-point for those who have not reflected on theological method, what is really happening is a peculiar act or state of amnesia. The Mystery of the Trinity is not being re-membered, but rather dismembered in the experience and expression of living faith. To fall an early victim to this kind of forgetfulness usually brings with it a later effort to over-compensate with a more refined and rigid dogmatism. One may end with an intense, defensive kind of verbal orthodoxy, but be left without the sense of the mystery of life and Love that the doctrine of the Trinity represents.[18] The mystery is replaced by a kind of intellectual puzzle. Presumably, it is designed to test the believing mind in its readiness to accept the unthinkable. But soon, the temptation is to dismiss the Trinity as irrelevant and of no practical value to Christian existence.

Needless to say, any trinitarian theology, if it is to be authentic, has to appropriate, in a critical manner, the great classical doctrines of Nicaea and Constantinople. Yet this can be done only by retrieving, and in a sense, repeating the experience out of which they were born. But such a retrieval can be blocked. If our preconceptions are composed of congealed abstractions related to faith only as tests of orthodoxy, then the church's living experience of God remains unexamined, either in its positive bearing of living the mystery of self-giving communal Love, or in its negative, dialectical struggle to demolish convenient idols and to exorcise rather familiar demons.

If an abstract dogmatism can distort the beginnings of trinitarian reflection, so, too, can philosophical or scientific preconceptions of God. For these can work to suppress the originality of the Christian data.[19] But this is nothing new in the history of theology. It has often, perhaps usually, been the case that Christian faith has been lumbered with philosophical preconceptions of what God is supposed to be, at the expense of what the Divine Mystery has been revealed to be in the living experience of the church. Needless to say, it is to

---

[18]This I take to be close to the main thesis of the very stimulating, J.S. O'Leary, *Questioning Back. The Overcoming of Metaphysics in the Christian Tradition* (New York: Seabury, 1985).

[19]See note 16.

the great benefit of theology when it subsumes, in a critical manner, the philosophical and scientific search for God. For instance, early patristic theology allied itself with the movement of Greek thought away from polytheism and dualism, to affirm the ultimate in terms of the Unique One, the Good, Being itself, the source of all *Logos* and order. In the same way, contemporary theology can make its own the affirmations of modern personalist philosophy in its apprehension of reality in terms of consciousness and communion, just as it can benefit from "Systems Theory" analysing and comprehending reality as a field of interaction, with the consistency of an interrelated whole, and as a total dynamic process. More dramatically, theology can make its own the insights of Social Analysis and thus locate the meaning of God as the foundation of human dignity and freedom, and as an inexhaustible movement towards liberation from all kinds of oppression. It is hardly possible to deny in any of these ancient or modern instances that the understanding of the trinitarian mystery of *Agape* can be greatly enriched.

But when these extra-theological conceptions of ultimate reality are uncritically absorbed into theology as unquestioned preconceptions, serious distortions occur. For example, if theology loses itself in the Greek tradition of understanding God as Unique all-perfect Being and Act, the specifically Christian data of God being Love, in a community of self-giving persons, can be minimized. Indeed, even if the modern notion of person is applied to the Trinity, the divine mystery can appear as a committee of consent rather than the One God in three persons. Similarly, our current sympathy with process and systems models might tend to a kind of divinization of the 'process' or 'system',—rather than being an exploration of the divine reality in these experiential or theoretical terms. And perhaps most seriously, as the best Liberation Theology knows, using religious notions simply as motives for social change with no sense of the context of Christian faith, risks both idolizing a social cause and destructively handing oneself over to the demons of violent revolution.

If, then, theology is not critically aware of the pre-theological preconceptions in the culture in which it works, it may find itself either unwittingly legitimizing the reigning ideology or cautiously re-issuing what to other disciplines has long been obvious. The responsibility of theology is both to appreciate what is distinctive and original in the Christian data, and to promote a creative interpretation of such.

6. The Role of Questions

Theological originality has its origin in questions. Such questions arise out of the faith, hope, and love of Christian commitment itself. New questions occur for the intelligence touched, unsettled, or transformed by the Christian experience of God, in an endless variety of historical and cultural contexts. How can God's Word, incarnate in Christ, be expressed as the meaning of all human meanings and remain liberatingly meaningful even in our encounter with absurdity? How can the Love of God, communicated in the gift of the Spirit, truly be the fundamental value integrating and transforming all human values and remain liberatingly so even in experiences of worthlessness and temptations to despair? How is the divine mystery of the Loving origin and fulfilling end of all related to everything we have found to be real? How does it remain liberatingly so even as we experience dimensions of God-forsakenness in the global dimensions of the evils with which we have to contend today?

Theology must make the attempt to answer such questions "from the inside out." This contrasts with a dogmatic extrinsicism: merely repeating dogmatic assertions with no sense of the questions that gave rise to them. It contrasts, too, with all the cultural preconceptions which may well be rooted in modern sensibility, but have foreclosed on the possibility or actuality of any transcendent answer.

In short, we have to begin with ourselves: with ourselves already caught up in the dynamics of shared self-transcending faith, hope, and love thrusting toward its unconditional fulfilment; with ourselves linked with everyone searching for ultimate meaning and value in this world, in a way that names, faces, and reacts to the threat of absurdity, cynicism, and despair; with ourselves, earthed and grounded in this universe collaborating in the explorations of art and science which reveal ever deeper and broader dimensions of mystery; with ourselves contributing to the self-directing history of our race towards a more human future.

It seems to me that such questions are condensed into two great interrogations. First, how, despite all the pain, separation, and evil of the world we share, do we belong ultimately together? And, secondly, before whom, in whom, with whom do we finally stand against the destructiveness which so obviously threatens us, from within and without?

In the horizon opened up by such existential questions, the mystery of the Trinity takes on a new light. It appears as that which founds, inspires, clarifies, and fulfils every dimension of our self-transcending selves. For it is Love communicating itself to other selves as Word and Spirit. This divine self-communication heals and promotes our self-transcendence. It offers healing to a rootless selfhood drifting with no bearings in the world, which too readily settles for lesser versions of human identity. It confirms and holds the expanding self on a higher trajectory of fulfilment: faith comes to the realization that "nothing in all creation can separate us from the love of God in Christ Jesus our Lord." (Rom 8:39) Hope entrusts itself to this Love that has found us, committing itself to the absolute future beyond all possible futures, when "God will be everything to everyone." (I Cor 15:28) A self-giving charity reaching out to others is the authenticity that this Love demands and inspires: this highest gift "bears all things, believes all things, hopes all things, endures all things." (I Cor 13::7) Deep calls unto deep: the self-communicating God provokes and fulfils the dynamism of human self-transcendence.

But this is to run ahead. At this point, I am merely stressing the point that we are not beginning with an abstract definition of God, elaborated in this or that philosophical tradition. Rather, we are beginning with the notion of God inscribed into the conscious dynamism of our self-transcendence. God is the Love that has found us, taken us out of ourselves into something limitlessly more, assuring the fulfilment of all human hopes, which, though lived, can never be fully brought to comprehensive expression. As it uses all the resources of Scripture and appropriates the variety of ecclesiastical and mystical doctrines, theology attempts its limited, systematic exploration. The basic notion of God evokes its images, its symbols; it inspires a tradition of prayer and teaching; in different crises it demands an authoritative interpretation if the originality of the gift is to be respected. It exacts in developing contexts of culture and history a fresher, more compelling articulation of what is present but has fallen short of expression. Thus it provokes the creativity of theology: the effort to mean, in the most telling way, the mystery present to our faith, hope and love.[20]

7. The Functions of Trinitarian Meaning

The more we attempt to articulate the meaning of the Trinity in relation to the questions we human beings are living, the more such trinitarian meaning will function in four recognizable ways.[21] The first is cognitive. There is a specific fulfilment for the mind in coming to a closer approximation to the truth of what has been revealed. False and inadequate conceptions of the Trinity are replaced by an understanding that respects the data and develops in the context of the resources and exigencies of a contemporary culture.

Secondly, such trinitarian meaning is constitutive: it deeply affects the identity of those who assimilate such an understanding of God. As the meaning of ultimate Love, the Trinity 'indwells' the hearts and minds of believers. They, in turn, become witnesses to such transcendent meaning in the conversation that forms the meaningful world. One grasps oneself and others as members of Christ, as temples of the Spirit, as sons and daughters of God.

Thirdly, this trinitarian meaning is communicative. The meaning of the "we believe" of Christian faith lives from the "we" of the Trinity. The trinitarian mystery of self-giving Love provokes both the formation of community and the outreach of mission. Further, it clarifies and promotes the shared field of Christian experience.

Fourthly, the meaning of the Trinity is effective. By exploring, elaborating, and celebrating the meaning of God in this way, we not only know something, become someone in so doing, and open ourselves to the deepest foundations of our mutual belonging, we are also inspired to transform the world in a certain way. It is to have a trinitarian agenda. For Christian authenticity, if it nourishes itself on the cognitive, constitutive and communicative meaning of the Trinity,

---

[20]See Bernard Lonergan, *Method in Theology* (London: DLT, 1972), pgs. 101-105 for the basic technical expression and Sebastian Moore's recent writings for very imaginative applications, e.g., "The New Life", *Lonergan Workshop, vol. V*, ed. F. Lawrence, (Chico, Calif.: Scholars Press, 1985), pgs. 145-161.

[21]Lonergan, *Method,* pgs.76-81.

necessarily begins to imagine the world and its possibilities in a new way. The absurdities and breakdowns of society are countered by the excess of Christ's redeeming grace, by the inexhaustible energy of the Spirit. The rights and dignity of our fellow human beings take on new significance against the horizon of an ultimate mystery, related to all as Creator and redeeming Love. How the trinitarian mystery is a liberating meaning depends, naturally, on the different contexts in which we consider it. Politically, it tends to subvert any monarchical or patriarchal ideology which underwrites oppression and injustice. Psychologically, it liberates religious imagination from those familiar manipulative fixations which block rather than promote self-transcendence. Missiologically, it inspires an outreach into other religious traditions of the world, in an adoring search for the incalculable ways of the Spirit, the presence of the Risen One to all peoples, and the universal Love of the Father of all. We will return, of course, to these matters.

So, to explore the meaning of the Trinity is to find it potentially meaningful in the four ways mentioned above: it is brought within the range of our knowing in some limited way; it dwells in our consciousness as something supremely significant for our identity; it establishes a community of shared meanings and values; and it directs us to change the reality of our world in accord with the conversion of mind and heart it inspires.

8. *Techniques of Theological Reflection*

How then can the meaning of the Trinitarian mystery be elaborated, so that it can function in the four manners we have just indicated? One classic answer, a good description of the Catholic theological tradition, is given in Vatican I's *Constitution on Divine Revelation, (Dei Filius)*:

> If human reason, with faith as its guiding light, enquires earnestly, devoutly and circumspectly, it does reach, by God's generosity, some understanding of the mysteries, and that a most profitable one. It does this by analogy with the truths it knows naturally, and also from the interconnection of the mysteries with one another, and in reference to the final end of man. Reason, however, never

becomes capable of such mysteries in the way it understands the truths that are its proper object. For divine mysteries, of their very nature, so excel the created intellect that, even when they have been given in revelation and received in faith, that very faith keeps them veiled in a kind of obscurity as long as we are 'exiled from the Lord' in this mortal life, for 'we walk by faith and not by sight'.[22]

There are four points directly concerning trinitarian theology here. First, the mystery of the Trinity can be partially known, even as it intrinsically transcends the scope of the finite mind. The mystery does not reveal itself to be ignored, but to establish communion with believers in a mutual love and knowledge. A fulfilment is envisaged when, as the Apostle says, "we know as we are known" (1 Cor 13:12).

Secondly, such "most profitable knowledge" comes within the range of human possibility when faith makes use of analogy. By extrapolating from the experiences, symbols, and models accessible within the limited horizons of mundane knowledge and relationships, theology can find terms in which to explore the divine mystery, even though it can never be exhaustively or immediately known. For instance, faith affirms the reality of God in terms of intra-mundane symbols, 'Father', 'Son', 'Holy Breath'. Such symbols themselves are embedded in a rich image-laden context where the divine is referred to as 'Word', 'Fire', 'Light', 'Living Water', 'Radiant Cloud of Glory,' 'Voice from Heaven', 'Descending Dove', and so forth. Then, there are all the characteristics of God brought home to human experience in the parables of Jesus. And, at the heart of such expressions, is the humanity of Jesus himself, the revelation of the Father.

More theoretically, there is a whole panoply of concepts arising out of human experience which are pressed into theological service: for example, 'person', 'nature', 'relationship', 'sending', 'procession', 'knowing', 'willing', 'indwelling', 'community', 'unity'.... Such analogical notions are the stock in trade of the theological tradition. And, as I have already implied in reference to the new paradigm of reality, theology is being challenged to develop its analogical capacities further. Further, the modern feminist critique of traditional

---

[22] DS 3019. For further comment, see Lonergan, *Method,* pgs. 355ff.

theological language provokes a further kind of analogical creativity. It criticizes the one-sidedness of patriarchal and masculine symbolism while provocatively pointing to the need to retrieve and develop analogies of God in terms of the experience of the feminine.

Thirdly, there is the theological technique of inter-relating the mysteries of faith to each other by establishing their interconnection in the One Mystery of Love. In this way, theology approximates to a *Gestalt* of the revealed God. Particular classic themes of theological reflection such as the unity and trinity of God, the incarnation, the paschal mystery, the sending of the Spirit, creation, grace, church, the sacraments, eschatology are correlated to one another in more and more rich configurations. A contemporary metaphor for these interconnections is the hologram. New techniques of lensless photography can produce a multi-dimensional image of the object. This results in being able to view it from different angles, in contrast to the standard flat image. The Trinity has especially suffered from monodimensional presentations. This occurs when it is identified with a purely doctrinal formulation, usually to be quickly schematized in the form of a triangle and compressed into a highly abstract "psychological analogy". So it was divorced from other theological themes, as these, too, were increasingly appropriated by specialists (as the names Christology, Pneumatology, Ecclesiology, Sacramentology, Eschatology suggest). The overall systematic enterprise came to be fragmented, to cause a special kind of "forgetfulness of mystery",—not unlike what Heidegger describes in a philosophical context as the "forgetfulness of Being". For each theme excuses a kind of amnesia in regard to the others; and, more particularly, a forgetfulness in regard to the source and centre and goal of all theological intelligence, the mystery of God as *Agape,* as self-giving Love.

When such atomism and amnesia go unchallenged, theology all too easily becomes a *reductio ad absurdum,* as each specialized theme is treated as 'the most important' to the depreciation of the rest. But the result is otherwise if theological reflection is more genuinely systematic in its concern for the "interconnection of the mysteries". It is the special glory of Karl Rahner to have exemplified this in a remarkable way. If a systematic theology manages to be more holographic in its technique and sensibilities, each of the particular themes finds its focus in the trinitarian mystery of the self-giving God. The result is an *introductio in mysterium.* The basic trinitarian symbol of God expands into the whole thematization and praxis of theology. If I have above stressed theological caution against reduction of the Christian data by cultural presuppositions, here I am stressing a similar caution against such reductionism from within. For this happens when a particular theme is absolutized in forgetfulness of trinitarian mystery, the *Theos* of which Theology treats.

The third technique of systematic reflection deals with "the truth that will make you free" (Jn 8:32). It seeks to understand the mysteries of faith as liberating human beings in the light of their true destiny in God. Trinitarian Love, in inspiring self-transcendence, promises its fulfilment in all the dimensions that human experience can identify: cosmic, social, historical, individual. In terms of trinitarian meaning, it seeks to express the mystery of the Trinity as the principle, form and goal of "life to the full" (Jn 10:10): it shows how the self-giving God enters into "man's making of man", as it contests our perverse self-projects with the promise of an absolute future in which "God will be everything to everyone" (I Cor 15:28).

This orientation of systematic reflection is related to the more precise and urgent contemporary concerns of Liberation Theology. How is theology not merely the product of Christian faith, but grounded in its conduct, both inspiring and being inspired by transformative praxis? In the interests of serving the hopeful, liberating conduct of faith, it necessarily has to wrestle with such questions as the following:

1. How can trinitarian meaning be a liberation of mind from all the ideologies that would reduce the universe to the "nothing but" of their dominant concern?

2. On the psychological level, how does trinitarian meaning liberate the psyche from the diseased affectivity of the religious type, with its infantile projections and manipulations? How does it promote conversion and personal integration on the psychological level?

3. How does this trinitarian understanding of God arise from and inspire solidarity with the poor, with the victims of history, with the prophets and martyrs of our time? How is the Trinity an agenda of liberation?

4. What is the meaning of the Trinity in terms of the current feminist critique of patriarchalism? How does it work against the oppression of women in both church and society and redeem us from the repression of the feminine in contemporary consciousness?

5. What is the meaning of the Trinity for the mission of the church in the contemporary context of the interfaith dialogue and collaboration occurring today for the first time? How is the Trinity not an esoteric Christian doctrine but a redemptive stimulus to appropriate humanity's global religious experience in a positive, hopeful manner?

The orientation of theological reflection which turns on understanding Christian reality "in reference to man's last end" must ask these and similar questions. It seems to me that it must be characterised by a keen sense of 'absolute eschatology', i.e., the really ultimate in human destiny, that it must deal with the realities of 'present eschatology', which is the manner in which the ultimate is already present as judgment and promise in the here and now. Examples of this are indicated in the above questions. For the indwelling presence of the Trinity is impetus to create the forms of the future within history. It inspires all the holistic and global values in the present, as these attract human freedom forward into a deeper collaboration with the God of the Kingdom.

These three classic techniques of theological reflections,—analogy, interconnections, eschatological liberation,—will shape our present effort to explore the meaning of the Trinitarian Mystery. For we will be dealing with analogies, images, 'vestiges', symbols, models of the Trinity. Also, we will certainly be trying to establish connections between Trinity, the human self in all its dimensions, creation, revelation, grace, the paschal mystery, the church, in an effort to form a hologrammic *Gestalt* of the Trinity. Further, I will have a concern throughout this treatment to present the Trinity in terms of hope, with all the implications of eschatological liberation that this offers. True, I will change the order of these three techniques somewhat. I am persuaded that it will be more profitable to treat the 'interconnections' first, to follow this with 'analogies', and to conclude with the theme of eschatological liberation. I hope the reason for this will become clear.

9. Risks, Demands, Advantages

In introducing his *De Trinitate,* St. Augustine pithily remarks that in the domain of trinitarian theology, "nowhere is the error more dangerous, the search more laborious, and the results more rewarding." A word, then, on the risks, the demands and the advantages associated with this type of reflection.

When all is said and done, the most dangerous error in trinitarian thinking is the most obvious one: irrelevant abstraction. The doctrine of the Trinity has been swathed in such a wrapping of mystery, philosophical complexity, austere doctrinal formulation that even the word 'Trinity' causes something like a mental block for preachers and theological students! When this most demanding concern of theology, a reverent exploration of the divine mystery, begins to look like an exercise designed to prop up an archaic metaphysical apparatus, then such a "metaphysics" has to be "overcome".[23] When the fundamental reality of the self-communicating God causes such a dissonance in the communication of Christian faith, there must be something wrong. The Gospel of God giving into the world what is most intimately "his own", the Son and the Spirit, somehow ceases to be "good news" about the fulness of life being offered. It has so often become a form of supercelestial mathematics designed to prove how three equals one—a kind of test to assess the credulity of the believing mind. Little wonder that this kind of 'error' takes all the fascination out of the mystery of the Trinity. There may be an austere trinitarian doctrine, but there is no creative imagination or passionate feeling associated with the divine mystery of God. Common-sense believers find it an irrelevant superstructure mystifyingly imposed on an already sufficiently complicated faith.

Modern reactions to this kind of distortion have, of course, tried to bring the Trinity more within the reference of human experience. This has resulted in allegations that new errors are being made, or, more often than not, old ones repeated. For example, the imposing trinitarian theologies of Barth, Rahner and Macquarrie, are suspected of being new forms of modalism: the three divine persons are

---

[23] At least to this degree J. O'Leary's *Questioning Back* ... can expect general agreement!

reduced to being merely modes of divine being, not subsistent, invocable 'persons', truly representing the communitarian reality of God. At the other extreme, the insightful theologies of, say, Moltmann and Muehlen are apprehended to be veering towards tritheism: the three are so distinct as to be all but separate in their respective consciousnesses, in their knowing, willing and acting, with the resultant reduction of the divine unity to something akin to the moral unity of a committee.

Such errors are, indeed, dangerous, if they are present, however implicitly, in the work of such leading theologians! Nonetheless, I suspect the real error here lies in forgetting what theology is all about. It is not trying to put some form of religious theory in the place of a living, passionate, active faith. Rather, its whole aim, given the fragmentary, provisional character of our thinking about God, is to liberate faith for its most inspiring vision and most energetic commitment. A further quotation from Augustine sums up the spirit of such an exploration:

> Let everyone who reads these pages proceed further with me where he is as certain as I am. Let him search with me where he is hesitant as I am. Whenever he makes a mistake, let him come back to me; and whenever the mistake is mine let him call me back. Thus, let us enter together on the path of charity in search of him of whom it is said, 'seek his face forevermore.'[24]

The risks are there, and search is certainly laborious. To elaborate a Trinitarian theology necessarily means going through the whole field of theology: all that we can know of the divine unity and Trinity, as Creator, Redeemer, and Consummation of all that is, all the particular mysteries of grace, incarnation, redemption, liberation, sacraments, the church in all its dimensions. This presupposes that such a theology is open, at least in principle, to all the data as these occur in the experience of the People of God, whether such data be found in scriptural, doctrinal or liturgical expressions, mystical experiences, theological theory, or manifold praxis.

Whilst the data are inherently unlimited, the contexts in which

---

[24] *De Trinitate*, 1.

they have been and must be interpreted are increasingly complex. There are contexts formed by particular historical situations where special problems have to be faced and resolved. There are contexts that emerge in accordance with the demands of different cultural situations and different historical imperatives, be they intellectual, moral, esthetic, or religious. Today, there is the emerging global context: the opportunities arising from world-wide communication and inter-faith encounter, the newly understood dimensions of world poverty, of self-destruction on a world-scale.

The difficulty of trinitarian theology resides in its being theology at its most vulnerable. It has to risk dealing with such inherent complexity, and yet tends toward that eschatological vision of God where all the mysteries of life come home. The trinitarian formulation, God as Father, Son, and Holy Spirit, is a language of faith bringing the universe of grace into focus. A trinitarian theology that does this runs the risk of being turned in on itself in sterile abstraction from any experience of faith, as the history of theology scandalously shows. If that happens, it is quite clear that the Mystery of trinitarian Love has been reduced to absurdity. If, on the other hand, theology keeps its nerve and so concentrates on the great central mystery implied in the realm of grace as it is made known in Christ, then we can rightly hope that such a theology will be an *introductio in mysterium,* a mystagogy of critical and creative reflection.

Though the risk is in reducing the understanding of faith to sterile complexity and monotony, nowhere does a genuine theology find the "results more rewarding". To promote a vision of faith where the articulations of faith interconnect in the one central mystery of God's self-giving Love, is no small service. It is the benefit of a truly sapiential theology. It suggests an ever-new paradigm of reality even in these days of momentous explosion of knowledge. Consciousness, community, inter-relationality, union in difference, life and love,— all belong to this paradigm as theology has always, in some sense, known. But in the complexity of the contemporary movement of culture and development of science, insofar as the Trinity can suggest a comprehensive paradigm for our understanding of reality, that reality will have a coherence and consciousness of personal presence inscribed into it, well able to give direction to the unsettling experience of "The Turning Point".

The meaning of all our obscurely meaningful fields of experience, the 'sufficient reason' of all our affirmations in science, philosophy, and religion, will find in a renewed understanding of the Trinity a luminous centre of synthesis and a point from which to expand into further search. The worthwhileness of all our efforts to create a global humanity of peace and justice will find its ultimate value in the Love that continues to give itself. Our limited horizons are expanded into an overarching horizon of hope, in adoration, even now, of the God who will be "everything to everyone".

Above all, when theology is single-minded about its true subject, it develops the ability to proclaim and delight in "The Good News of God" (Rom 1:1).

2

The Scriptural Foundations

The scriptures are of absolutely fundamental importance to both church doctrine and theology. Nonetheless, such sacred writings are primarily neither doctrinal nor theological texts. They are far more immediately related to living faith: the New Testament texts are the fundamental literary expression of the church's original experience of the mystery of Christ. Out of that original experience they arise; and that original experience of gracious reality is what they witness to and intend to promote for the benefit of later generations of faith.

1. The Trinitarian Meaning of Scripture

Because they document the irreversible, culminating experience of God in Christ, the scriptures are a vivid expression of living meaning. These early Christian writings, in all the variety of their rhetoric, are trying to make sense of what has been overwhelmingly and convincingly given in Christ. There were, of course, resources available to these early writers, above all those they inherit from the faith of Israel. Still, their task was not to repeat what had gone before, but to announce the radically 'new' in their religious experience.

This effort to mean Christian reality was first of all effective. The scriptures witness to and inspire nothing less than the transformation of human existence in Christ. Their intention is urgently practical: for they suppose a life of searching faith,—asking, seeking, knocking on the door for the fulfilment of the Kingdom; they call to conversion and continually repeat the new commandment of love; they impel to the mission of baptising all nations in the name of the Father, Son and Holy Spirit.

The scriptures evidence a communicative meaning, too: they are the expression of a community alive to the realities of "one Body, ... one Spirit ... one hope ... one Lord, one faith, one baptism, one God and Father of us all" (Eph 4:4ff).

Further, the sacred writings form the consciousness of the church into a distinctive sense of identity. This constitutive meaning shapes Christian awareness of how God is now present in and to them in Christ. This is expressed in terms of an identity as members of Christ, temples of the Spirit, sons and daughters of the Father. It promotes a life transformed into a new capacity for freedom and relationship: "anyone who is in Christ is a new creation; the old has passed away, and behold, the new has come" (2 Cor 5:17).

Such varied 'meaningful' creativity turns on the realist convictions of early Christian witness. Quite simply, they were intending to tell the truth, and usually in a way that cost them much, even their lives. In short, there were cognitive meanings at stake. Whether the world accepted what has happened or not, whether or not it was all a scandal to Israel, a folly to the Greeks, or subversive for the Romans, whether or not Christians themselves could live up to the whole thing, this was how the real God had acted, and what the real God is. To back off from the objectivity of faith, essentially evidenced in the resurrection of the Crucified, is to make preaching vain, faith futile, to leave the guilty with no hope of forgiveness and to misrepresent God himself (1 Cor 15:12-19).

This original meaning-making is, in the terms of Christian tradition, "inspired by the Holy Spirit". The scriptures are revered as "inspired writings". As such they enter into all consequent reflection as an irreplaceable foundation. To minimize this scriptural witness would amount to denying the uniqueness of the Christian event as it was originally recognized, expressed, and assimilated in its historical actuality.

The scriptural data not only present faith with the reality of God's presence in Christ. They also inspire ways of thinking about it as we observe the original patterns and processes of presenting Christian meaning. If, at one extreme, the special achievement of later doctrinal definition would be to state what was at stake, the peculiar richness of modern scriptural scholarship is its exploration of how, why, and in what forms, scriptural meaning took shape.[1] In short, the scriptures are the foundation for theological meaning not only in what they present, but in the manner in which they present it.

As such a foundation, the New Testament documents provide data for trinitarian theology in four ways. First, in the way they word the experience and meaning of God revealed in Christ they exhibit a *rhetoric* of trinitarian faith. Secondly, the scriptures *narrate* the meaning of the divine mystery in terms of the *dramatis personae,* Father, Son and Spirit. Thirdly, in this rhetoric and narrative, one can observe the presence and interplay of the various key *symbols* evocative of the divine character. And, fourthly, biblical rhetoric, narrative and symbolism articulate different levels of *experience,* that of the church, that of the early disciples, and that of Jesus himself.

Rhetoric, narrative, symbolism, experience: such is the richness and complexity of the biblical data regarding the Trinity. A note, then, on each of these four inter-related areas.

2. The Rhetoric of Trinitarian Expression

Here I am using the word, 'rhetoric', in a very basic sense. It is that creative effort of the biblical writers to 'word' their experience of God in Christ.[2] A verbal creativity arises out of their awareness of the 'new' with which the whole New Testament deals.[3] The awareness of momentous events provokes a search for the right words in a kind of verbal celebration of the transformation that has occurred, and to give it enduring public meaning. The wording of the 'New' reality that has taken place in Christ is a complex linguistic event. Though the old categories are surpassed, these, and the terms deriving from

---

[1] A monumental effort to document the variety of early Christian contexts and the forms of Christian meaning which they provoked is E. Schillebeeckx, *Christ. The Christian Experience in the Modern World,* trans. John Bowden (London: SCM 1980), especially pgs. 112-445.

[2] See especially Amos Wilder, *Early Christian Rhetoric* (New York: Harper and Row, 1964); Franz Josef van Beeck, *Christ Proclaimed. Christology as Rhetoric* (New York: Paulist Press, 1979). The early chapters of this latter work are most useful.

[3] Joseph Sittler, *Essays on Nature and Grace* (Philadelphia: Fortress Press, 1972), pgs. 23-50. Also Cf. Robert W. Jenson, *The Triune Identity* (Philadelphia: Fortress Press, 1982), pgs. 21-51.

them, are all that is available to express what now must be proclaimed: "In many and various ways, God spoke of old to our fathers by the prophets; but in these last days, he has spoken to us by a Son." (Hb 1:1f) The many and varied communications of God in the past now look to a reinterpretation in the light of what has occurred in "these last days".

This rhetoric of the 'New' is first of all one of fulfilment regarding what the past has promised or hoped for. The New Testament understands it as deriving from the Risen Lord himself. Such a way of speaking certainly affirms that Jesus Christ is the fulfilment of all the religious hopes that preceded him. But it words the meaning of faith not only terminating in Christ as an 'object'. It is also communion with the Risen Lord as a 'subject'. Not only is it a matter of believing in Christ, but, more deeply, of being 'in Christ'. For the disciples' faith enables them to enter into the mind of Christ. They are in contact with him as he "opens their minds to understand the scriptures" by exegeting the meaning of the biblical hope that looked to his coming: "everything written about me in the law of Moses and the prophets and the psalms must be fulfilled." (Lk 24:44-47) The mystery of Christ is a world of meaning, of Logos and Spirit, in which all the words of faith and hope have new significance.

The consequent New Testament rhetoric works to extend Christ's fundamental exegesis of his own meaning. The 'inspired writers' readily present Christ as the fulfilment of everything that has gone before. Christ is the 'Yes' to all God's promises and the 'Amen' to all our prayers (2 Cor 1:20). In Christ there occurs the 'new' in relation to covenant, commandment, creation, temple, law, and so on. The Word has been definitively uttered, embodied in him. And, through him, has occurred the final outpouring of the Spirit.

Most notably, Paul and John speak of Christ as the one in whom the meaning of the divine Name is realized. In giving his name, God has rendered himself invocable as the God of his People's liberation. An historical promise is intimated in the literally provocative character of this name, "I will be who I will be" (Ex 3:14).[4] Paul hymns the glorification of the self-emptying of Jesus as a conferral of the name

---

[4] I find J.C. Murray's account of the meaning and significance of the divine name persuasive in *The Problem of God* (New Haven: Yale University Press), pgs. 6-16.

which is above every other name (Phil 2:9f). More concretely, John presents Jesus as the embodiment of the divine name in the numerous instances that resonate with references to it (Jn 1:18; 3:32; 8:24, 28, 58; 13:9)[5]

Within this context, a variety of terms are employed to convey the unrestricted and irreversible character of God's self-communication in Christ.[6] For there are a variety of ways in which the Jewish scriptures speak of God's special presence in Israel's history. These are taken into the rhetoric of the New Testament writers. For example, as Spirit, God is recognized as the life-force of creation, as a holiness which indwells Israel, as the inspiration of the prophets, and as the anointing which empowers the Messiah. It is this Spirit which will be poured out on all peoples, as Joel prophesied and Peter proclaimed (Joel 12:28-32; Ac 2:14f).

As the all-powerful Word and all-engendering Wisdom, God is present as the sovereign agent of creation and history. For the Word is spoken and the Wisdom comes forth to accomplish the purposes of God's saving work.[7] It is addressed to human conversation, but is not conditioned by it (Is 55:10f). In the rhetoric of the New Testament the Word, in which all things were made, was made flesh to dwell amongst us (Jn 1:14). Likewise, Christ is the divine Wisdom, "the image of the invisible God, the firstborn of all creation . . . all things were created through him and for him . . . in him, all things hold together." (Col 1:15ff)

In the Jewish scriptures, Christian theology found the terms by which to express the culmination of God's saving presence. Spirit, Word, Wisdom are the great classic categories that are employed. Christian faith makes its own the vocabulary forged to express how God is involved in the history of Israel. Christian usage will necessarily show discrimination in its employment of the available terms, for it is concerned to express the uniqueness of Christ. For example, the symbolic terms, 'Father' and 'Son', though not unknown in the

---

EM[5]See Raymond E. Brown's commentary on John, *The Anchor Bible. The Gospel according to John I-XII* (New York: Doubleday, 1966), Appendix IV: *Ego Eimi*—"I am", pgs. 533-538.

[6]For a concise account of this and related material, see John J.O'Donnell, *Trinity and Temporality* (Oxford: Oxford University Press, 1983), pgs. 28-32.

[7]For the New Testament usage of 'Word' in relation to its various Old Testament antecedents see R.E. Brown, *The Gospel according to John I-XII,* Appendix II: 'The Word', pgs. 519-524.

Jewish scriptures, are transformed into a new range of expression in the New Testament.[8]

Against this background, the New Testament sets forth its testimony in a vivid awareness of God's self-involvement in history. Though this is expressed in a variety of ways, the fundamental impression is that the One God, the Uniquely Saving One, is really present in a self-disclosing relationship and activity. The Word, the Wisdom, the Spirit, the Angel of the Lord are not intermediaries leaving the reality of God concealed. They are mediations of the divine reality which made it revealed. As such, these mediations are presented as leading to the definitive mediation of Christ and his Spirit.

The uniqueness of this saving God is not set over against a trinitarian conception as though the Son of Israel were one, and the God of Jesus Christ somehow three. Expressions abound in the Jewish scriptures which indicate that God is not a solitary remote deity, somehow needing to make contact with the human other as though from the outer space of an isolated transcendence. The vivid symbolism and the concreteness of many of the expressions of the character of this God suggest a fulness of life, indeed, of communal life. Here I have in mind especially the 'we' passages of Genesis, where the image of God is realized in the communion of male and female (Gn 1:26), the appearance of the Lord to Abraham as "three men" (Gn 18:2), and the transcendent vision of the divine community expressed in Is 6:1-5. Exegesis gives different readings of the significance of this plurality in God. But in no way is it suggested that such a God is in need of human companionship to fulfil his life. Rather, it is God who fulfills the needs and hopes of his people. Relationship to this one God makes human companionship, human community, possible. To break from such a relationship brings violence and disunity into the human race, as it did with Adam and Eve, with their sons Cain and Abel, and their descendants as they built the tower of Babel. This was also continually instanced in the prophets' denunciation of human selfishness.

---

[8]See Walter Kasper, *The God of Jesus Christ* trans. M.J. O'Connell (London: SCM, 1984), pgs. 138ff; 163-166.

As one well-recognized authority puts it, "the idea of plurality within unity was already implicit in Jewish theology".[9] It was this sense of plurality, so different from the Greek conception of the Transcendent One, which remains a given for later Christian theology. But as it used the terms of such plurality in unity, it extended them to mean what was distinctive to its faith. And at that juncture a different kind of unity began to be expressed which would be, in fact, a scandal to Jewish religious thinking. Christ was not merely an extension of the divine personality, nor merely a prophetic mediator of the divine presence. That could be tolerated, and in large measure, accepted into the logic of Jewish theology. But what broke this logic was what Christians have come to call the incarnation. This was the point where the new wine burst the old wineskins. It is well summed up in the following words:

> Although Jewish concepts were used in an attempt to explain Jesus' relationship to the Father, these concepts were not sufficient for the task. Jewish thought did not admit of this kind of plurality within the Godhead. It has no room for a second person within the Godhead, who not only did the will of the Father, but conversed with him, took counsel with him and pleaded with him. .... This idea of extension of the divine personality is Hebraic. The idea of interaction within the extended personality is neither Hebraic nor Hellenistic but Christian.[10]

So here began the second, distinctive phase of New Testament rhetoric. The newness that it sought to bring to expression was affirmed first of all in terms related to the Old Testament. It worked with its Jewish inheritance, that sense of God, self-involved in history, leading his people to salvation. But then it proceeded to elaborate the meaning of its own distinctive experience. The grace of the Christian mystery was the definitive self-revelation and communication of the God who had been involved in all Israel's history. The new and final had arrived. In "these last days", God has spoken through the Son: the Word had become flesh.

---

[9] A.Wainwright, *The Trinity in the New Testament* (London: SPCK, 1962), pg. 37.
[10] Wainwright, *op.cit.*, pgs. 39f.

The surprising thing, textually and rhetorically, is the pervasive presence of triadic formulations. Even the earliest New Testament document, I Thessalonians (A.D. 58?) speaks in a straightforward uncomplicated manner about the threefold character of God (1 Thes 1:1-5). It is assumed that everyone will understand what is meant in such expressions. Without wanting to be uncritically maximalist in regard to trinitarian references, it is hard not to be impressed by the seemingly spontaneous use of triadic rhetoric as the various dimensions of the New Testament experience of God's presence are 'worded'. The way such a triadic rhetoric issued so spontaneously in Christian expression requires an explanation, especially given the long struggle for adequate doctrinal formulation which would occupy the next centuries. For this triadic manner of speaking imposes itself, for example, in Paul's discussion of the law (Gal 3:11-14) and of Christian freedom (Gal 4:4ff). It pervades his expressions of thanksgiving (2 Thes 2:13; Col 1:3-8). It is present in the spontaneous movement of his expression of prayer and worship, (Rom 15:30; Phil 3:3ff;Eph 3:14ff), just as the Christian community's unity and manifold giftedness is presented in trinitarian terms (1 Cor 12:4-8).

Then there are more explicitly formal credal and liturgical formulations. At the conclusion of Matthew's gospel, the Risen Lord commissions the disciples to go forth and baptize the nations "in the name of the Father and of the Son and of the Holy Spirit" (Mt 28:19). Then there are other expressions where a more deliberately ordered triadic pattern is evident. The most likely explanation of this is a settled liturgical usage. The most memorable of these is 2 Cor 13:14.

Yet there is another kind of rhetoric more strongly indicative of the deep structure of trinitarian consciousness. It is not a matter of triadic formulations even if there is no formulation of a trinitarian doctrine as it would emerge in the later problematic. Rather, the kind of rhetoric I am referring to is more explicitly doxological, concerned only to give expression to the experienced reality of God. It appears, it seems to me, in two ways. These can be termed the 'iconic' and the 'schematic'.

By 'iconic', I mean those instances where New Testament language works to construct an image of the divine mystery as it is involved in our salvation. Such iconic rhetoric is found principally in the synoptics. The notable instances are the various depictions of the baptism of Jesus: the Spirit descends in the form of a dove, the heavens are opened, the divine voice proclaims Jesus as his beloved Son (Mt 3:16ff; Mk 1:9ff; Lk 3:21ff; Jn 1:32ff). Then there are the Infancy Narratives, especially that of Luke: it gives something like a hologrammic impression of God's saving presence: the Holy Spirit is the divine power at work, Jesus is uniquely the Son of the Most High (Lk 1:32-35). Then, too, there are the transfiguration passages, the cloud of glory, the voice from heaven, the proclamation of Jesus as the Beloved Son (Mt 17:1-8; Mk 9:2-8; Lk 9:28-36). Of similar iconic value is the description of Jesus rejoicing in the Spirit, to express the intimacy of his communion with the Father and his role in inviting others into it (Lk 10:21f). Even the event of the Ascension is iconically expressive of trinitarian meaning (Lk 24:50-53; Ac 1:6-12): the Risen Lord ascends to the divine realm, from which he will send the Spirit, as "the promise of my Father" (v. 49).

In contrast to this iconic descriptive type, there is a less symbolically portrayed form of rhetoric in evidence. Here the accent is on the schematic presentation of the fulness of salvation in Christ. True, these two rhetorics, the iconic and the schematic, are often interwoven as, say, in Acts: the events of the Ascension and Pentecost, of their very nature, provoke a particular kind of schematic presentation of the divine three in their respective roles (Ac 1:4, 8; 2:23, 28; 9:17; 10:38; 11:15ff ...).

But, when we turn to the Pauline writings, a more coordinated theology is apparent. The conceptuality is stronger. It approaches a systematic presentation of the divine mystery—though without theory or any special awareness of the problematical nature of what is presented. Here the best examples are the way major sections of Romans, Galatians, 1 Corinthians and Ephesians are constructed: there is a strong emphasis on three aspects of the mystery of salvation; the originating mystery of the Father's gracious love; faith in, and conformity to, Christ; and life in the unity and power of the Spirit. These aspects are coordinates for the presentation of the grace of salvation. The incipiently trinitarian meaning is brought to a notably concentrated expression, for example, in Rom 8, 1 Cor 12, Gal 3, Eph 1. To give one example of this kind of schematic structure,

> There is one body and one Spirit, just as you were called to one hope that belongs to your call, one Lord, one faith, one baptism,

one God and Father of us all, who is above all, and through all and in all. (Eph 4:4-6)

The best example of this schematic trinitarian rhetoric is found in John's Gospel. Here the evangelist is not only giving a coordinated account of the fulness of grace and truth now present to the world in Jesus Christ (Jn 1:14), but is evidently attempting something more systematic. He is inculcating a way of understanding the divine three in the one mystery of God. John expresses this as one aware of the problems latent in the triadic presentation of the divine mystery in the Gospel. In the four centuries to follow, the church will eventually face the major, inherently problematical points in its presentation of God as Father, Son and Spirit. Nonetheless, it is not anachronistic to notice that John is already beginning to face this challenge. If it is all because the Father has so loved the world (Jn 3:16); if the Son is to be confessed as "My Lord and my God"; if he departs to send the Spirit from the Father, then it requires no imagination to expect the question to arise, how are these divine three related to one another?

One very significant aspect of the Johannine rhetoric is the manner in which it expresses the communion existing between the Father and the Son. To this degree, it points to a dialogue or conversation going on between them. The Word made flesh is dialogical: his origin is from the Father, his identity is to be this Father's Son; his mission is to do the Father's will. Existing from and for the Father, he is sent from the Father, receives everything from him yet is one with him. Yet the Father is greater, the origin and goal of all that Jesus is. No one goes to the Father but by Jesus, but no one can come to Jesus unless the Father attracts. The speech of the Son and the silence of the Father who speaks only in this Word, express the character of the transcendent mystery into which all believers are drawn. The prayer of Jesus in Jn 17 is the climax of this kind of rhetoric:

> ... that they may all be one even as thou, Father, art in me, and I in thee, that they also may be in us ... (Jn 17:21).

Compared to the interaction of Father and Son, the presence of the Spirit is not as directly expressed in John's Gospel. On the other hand, as we will stress later, the whole wording of the Word depends on the presence of the Spirit. For this other Paraclete, the Spirit of Truth, whom the Risen Jesus sends, "will teach you all things, and bring to mind all that I have said to you" (Jn 14:26).[11] The Gospel can speak of the Father and the Son because the Spirit gives and continues to give his testimony (15:26). The Paraclete guides successive generations of believers into all truth (16:13). Implicitly, the Spirit is a pervasive presence in John's Gospel. He inspires understanding of Christ, and guides its development. The problem seems to have clearly occurred to the evangelist: how was he to correlate the presence of the Spirit to the dialogical relationship existing between the Father and the Son? How was he to insert the Spirit into the symmetry of the communication taking place between the Father and the Son?

At this point the Gospel shows an almost scholastic precision. Rhetorical expression becomes a precise statement of relationships:

> I have many things to say to you but you cannot bear them now. When the Spirit of truth comes, he will guide you into all truth, for he will not speak on his own authority, but whatever he hears he will speak, for he will declare the things that are to come. He will take what is mine and declare it to you. All that the Father has is mine; therefore I said, he will take what is mine and declare it to you. (Jn 16:12-16)

In this presentation, the Spirit of Truth is the one who hears and receives what is going on between the Father and the Son, that totality of communication that comes from the Father to the Son, and from the Son to the Father. He is the Spirit of Truth in as much as he makes this communication open to believers, and draws them into it.

The least that can be said is that John is aware of the problem in the rhetoric of faith. He begins to face it by presenting the mystery of the whole in the form of a logic which at least structures a way of thinking about the divine Three. The logic draws its force from a sense of the divine as a field of loving communication that finds its

---

[11]For an excellent treatment of the Holy Spirit in John, see Gary M. Burge, *The Anointed Community. The Holy Spirit in the Johannine Tradition* (Grand Rapids: Eerdmans, 1987).

expression in self-surrender to and for the sake of the other. The Son lives for the Father. The Father gives everything to the Son. Father and Son give everything over to the activity of the Spirit. The Spirit speaks not on his own authority, but from what he has heard from the Son, and by implication, from the Father, to glorify them both.

The dynamics of trinitarian theology have begun. In the wording of this gospel, the divine Three are being presented as a unity which is at once a communion of life, and a community of inter-related divine 'personalities'. Subsequent doctrinal formulation and systematic theology will try to do justice to the Johannine rhetoric.

3. The Trinitarian Narrative

As we have seen, the rhetoric expressive of the divine mystery is varied and complex. Yet behind all this wording in terms of fulfilment, of novelty, of spontaneous celebration, or dramatic image and carefully stated order is something deeper and simpler. It is the story of God.[12] This narrative of the divine mystery and its self-investment in the world's redemption provides the fundamental disclosure of the character of God. For the mystery of the saving God is told essentially in terms of God so loving the world, it is narrated in terms of the *dramatis personae* of Father, Son and Spirit. However, abstract trinitarian theology may have become in its doctrinal mode, there is, at its heart, the simplicity and complexity of a love-story. It tells of how God, out of love, gave what is most intimate to himself, his Son and Spirit, to be involved with this human world as saviour and redeemer.

This fundamental story of grace is told and retold in a variety of contexts: creation, election, liberation, covenant, promise,—all culminating in "these last days", with the sending of the Son and the consequent outpouring of the Spirit. The telling point is always the manner in which a transcendent divine love is going beyond itself in an initiative to form, heal, enrich and finally transform all creation. "In this is love, not that we loved God, but that he loved us . . ." (1 Jn 4:10).

---

[12]For a somewhat similar approach, see R. Jenson, *Triune Identity*, pgs. 1-13.

This narrative contains three stories,—or better, three versions of the one story. Most obviously it is the history of the People of God, the religious biography of Israel and of the Church. Yet there is a second level, explicative of the first; this I would call the "biography of God". Thirdly, as the telling point of both these accounts, there is something far more disclosive: the "divine autobiography". A word on each of these.

First, then, the biblical story is an account of the religious history of God's People. Their story comes to our hearing as it tells how scattered and enslaved groups became a People with a unique historical identity and mission. For they heard the call of the one, true God. They were the Chosen; they knew God by name. They invoked him as their God as he led them to freedom and the land of promise. On this journey they were established as God's own in the covenant of Sinai. It is, of course, a human story of many detours, of faithfulness and failure, of hearts now open, now shut against God's word. The prophets of this Word continually recalled the unfaithful and the wavering to the integrity of the covenant.

This story of the covenant is told in terms of a promise looking to its fulfilment. The New Testament celebrates the culmination of this story when "God visited and redeemed his people." God's People have reached an historical climax in Christ. For God "has raised up a horn of salvation for us in the house of his servant David . . .", in accord with the word spoken by the prophets, the mercy promised to the patriarchs, the oath sworn to Abraham, the promise expressed in the covenant (Lk 1:68-73). The tender mercies of their God lead them to "the dawning of the day from on high" to shine into the darkness of despair and to open the way of peace (78f).

In an obvious sense, this first version of the story is the most broadly accessible. It occurs within the wider world of religious experience, and has a classic status within the great religious experiences of the world. The religious experience in question here is made up of many life-stories . . . Abraham, Moses, David, Isaiah, Jeremiah . . . Mary, Jesus, James, Paul . . . . Yet these are told and retold in the broader sweep of the unfolding communal history of God's People: the twelve tribes of Israel, the holy remnant, the twelve apostles, the disciples, the church . . . . The inner criterion for the meaningfulness of this narrative, the whole reason for its telling, is that it deals with the activity and character of the one, true God.

The story of God's People is tellable because it tells the story of God: the history of the People lives from the 'biography of God'.

The elements of this biography of the gracious God can be quickly recalled, for they are implicit in the history and self-understanding of those who follow his ways. "In the beginning, God created heaven and earth" (Gn 1:1). He transcends all nature and history; and everything that comes from his hand is good. Such a God is not thwarted by evil. The promise of deliverance is always there. He sees the affliction of his people and desires to bring them into the good and broad land flowing with milk and honey (Ex 3:7f). In this process of liberation, he will be "who he will be" (Ex 3:14). What he is doing, and who he is, he reveals in "many and various ways" as he speaks to our fathers by the prophets, but "in these last days", he has spoken to us by a Son (Hb 1:1f). This Son is the revelation of how God so loved the world of his creation (Jn 3:16). The 'Gospel of God' is "the gospel concerning his Son, descended from David according to the flesh, and designated Son of God in power according to the Spirit ... by his resurrection from the dead" (Rom 1:1-4). The "Spirit of him who raised Jesus from the dead" will be the principle of new life for believers in their present experience of mortality (Rom 8:11). To be led by such a Spirit is to enter into a new relationship with God, and know the divine mystery in a free, intimate way, as the invocation, "Abba, Father" expresses it (Rom 8:14f). God is revealed as the one who has destined us in love from the foundation of the world, to be his sons and daughters through Christ Jesus. The story of God is told as the source of "glorious grace" (Eph 1:3-13).

Though this story of God is told in terms of glory and grace, it is not a story of God who is removed from the darkness of human existence. There is no implication that God is ignorant of our sense of distance from the divine. For it is in the human experience of death, guilt, powerlessness, and oppression that this divine story is most telling. This story of God's grace is most striking as it triumphs over the disgrace of the human world. God's Love keeps on being Love, grace is the more radiantly revealed as grace, precisely where the power of sin and evil seems strongest:

> While we were still weak, at the right time, Christ died for the ungodly ... God shows his love for us in that while we were yet

sinners, Christ died for us ... while we were his enemies, we were reconciled to God by the death of his Son. (Rom 5:6-10)

This gracious story, be it simply overheard as 'their story' or variously appreciated as 'the story of God', resonates in different degrees in human consciousness. We might find no telling point where it personally engages us. Nonetheless, for most of us, it is given a hearing as one more good story worth the telling from time to time, at Christmas, perhaps Easter, on the occasion of the death of a loved one, in time of national or social crisis. It is entwined in our lives as part of the religious roots that somehow keep on nourishing our lives. To neglect it would be to risk falling more deeply into spiritual and cultural amnesia. Such a story has its place.

... And it is often kept in its place. It is too good to be true, given the reality of a world that is too disillusioned in its failures and too secure in its achievements to allow for such excesses. Yet there are those who continue to hear this story as The Story. For it alone redeems and fulfills all good human stories.[13] Christians find in the Gospel an intensely involving personal communication. It is 'our story' because in the communion of faith it is 'Your story': The 'You' here is the Universal Lover who has given what is most intimate to himself, the Word and Spirit, to be the form and movement of our human stories. God is no longer the removed 'He' or 'She' or 'It', but the 'I' who speaks and the 'You' who is addressed: "This is my beloved Son. Listen to him." (Mk 9:7) "I am the way, the truth and the life ... " (Jn 14:6). "Father, ... all thine are mine, and mine are thine, and I am glorified in them ..." (Jn 17:10).

Faith means that we hear this story as God's own Word. In this way, the Gospel becomes a kind of divine autobiography, narrating, in the first person, God's self-involvement in the world's salvation. Faith hears this Word 'in the right Spirit', as it is uttered into the human conversation: "You did not receive the spirit of slavery to fall back into fear, but you have received the Spirit of Sonship. When we cry, 'Abba, Father!', it is the Spirit himself bearing witness to our spirit that we are the children of God." (Rom 8:15f) In hearing the

---

[13]See J.R.R. Tolkien, *Tree and Leaf* (London: Unwin, 1964). For a more general treatment, J. Navone and T. Cooper, *Tellers of the Word* (New York: Le Jacq, 1981).

divine story, the believer is drawn into communion with God and made part of this autobiographical unfolding of the divine identity in the world: Jesus rejoices in the Spirit as he says, "I thank thee, Father ... all things have been delivered to me by my Father; and no one knows the Son except the Father, or who the Father is except the Son, and anyone to whom the Son chooses to reveal him." (Lk 10:21f) Thus, the Gospel is the autobiographical unfolding of the Name of God, "I am who I am" (Ex 3:14). The divine identity is communicated to the immediate hearing of faith. The autobiographical character of the Gospel can be illustrated by so much of John's Gospel. Let me give some indication.

First, the Word of the prologue. It is in the beginning with God, and "was God" (Jn 1:1). It reveals the truth of what God is. For this Word becomes flesh and dwells amongst us, full of grace and truth (1:14). In so becoming flesh and dwelling amongst us, this Word enters the narrative form of human existence. The Word in becoming flesh becomes a story: it is spoken and heard in the time and space, in the light and darkness, in the midst of the conflicts, movements and limits of human history. Though "no one has ever seen God, the only Son, who is in the bosom of the Father, has made him known." (1:18)

Secondly, through the Spirit, we hear the divine story as involving our own life-stories: "I have yet many things to say to you but you cannot bear them now. When the Spirit of truth comes, he will guide you into all truth ... he will declare to you the things that are to come." (Jn 16:12ff) The Spirit is the power of the Word-Story to involve all life-stories ... "all truth ... the things that are to come".

Thirdly, there is a vital union existing between Jesus and his disciples. The story of the vine includes the story of the branches (15:1). God's 'autobiographical Word' not only becomes the new commandment, "Love one another as I have loved you" (v. 12), but the great prayer that all will be included in the communion existing between the Father and the Son:

> I do not pray for these only but also for those who believe in me through their word, that they may all be one, even as thou, Father, art in me, and I in thee, that they also may be in us ... (Jn 17:20-24).

If Christian faith is to appreciate the Gospel as the autobiography of the Father expressed in the Word and communicated in the Spirit, Christian ministry invites the ever wider circle of potential hearers to hear this story as their own:

> That which was from the beginning, which we have heard ... concerning the word of life,—the life was made manifest and we saw it and testify to it and proclaim to you the eternal life which was with the Father and which was made manifest to us,—that which we have seen and heard, we proclaim also to you, so that you may have fellowship with us; and our fellowship is with the Father and his Son, Jesus Christ. We are writing that our joy may be complete. (1 Jn 1:1-4)

The joy in question is that of being included in the original story of the oneness existing between the Father and the Son. It results from the praxis of *koinonia* as it narrates the meaning of the divine communion in a way that includes all who will come to believe throughout the whole of human history. Just as Paul can write representatively, "he loved me, and gave himself for me" (Gal 2:20), the Johannine community lives with the assurance that, though "it has not yet appeared what we shall be ... when he appears we shall be like him." (1 Jn 3:2) It is evident that the Gospel is an original love-story opening out to involve all who hear it: "whoever confesses that Jesus is the Son of God, God abides in him and he in God." (1 Jn 4:15) Believers are caught up into the drama of this story of the Father and the Son as they yield to the witness of the Spirit: "By this we know that we abide in him and he in us because he has given us his own Spirit." (1 Jn 4:13)

The basic trinitarian terms of Father, Son and Spirit derive from the 'first person' narrative of the God who so loves the world. They remain the most telling terms of the divine autobiography as it is expressed in the Gospel and intimated in the Spirit. Since it is the story of the eternal life which was with the Father (1 Jn 1:2), of "life to the full" (Jn 10:10), it is told and retold in all the variety of cultural, communitarian, and individual contexts. Taken together, these make the larger story of the pilgrim church, and its journey to the answer of that prayer, "that they be one".

In short, the names of the divine Three which a later doctrinal theology will confess as 'the three divine persons', are first of all the names of the *dramatis personae* in a multi-layered narrative. For the Father, Son, and Spirit determine the identity and story of the People of God, just as they are necessary referents in narrating the gracious story of God. Most of all, they are disclosive terms for God's own self-expression as Love.

Such a story employs, of course, a distinctive range of symbolism. We turn now to this.

4. Trinitarian Symbolism

We will be returning to this point in a later chapter. Here I shall confine myself to a few remarks about the biblical data. In the first place, the most obvious point of all is that we are dealing with symbols when we speak in terms of 'Father', 'Son', and 'Holy Spirit'. This simple point counters the tendency to become dogmatically fixated on a precise dogmatic elaboration of theological meaning. As we shall see, the dogmatic definition of the Trinity resulted from a far more theoretically refined mentality than that found in the world of the New Testament, even granted that John's Gospel begins to face the 'trinitarian problem'. For good or ill, this theoretical 'differentiation of consciousness' led to certain levels of abstraction from the living momentum of the biblical symbols which here concern us. It would be good, of course, if it led to a deeper, clearer, more critical appropriation of the biblical symbols. It would be for ill if it simply replaced this affectively-charged symbolism embedded in the immediacy of experience with dogmatic concepts. Such a paper-thin dogmatism would be caught midway between the first naiveté of undifferentiated thought and the 'second naiveté' (Ricoeur) of an intellectually integrated faith.

Secondly, the three biblical symbols of Father, Son, and Spirit are correlated in a dramatic interplay. They exist in a unified symbol-system meant to disclose the identity and saving presence of the One God. The Father/Son symbolism is most clearly correlated. It discloses a communion of life, mutual knowledge, common will and reciprocal revelation as the Son reveals the Father (Jn 14:9), and the Father acclaims the Son (Mk 9:7) and draws all to him (Jn 6:44, 65).

The Father and the Son, in different but related ways, give the Spirit (Jn 14:26; 20:22f). And the Spirit inspires new relationships to each of them (Rom 8:14ff; Jn 16:12-15). In this dynamic interplay of the symbols of God, the one relational and communitarian divine mystery is evoked.[14]

Thirdly, this interplay of symbols occurs in a dramatic and practical context. Jesus was not a professor of theology, but the agent and embodiment of God's Reign. Even in the conflicts described by the biblical writers, the issue was not whether or not God was merciful or loving, since everyone believed this. It was rather how God was truly present as loving and merciful to his people, and how that presence should be practically honoured. It was at this point that Jesus and his followers were recognized as subversive of the politico-religious structure of society: the sabbath was made for humans, not humans for the sabbath (Mk 2:27; 3:1-6). The sacred symbol of the sabbath was meant to be a sign of God's healing, freeing presence, not a harmful religious imposition. To "be perfect as your Heavenly Father is perfect" (Mt 5:48) was not meant to justify a more exquisite application of the Law; it had to do with acting in the same manner as God acts,—in uncalculating love, forgiveness and generosity (Mt 5:21-47). Such perfection looks to a new realm of praxis in which God is not simply a cultic symbol legitimating an inhumanly structured world. Rather, to invoke the real God is to commit oneself to laying that inhuman world open to the judgment of God's Reign.

In his association with sinners, his works of healing and exorcism, in his call to risk all for the sake of the Kingdom, in all his works and words, Jesus is involving God as the One who legitimizes his activity. He acts in the power of the Holy Spirit. Yet he is accused of flouting the Law, of making himself equal to God,—even of being possessed by the evil spirit (e.g., Mk 3:22-30). The force of his life is interpreted as a threat to the religious and social organization of his society. For Jesus is freeing religion from the sense of God as an oppressor sanctioning the deification of the Law. The God of Jesus, the God who works in him, is intent on the healing and liberation of human beings.

---

[14]For a very suggestive treatment of trinitarian symbolism, see Christian Duquoc, *Dieu différent. Essai sur la symbolique trinitaire* (Paris: Ed. du Cerf, 1977).

In this experience of the liberating presence of God, the interplay of the symbols of the Father, Son, and Spirit occurs. The unredeemed religious imagination is quite content with a patriarchal 'father figure' legitimating established authorities. It manifests itself in the sentimentality of an infantile 'son' ever dependent on such authority, just as it finds a convenient source of rationalization for self-indulgence in an always consoling 'spirit'. Thus unredeemed imagination is challenged by the biblical symbolism of Father, Son, and Spirit, especially as it is so dramatically focused in the cross. By invoking God as "Abba ... Father", with all the implied sense of familiarity and immediacy with God, Jesus is implicating God in his subversive liberating action. His opponents deem his action blasphemous and diabolic. But Jesus claims he is acting in the Spirit's power. The ultimate sin was to confuse the liberating activity of God with the destructive power of Satan (Mk 3:28-29).

In such an interplay of symbols in the context of Jesus' liberating activity, the seeds of a new knowledge of God are planted. The fundamental trinitarian symbolism indicates the liberating character of God. It evokes the manner in which God is personally involved in the drama of human existence as a force for freedom and the giver of life. The immediate expressiveness of such symbolism is far richer than can be expressed in the necessary dogmatic affirmations that will be made later. For the two obvious things are in danger of being forgotten: first, the symbolic character of these designations of God; and secondly, their interplay in illuminating the experience of the liberating presence of the One God. A later chapter, and the section immediately following will throw more light on this trinitarian symbolism.

5. *Trinitarian Experience*

Trinitarian dimensions of Christian experience are implied in each of the three matters so far treated: the rhetorical movement, the narrative structure, the play of symbols. Each of these mediates the fundamental New Testament experience in a distinctive manner. This decisive experience, in turn, stimulates the continuing effort to make it meaningful: cognitively, as a new truth to be known; constitutively, as a new identity to be appropriated; communicatively, in the new community to be formed; effectively, as a new orientation to the whole conduct of life.

This attempt to be fully meaningful works to clarify, promote and communicate the basic experience of God's saving and self-giving presence. For then, as now, it is possible to have the experience but to miss the meaning, or to have the meaning and miss the experience. Theology's task is that of "approaching the meaning so as to restore the experience" in the contribution it can give.[15]

But whose experience is in question? Any response must be rather complicated. For there are at least three inter-related levels of experience brought to expression in the New Testament writings. First, there is that of the early church, in all the variety of its contexts. Secondly, there is the experience of the disciples of Jesus, those who were the first witnesses to his life, death and resurrection. Thirdly, and most mysteriously, there is the experience of Jesus himself. Each of these levels of experience presents complex hermeneutical problems. Nonetheless, a brief suggestion on each might throw some little light on the matter.

A. THE TRINITARIAN EXPERIENCE OF THE CHURCH

It is always problematical to talk about experience as though it were an electric current flowing from one age to another. In fact, all that remains is the living experience of the church now, with its origins in the past. This contains various documents, verbal and symbolic expressions of what was going on 'in those days'. This is not to say that we are locked in an impermeable present unrelated to what went before. For the documents of the past, precisely as they resonate in the present consciousness of Christian faith, disclose a very decisive way of 'being in the world'. They emerge out of a way of feeling, believing, loving and hoping; a way of acting within, for, and even against, that past world. In what they said and did, believed and prayed for, these people who have now gone from the earth, manifested a hope that what they found to be wondrously and liberatingly true might have similar significance for later generations, such as ourselves, so many centuries later. In trying to recapture the quality of their experience as an inspiration for our own experience and reflection, we ask, to what degree was their experience trinitarian?

---

[15]With apologies to T.S. Eliot's *The Dry Salvages!*

In short, how do these documents evidence a religious way of life significantly marked with a trinitarian character? To what degree is there an "historically transmitted pattern of meanings embodied in symbols" by which the believers of that time could be said to "communicate, perpetuate and develop" their experience of life?[16]

The following celebrated definition of the religious components of experience strikes me as valuable for any exploration of the trinitarian dimensions of the experience of the early church. For religious existence is

> A system of symbols which acts to establish powerful, pervasive and long-lasting moods and motivations in men, by formulating conceptions of a general order of existence, and clothing these conceptions with such an aura of factuality that the moods and motivations seem uniquely realistic.[17]

Such a description indicates the four headings under which one might investigate the trinitarian dimensions of early ecclesial experience:

1. *A system of symbols:* here I would point out the interplay of the key trinitarian symbols, Father, Son, and Spirit, as I described it above.

2. *Moods and motivations:* the basic mood is a sense of the 'new'. To believe is to be convinced that a definitive self-manifestation of God has taken place. "In these last days", God's dealings with the world have culminated in the coming of the Son, and in the outpouring of the Spirit. The divine communication, occurring in the Son and Spirit, inspires powerful motivations: we must love as we have been loved and give thanks to the Father through the Son and Spirit as faith reveals a universe of grace, e.g., Col 1:3, 12; 2:6; 3:16f.

3. *Conceptions of a general order of existence:* These are obviously instanced in the initiative of the Father's loving design to unite all things in Christ (Eph 1:3-14). Then, there is the Son who comes as the fulfilment of all God's promises: he is the firstborn of all creation,

---

[16]See Clifford Geertz, "Religion as a Cultural System", *Anthropological Approaches to the Study of Religion,* ed. Michael Banton, ASA Monographs 3, (Tavistock, 1969), pgs. 3ff.

[17]Geertz, *op.cit.,* pg. 3.

the firstborn from the dead, the one in whom all creation coheres, the one in whom the fulness of God dwells (Col 1:15-20). Finally, the Spirit as the principle of Christ's resurrection, will bring about the resurrection of all who believe in him (Rom 8:9ff).

4. *The aura of factuality and unique realism:* Here I would point to the conviction that the Father has been uniquely and exclusively revealed in Christ (Jn 14:9). Then there is the reality of the Spirit: first, a clear sense of having to wait for the Spirit (Jn 14:25ff); then the subsequent assurance that the Holy Spirit has been given as dramatically expressed in Acts 2.

Questions framed in terms of each of these four headings can uncover a great amount of pertinent data in the New Testament documents.[18] Within such a complexity, however, three vivid, quite definite and related impressions of the original biblical experience are evidenced through the symbols, moods and motivations, conceptions of universal order, and convictions of the ultimate truth.[19]

The first is that of 'Spirit'. This is implied in a sense of corporately conscious involvement in a new level of life. This manifests itself in a range of new relationships: to the Father, to Jesus, to the Christian community, to the larger church, to the universe itself, to one's neighbour, to strangers and enemies, to suffering and death.[20] It inspires an exhilarating sense of mission as *The Acts of the Apostles* indicates. For the community of that time shared in the gift of a vital, liberating presence. In this, they find themselves with special gifts and fresh energies, as "to each is given the manifestation of the Spirit for the common good." (1 Cor 12:7) They seem to be breathing a common breath of fresh air, a pervasive atmosphere in which their new being in Christ can grow to its fullest proportions.

The second vivid impression of this original ecclesial experience is that of being addressed through the 'Son'. God's communication "in these last days" culminates in him (Hb 1:1f). The "many and various

---

[18]See Schillebeeckx, *Christ...*, pgs. 112-45.

[19]For a good expression of this point see Bernard Cooke, *Beyond Trinity* (Marquette: University Press, 1969). For an impressive philosophical analysis of scriptural data, see David Brown, *The Divine Trinity* (London: Duckworth & Co., 1986), pgs 52-159. For an alternative view, James P. Mackey, *The Christian Experience of God as Trinity* (London: SCM, 1983).

[20]This world of new relationships is classically expressed in Rom 8-10.

ways in which God spoke to our fathers" have led to the final address. The reality of such a fulfilment breaks out of all the categories available to interpret it. The old wineskins will not hold. The scandal of the cross and surprise of the resurrection leave all available notions such as Son of God, Son of Man, Messiah, prophet, Lord, priest, stretched to the breaking point. For "no one knows the Son except the Father" (Mt 11:27). The unheard of Word has been spoken; the inexpressibly new has happened.

The third vivid impression concerns God as 'Father'. This is the most difficult to express, combining as it does the suggestion of a liberating intimacy with God (Rom 8:15f; 1 Jn 4:7) with an 'unknowing' of the ultimate mystery (Jn 1:18; 1 Jn 4:12; 1 Tim 6:16). Yet such a paradox functions to illuminate an overwhelming positive sense of relationship: in his Spirit, through his Son, Christians know the Father. In the freedom of love (Rom 5:5), they invoke the primordial mystery as 'Abba' (Gal 4:6; Rom 8:15f).God is not seen, but is known as Love in the measure that Christians participate in the loving reality of what God is: "Let us love one another for love is of God; and he who loves is born of God and knows God" (1 Jn 4:7). God's loving relationship with believers is such that nothing in all creation can sunder or impede it (Rom 8:37ff).The dreaded ambiguities of humankind's relationship with the divine now yield to a liberated sense of intimacy, union and invitation: "To have seen me is to have seen the Father" (Jn 14:9).

These three vivid impressions, of 'Father', 'Son', and 'Spirit' respectively, shape any approach to the New Testament data concerning the early church's experience of God. To omit any of these three impressions would do violence to what is documented: God is 'with us' in the Son, 'within' us in the Spirit, all-embracingly 'around' us as the Father. It is true that such experience is mediated by various kinds of witnesses. Here I refer to the experience of the original disciples, the 'eye-witnesses', the living sources of first-hand accounts of what had been seen, heard and touched (1 Jn 1:1-4; Ac 1:21f). To that level of experience we now turn.

B. THE TRINITARIAN EXPERIENCE OF THE DISCIPLES

A recent reconstruction of this fundamental experience seems to me not only to be imaginative but also reasonable. Sebastian Moore [21] deftly suggests the psychology of these first witnesses. In his analysis of human consciousness, he evokes the manner in which the person experiences a longing for the ultimate other as the fulfiller of our search for worth of the individual identity.[22] He then describes the dynamics of guilt as it casts its shadow on our sense of God.[23] The other is then experienced "not as a presence but as a pressure." For the guilty project onto God associations of vindictiveness, domination and threat. The perverted psyche projects a diseased image of God.

Against this horizon, Moore interprets the New Testament data concerning the disciples' experience.[24] The following five points will give some indication of his line of approach.

i. The Ministry of Jesus and the Reality of God: the effect of Jesus' presence and conduct was to free his disciples from their diseased, dehumanizing conceptions of God. What Jesus did and said and was, invited an appreciation of the genuine reality of God:

> They caught from him that sense of the goodness and beauty of nature, of the world, of life, of people, which is part of a guilt-free open relationship with the mystery. Instead of a God who was remote and enigmatic ... there was a loving presence in everything; it brought people together; it promoted human flourishing everywhere.[25]

ii. The Vacuum of the Cross: the Jesus movement collapsed with his execution. In the darkness of the cross, the disciples experienced something far worse than the mystical dark night of the soul, for it was more like the death of God than the divine absence. All the promise contained in their recent perception of God as truly and lovingly involved in human life, came to nothing. Such a God was proven to be powerless in the death of Jesus. Still, the experience of utter darkness created its own possibility. The ground was cleared,

---

[21] *The Fire and the Rose are One* (London: DLT, 1980).

[22] *Op.cit.*, Part One, EROS (2-54). Throughout, this treatment is a striking application of Lonergan's "intentionality analysis."

[23] *Op.cit.*, Part Two, THE SHADOW, pgs. 55-73.

[24] Pgs. 80-96.

[25] Pg. 80.

as it were, to receive a new divine revelation and to have an 'original experience' of the divine reality. Their former distorted sense of God would be brought to nought, for in a psychological sense, as Moore dramatically says, Jesus "buried" God for them: the collapse, the darkness, the emptiness was the space in which the radically new could appear.

iii. The Displacement of the Divinity into Jesus: when Jesus reappears as the Risen One, he becomes the centre of a new God-consciousness. As a power stronger than defeat and death, he is the focus of a radically new experience of God. In him the true reality of God is unveiled. This aspect of the disciples' experience is at the root of the subsequently formulated belief in his divinity.

iv. The Extension of God into Jesus: the Risen Jesus is not merely the focus of the new God-consciousness. The original mystery of God soon reappears after the initial displacement. For God is now revealed as the loving and life-giving force that raised Jesus—as the Father revealed in the Son, as the God who by extending what he is into Jesus, now enters human consciousness as the Love that keeps on being Love, despite, and in, all human limits. Thus, the crucified and risen One begins to appear in the light of this God.

v. The Cyclic Life-Flow: the new consciousness of being involved with God-in-Jesus results from an experience of mysterious vitality. It connects God with Jesus and becomes the field of shared life in which believers are united with him. This experience of a wonderfully new vitality grounds the disciples' awareness of the 'Holy Spirit', uniting Father, Son, and themselves.

Thus, Moore imaginatively evokes the disciples' experience of the death and resurrection of Jesus as a displacement and extension of God, and as a field of dynamic oneness. He feels he is indicating an approach "to a grassroots derivation of the Trinity". The following words are a good summary:

> This grass-roots derivation of the Trinity depends on the pre-understanding of the God-connection. For the understanding, the meaning of 'God' is shaped by a person's psychological state. Thus, while a person is still in guilt, 'God' is to him the jealous, all-dominating one, the threat to man's fragile existence. For the

disciples of Jesus, this 'God' dies with the collapse of the Jesus movement. The 'God' they next encounter, the next divine affective focus, is Jesus as a power stronger than death. As the meaning of this sinks in, they are able to experience the original God not *as* jealous or domineering, but as loving, as bringing us into immortal life. Finally, the sense of the sheer vitality of God can burst upon the soul and be named 'Holy Spirit'. Thus the matrix of the images of the divine persons is the 'infinite connection' as it undergoes the transformation of the encounter with the risen Jesus.[26]

Though such exegesis is evocative rather than textually analytical, it does seem a reasonable account of what was going on and well-attuned to the biblical data. As an effort to retrieve the interiority of the disciples' experience, it goes some way in showing how such an experience is foundational for the wider and later community of the church. The experiential impetus which created the New Testament trinitarian rhetoric and found expression in the narrative structure and interplay of symbols is implied.

But there is a third factor, the most basic of all to the Trinitarian character of the New Testament experience. This is the experience of Jesus himself.

C. THE TRINITARIAN EXPERIENCE OF JESUS

Jesus' own 'experience', in a general sense, has been touched upon in the different ways we have approached the scriptural foundations of trinitarian faith. The New Testament rhetoric of the first section draws its creativity from the explanation of the Risen One as "he interpreted to them in all the scriptures the things concerning himself" (Lk 24:27). Then, the narrative structure is most intense as a kind of divine autobiography, with Jesus as the 'telling point' (Mt 11:27ff; Jn 1:14, 18). Further, the trinitarian symbols of Father, Son, and Spirit interact in the conduct of his life as he proclaims and makes present the Reign of God. Finally, the manifold experience of the church has its origins in his sense of himself as uniquely related to God in the advent of the Kingdom.

[26]Pgs. 83ff.

But since Jesus himself wrote no New Testament text, it is the interpreter's task to discern how the subjectivity of Jesus' experience of God is expressed in the words of those who did write those texts. Out of their own experience, as they remembered the whole reality of his presence to them, they do give a number of indications of what they knew or presumed his experience to be. What are these?

The short answer points to the New Testament data concerning Jesus' exclusive communion with God as "my Father" (e.g., Mk 14:36), and, as relative to this, his sense of being possessed by the Holy Spirit (e.g., Lk 4:18). These two facets of his experience are inter-related; his sense of identity and mission, as, for instance, the baptism pericope of Mark expresses it: " ... Immediately he saw the heavens opened and the Spirit descending on him like a dove; and a voice came from heaven, 'Thou art my beloved Son.' "(Mk 1:10-11).

Though Christian experience is marked by a share in this Sonship and by a possession of this Spirit (Rom 8:14ff), it is never at the expense of the exclusive, unique quality of Jesus' place in the mystery of God, nor of his experience of this. For the shared Christian experience depends on what is utterly unique in Jesus. Although his distinctive style of addressing God as "Abba" carried over into the prayer of the early Christian communities (Gal 4:6; Rom 8:15), his experience and his relationship to the Father is consistently recalled as original and distinctive. The evangelists indicate features of this distinctiveness in the disjunction, "My Father" and "Your Father" (Mt 11:27; Jn 20:17; Lk 6:36; 12:30ff; Mk 11:25; Mt 23:9). Not even when he is teaching his disciples to pray does he say, "Our Father" (Lk 11:2; Mt 6:9). The incommunicability of his relationship to the Father, and his experience of this, are thus suggested.[27]

Behind such exalted instances of theological expression is a memory and interpretation of the prayer of Jesus. Luke documents this in a remarkable way. It is precisely as he prays that Jesus is caught up in the experience of the descent of the Spirit, and the Father's claiming him as "my beloved Son" (Lk 3:21f). His works of healing and his gestures of forgiveness lead to or derive from his prayer (5:16). A night in "the prayer of God" (6:12) preceded his choice of the twelve. Likewise, his solitary prayer provokes the

---

[27]W. Kasper, *The God of Jesus Christ*, pgs. 173ff.

conversation with his disciples about his identity and leads to the prophecy concerning his suffering and glorification (9:18). While he prays, the mystery of his identity radiates forth in the transfiguration (9:28-36). From the depths of his prayer, he teaches his disciples to pray (11:1). In prayer, he surrenders to the Father's will (22:42ff). Through his prayer, he mediates his Father's forgiveness (23:34); and in the prayer of abandonment to the Father, he dies (23:46).

If such instances of praying indicate the evangelists' interpretation of the interiority of Jesus' experience of his identity, of his mission, of his relationship to the Father, so too are other features of his life.

The world of the parables is the product of his unique consciousness. He translates in the routine symbols of everyday the mystery that is at work in him. The Kingdom is at hand as an impossible new chance for all. The times have reached their fulfilment. The presence of limitless mercy and self-giving love affects seemingly solid realities of the previous world with the unutterably new. The horizon in which his experience of the world occurred, the distinctive parabolic expression of such experience,—both disclose the deepest mystery of his consciousness. The parables are deeply ironic invitations to see the world as he sees it: a strange world no doubt, to his fellow Jews, when Samaritans could be good, when bankers could write off debts, when a patriarch could make himself ridiculous by feting the return of a worthless son, when a shepherd could leave the ninety-nine sheep to look for the one that was lost . . . .

In this world of limitless grace, Jesus moves with complete assurance and authority. He does not hesitate to contest the teachings of the accredited religious authorities (Mt 7:29; 12:1-14), even when it dealt with the intensely sacred symbols of law, the temple, the Sabbath itself. The authority of his presence was such that he could call the disciples he desired (Mk 3:13), to leave everything, even to the point of risking degrading execution (Mk 8:34; 10:28). The unique relationship he enjoyed with the Father, involved him in compassionate solidarity with outcasts,—with all who were offered no hope by the religious and political institutions of his day (Mt 9:10-35). His exclusive relationship with God involved him uniquely in the lives of others. If Jesus' experience as Son was founded on an exclusive communion with the Father, it led him, step by step through his life, to an inclusive relationship with all. He experienced his identity involving the ultimate destiny of "the many" in the formation of the New Covenant.

The Gospels record, as correlative to Jesus' exclusive relationship to the Father, his awareness of being possessed and guided by the Spirit. As we mentioned, the baptismal narratives most vividly portray this. The presence of the Spirit in his life is, in fact, suggested in a number of ways. A valuable instance occurs when he is accused of being possessed by the evil spirit. He repels this accusation as at least running very close to blaspheming against the Holy Spirit working through him, with its irredeemable consequences (Mk 3:22-30; Lk 11:20; Mt 12:28ff). Further, Jesus is depicted as "full of the Spirit", coming "in the power of the Spirit", as declaring that the Spirit is "upon him" empowering him to proclaim liberation for the oppressed (Lk 4:1-19). In this Spirit, he rejoices and celebrates his unique intimacy with the Father (Lk 10:21f). In this Spirit, he casts out evil spirits (Lk 11:20). His consciousness is that of the one in whose very conception the Spirit was active (Lk 1:35), whose whole life looked to the communication of the Spirit (Lk 24:49; Ac 1:5-8), which he himself fully possessed (Ac 2:33).[28]

One author summarizes his lengthy investigations into the experience of Jesus in these words,

> Jesus thought of himself as God's Son and as anointed by the eschatological Spirit, because in prayer he experienced God as Father, and in ministry he experienced the power to heal which he could only understand as the power of the end-time and as inspiration to proclaim a message which he could only understand as the gospel of the end-time.[29]

The trinitarian conception of God is, then, not implausibly related to the experience of Jesus himself. At the heart of trinitarian doctrine is not Jesus' unconsciousness or ignorance of himself, even if he was not teaching trinitarian theology! Rather the doctrine is the conceptual unfolding of his conscious identity and of the mystery enacted through him.

---

[28]See James D.G. Dunn, *Jesus and the Spirit* (London: SCM, 1975).
[29]*Op.cit.*, pg. 67.

And so, in three different but related ways, we have spoken of the 'trinitarian experience',—that of the church, that of the disciples, and that of Jesus himself. Such experience underlies the interplay of trinitarian symbols as Father, Son, and Holy Spirit, just as such an interplay lives from a narrative of what God is, and what God wills, with its reference to the three *dramatis personae* in the 'autobiography' of God. And this is set in the larger context of rhetoric through which the early church, in a creative and consistent manner, sought to word its perception of the God of Love.

3
Mystery and Definition

In the last chapter I tried to indicate how the rich fund of the original Christian experience blossomed into a special kind of trinitarian rhetoric. Such rhetoric was deeply marked by the dynamic structure of the narrative of God's Love, expressed in the Son and communicated in the Spirit. This story of grace was, in turn, deeply affected by the interplay of the trinitarian symbolism.

1. The Doctrinal Mode

To move now to the consideration of trinitarian doctrine gives the impression of entering rather suddenly into a different world of feeling, thought, and expression. It is a different religious tone. The expression is far more austere and technical. For the church was then feeling the need to word its convictions of the culminating self-disclosure of God with the precision befitting a precise answer to newly formulated, precise questions. The style of the biblical rhetoric which appeared so spontaneous and creative, so expansive in different directions, is now disciplined into an intellectual pattern of expression. The Gospel story of God's self-giving Love can appear as almost having stopped until the terms are clarified,—or, as some have feared, replaced by an abstract, alien vocabulary. The interplay of the threefold symbolism of Father, Son, and Spirit, which had been so evocative of the sense of communion, self-giving, and the intimate and dramatic dialogue between Father and Son, is now pinned down in the technicalities of person and nature, procession and relationship. The experience of what God so evidently was "for us and our salvation" has now yielded to questions concerning what the divine reality is in and to itself. The sense of God's self-communication has ended by provoking questions about the kind of self that God has to give, and how the giver is truly in the gift.

Why was this new mode of thought and expression necessary? The short answer can be easily given: the first simplicity of the original confession of faith had to become acquainted with the complexity of definition if it was to keep its original meaning. Such definition aimed to overcome confusion, actual or potential, if the essential Christian conviction of God's Love in Christ—which nothing in all creation could impede or diminish—was to be protected. For faith was not to be spared the challenge of its history. It has to pay the price of obeying the Lord's command. "Go, therefore, and make disciples of all nations, baptizing them in the name of the Father and of the Son and of the Holy Spirit." (Mt 28:19)

The first missionary expansion of the church was in the Greco-Roman world. Historically speaking, it could hardly have been otherwise. Theologically, one may well discern the hand of providence. Culturally speaking, it was a matter of mind catching up to faith to demand its own authenticity. The Greco-Roman world had at its disposal systems and techniques which would enable the early church to clarify its essential truths, to break free of mythological distortions, and to begin a statement of its meaning which eventually would be a classic resource for the expression of faith in all cultures. Other cultures, if Islam had not prevented an expansion eastward, may have made a different option when confronted with the Johannine triad, of Christ "the way, the truth and the life" (Jn 14:6). For example, a culture deeply marked by Buddhism or Taoism would presumably have explored the Gospel and tested the truth of it by assimilating it first of all as "the way". If, perhaps, it had come to expression in a more animist setting, say, in Africa or Oceania, the leading notion might well have been "the Life". But in the dominant concerns of a more philosophically differentiated culture, the Gospel and the mystery of God it communicated, emerged fundamentally as "the truth". To this purpose, two major literary languages offered a rich and subtle vocabulary as a resource; the skills of rhetoric had been cultivated; the laws of logic had been formulated. Above all, there was in existence a philosophical tradition, the creation and vehicle of that intellectual curiosity which was the special glory of the Greek mind. Take all this together with the profound sense of political crisis in the Roman Empire itself, threatened from within and without, and you have the context in which Christianity was impelled to articulate its fundamental vision.

2. The Problematic Character of Trinitarian Faith

In the light of the questions which would now be put to Christian faith, the mystery of the 'Three' emerged as problematical. Was it a perversion of the essential faith of Israel in the oneness of God? Was it a relapse into the old polytheism from which the great philosophers have broken free? How could the One absolute reality allow within itself that kind of origination and distinction implied in the very terms Father, Son, and Spirit? How could this Jesus, the focus of the Christian experience of God, be the true revelation of God in a way that would neither dissipate his genuinely human reality nor undercut the Christian claim that he is God's eternal Son?

Answers to such questions had to be found if the integrity of faith was to be kept. Without some kind of definition of terms, the original, traditional rhetoric of faith would become inflated to the point of being merely 'rhetoric' in the weakest sense, increasingly at a loss to assure the experience and the meaning of God's self-gift. Without a concentration on these issues and clarification of them, the fundamental narrative of faith would not be worth the telling— or be benignly accepted as one more interesting version of the immemorial accounts of how the gods had visited the earth.

To refuse to pose the most radical questions and to answer them by affirming what was understood as true and by denying what was not, the formerly inviting symbols of God's living presence amongst us would slowly become mere ciphers, human ways of speaking or the divine ways of appearing which have nothing to do with what God really is like in terms of the names in which Christians were baptized. The real God would remain undisclosed and, more importantly, uninvolved. Without this effort to clarify, to affirm and define, the living experience of faith would turn in on itself to become merely a loftly emotion nourished by a noble myth, leaving the enquiring mind unconvinced that there was anything special in the revelation of faith.

So Christian wisdom had to find a new mode of discourse. Without renouncing the original, vivid, rhetorical, narrative and symbolic expression, it had to go beyond it—in some way. The kerygmatic and the doxological had to make room for orthodoxy. This would come to expression in the dogmatic statement if the preaching and prayer of the church were to be protected and promoted. For the reality which the faith of the church witnessed to was not just any kind of truth. It was the saving mystery of God's self-giving Love. To celebrate that demanded, first of all, breaking away from the confusions of mythological expression by employing the techniques of a philosophical control of meaning. Only in that way would what was meant be clearly stated. But this would lead eventually to the point where faith would have to break out of the prevalent techniques and terms of philosophical meaning to express the distinctive reality of its own vision. For such faith dealt with a divine Lover involved in a divine self-giving. This, in turn, looked to the self that God had to give. Here was the final mystery, the realm that no human philosophy could pretend to explain nor human concept express.

The situation is well summed up in the words of an eminent patristic scholar:

> From the earliest moments of theological reflection it was assumed that Jesus Christ was true God as well as true man ... the problem which the Fathers had to solve was not whether he was God, but how, within the monotheistic system which the church inherited from the Jews, preserved in the Bible, and pertinaciously defended against the heathen, it was still possible to maintain the unity of God while insisting on the deity of the one who was distinct from God the Father.[1]

The dawning doctrinal responsibility of the church of the first few centuries did not mean a gradual abstraction from the concrete living of Christian faith. The Bible was still the fundamental document. The baptismal liturgy was celebrated "in the name of the

---

[1] G.L. Prestige, *God in Patristic Thought*, (London, SPCK, 1952), pg. 76.

Father, Son and Holy Spirit" (Mt 28:19; Didache 7). It was a common enough argument against Christians of heterodox Gnostic, Modalist, and later Arian tendencies, to point to their practice of baptism in the threefold name. Then, too, the early trinitarian forms of the Creed, used in such baptismal liturgies, the most familiar being the so-called 'Apostles' Creed', stressed the trinitarian character of God. Certainly in the second century, there is evidence of a settled type of trinitarian doxology, as Justin's *Apologia* (1:65) and *The Martyrdom of Polycarp* indicate.[2]

The presence of the divine had been experienced in Jesus; his identity was understood as divine: he was understood to be uniquely "from God", the Father. The problem was that of extending the inherited notion of the unity of God to include what had been revealed in Christ. The Christological point was understood to be the crucial issue. This would have inevitable consequences for understanding the divinity of the Spirit. Once the revolution in theological conceptuality had been tested in the confession of Jesus as Son, and one with the Father, the case of the divine status of the Spirit could be dealt with.

In the post-apostolic writings, there is no evidence of Jesus being gradually elevated to divine status. He is always presented on the inside of the divine sphere, as belonging to the divine realm and descending from it. Indeed, there is the perverse witness of the early phenomenon of Docetism: Jesus was so demonstrably divine that, it was alleged, he could be human only in appearance. Ignatius of Antioch in his Letter to the Trallians firmly underscored the true humanity of Jesus as he wrote, "Christ was really born, ate and drank, was really persecuted by Pontius Pilate, was really crucified and died, really rose from the dead . . ." Again, despite the pervasive Gnostic conviction of innumerable mediators of and gradations in the divine, the early Christians were quite sure that their redeemer did not belong to some lower order of reality. Indeed, the oldest surviving sermon of this era (Clement 2, 1, 1f) exhorted believers to think of Jesus Christ "as of God" so as not to belittle their salvation. In *The Martydom of Polycarp,* the oldest surviving account of martyrdom, we read, "It will be impossible for us to forsake Christ

---

[2]See B. de Margerie, *La Trinité chrétienne dans l'histoire* (Beauchesne: Paris, 1973), pgs. 90-98.

... or to worship any other. For him, being the Son of God, we adore, but the martyrs, we cherish." This sense of the divine status of Christ is even expressed in the earliest pagan report we have, for it describes Christians in liturgical prayer singing "a hymn to Christ as though to God" (Pliny); whereas the earliest Christian record of such prayer is addressed to Christ, "Maranatha, our Lord, Come!" (1 Cor 16:22).[3]

3. Faith Seeking its Appropriate Expression

In the centuries that followed, a grammar and vocabulary had to be devised to protect and promote the original simplicity of the church's faith. In the increasingly complicated context, three types of dialogue are clearly distinguishable.

The first results from the missionary outreach of the early church. It was essentially apologetic. For it had to explain itself within the Jewish tradition so as not to deny the oneness and unity of God. At the same time, it had to witness to the reality of the Son as the fulfilment of all that had gone before. Linked to this first phase and type of dialogue is a similar relationship to the profoundest currents of the Greek philosophical tradition (the Platonic and Neo-Platonic philosophies) and to its more superficial manifestations (Gnosticism). Here, Justin Martyr is a paradigmatic figure.

The second phase of dialogue occurred more within the church. This is the dogmatic period. The principal concern now would be to define authentic faith within the context of its own inner problematic. As this context of Christian reflection grew more sophisticated, questions were posed that must be answered if the communication of faith was to be honest and alive to its own reality. A variety of theological positions emerged in the discussion. Some of these would be identified as essentially destructive to the faith and divisive of the unity of the church. Here the paradigmatic figure was Athanasius.

The third phase, which I will term 'theological', is marked by the emergence of a Christian system of theology. Now the faith of the

---

[3]See the very valuable work, J. Pelikan, *The Emergence of the Catholic Tradition* (100-600) (Chicago: University of Chicago Press, 1971), pg. 173.

church is not only reflecting on the data of Scripture, but also on another type of data, those definitions of its own truth expressed in the Councils, especially those of Nicaea, Constantinople, and Chalcedon. Here the paradigmatic figures are the Cappadocians in the East and Augustine in the West.

I will make a brief remark, then, on each of these three phases, the Apologetic, the Dogmatic and the Theological.

4. The Apologetic Phase

As I mentioned above, in this early phase which extended practically to the end of the third century, the vitality of Christian faith manifested itself on many fronts. It was expanded through its confrontation with Judaism and Gnosticism and through its conflicts with various other external adversaries.

The first point is largely terminological. A very early Jewish-Christian way of speaking about the reality of the Son and the Spirit in the Christian experience of salvation was to term them 'angels'. Such a term connoted beings uniquely sent by the one God for his saving purposes. Various scholars have underlined the concrete meaning of such a term. It was not necessary to conceive of such beings as created. That would have been an answer to a question that had not been asked. Rather, the meaning of such angelic realities was that they were 'personal' communications of God, uniquely revelatory of the divine saving action. As an available general terminology, 'angel theology' served a purpose within the Jewish theological tradition. But it was necessarily provisional. For it could survive only as long as it permitted an ambiguity which, in the exchanges of Greek dialectic, would be more and more exposed.[4]

Understandably, this kind of expression disappeared from the Christian discourse quite quickly. It was never quite clear whether these angels were divine or not; indeed, the inescapable implication was that, as angels, Word and Spirit were always on a lower level of

---

[4]For example, in this early theology, Michael was sometimes identified with the Word, and Gabriel with either the Word or the Spirit. In the Shepherd of Hermas [VIII, 1, 1-2], we find one of the clearest expressions of this terminology: the "glorious angel" means the Word of God.

divine reality than God himself. Most of all, such terminology allowed for no meaningful distinction between Word/Son and Spirit. Though it allowed for the New Testament datum that Word and Spirit were 'sent' from God, it looked to the invention of another term which could be applicable to the Father as well. Three what? Not angels, ... then what? Three hundred years would go by before that term, 'person' would be found with its Latin and Greek equivalents.[5]

But while some archaic terms were being tried and found wanting, others were being increasingly exploited in the development of a genuine trinitarian theology. Most notable of these is that of *Logos* (Word) and its most notable exponent was Justin Martyr (+165). He took the term from John's Gospel and aligned it to both the manifestations of the Word of God in the history of Israel and the classic philosophical expositions of Logos in Platonic, Stoic and Jewish-philosophical (Philo) reflection. Through such a move, he could both commend the essence of Christianity as the knowledge of the Word Incarnate and relate it thereby to the Word by which everything was made, the Word which is intimated in all truth, which contains the whole of the moral law, and mediates all knowledge of God, the Word that had instructed the prophets of Israel and illumined the philosophers of Greece, and become incarnate in Jesus Christ. Such a theology was in the most literal sense 'dialogical'. The Word Incarnate was presented as already the essential element in a conversation linking Jerusalem and Athens. Christianity was necessarily a universalizing religion. And even if the presentation of Christ as God's Son struck pagan contemporaries as regressively mythological, Logos theology had its answer in that the divine sonship was linked to the presence of the logos within the divinity, in a derivation which was not physical but spiritual and on the level of mind.[6]

This type of theology was not without its risks. Logos theology linked the biblical doctrine of creation with the prevalent Middle Platonism. In this brand of Platonic thinking, the divine is so transcendent that it could be related to the created world only through a hierarchy of mediators. The Logos might be pre-eminent

[5] De Margerie, *La Trinité chrétienne*, pg. 99f.
[6] Alois Grillmeier, *Christ in the Christian tradition*, vol I, (Oxford: Mowbrays, 1975), pg. 109.

in this mediating role, but there lies the question: does it belong to the sphere of God or to the domain of creation? If it belongs to the divine sphere, the gap between God and creation remains. If it belongs to the created realm, the Logos is not divine in any real sense, and Christian faith is essentially undermined.[7]

In many ways, this would be the basic dispute occupying the dogmatic phase of reflection that would follow. How could the Word be from God without being less than God? The development of Logos theology clarified the question and cleared the ground for the answer that would be given.

The philosophical confidence of the early Apologists was replaced by a more conservative turn with Irenaeus of Lyons (+202). This is not to deny the brilliance of his sense of the 'economia' as the divine 'datum' with its own unity and development focused in the mystery of Christ. His profound Christocentric emphasis was perhaps his greatest contribution, (and the most neglected in the subsequent history of theology). His principal apologetic aim, as we see it instanced in the *Adversus Haereses,* is to counter the Gnostic influence that had begun to contaminate Christian thought in increasingly subtle forms.[8]

It is wrong to give the impression that Gnosticism was a homogeneous body of thought. Some of its features, however, do stand out: it seems to have arisen out of a sense of a deeply disrupted world-order. The individual self was experienced as lost in a universe which offered, of itself, no coherent meaning or value to life. This experience of lostness was deeply marked by a sense of dualism. The lower realms of existence were in the thrall of an evil, dark, material principle which works to keep the individual separated from the true self. This true self is attained only by rising, step by step, from the darkness and materiality of evil to the light, the divine, the good principle.But the realization of this true self is conditioned by a vast, gradated system of intermediaries emanating from the unknown and unreachable first principle. The gradual ascent to self-fulfilment was understood to be through a special kind of esoteric knowledge, a

---

[7]A very useful and concise reference in this whole area is John J. O'Donnell, *Trinity and Temporality* (Oxford University Press, 1983). See especially pgs. 33ff.

[8]See de Margerie's judicious comment in *La Trinité chrétienne* . . . , pgs. 100-111.

gnosis revealed to the initiate through the activity of some higher agent: through successive illuminations, the true gnostic escapes imprisonment in a degraded kind of existence and achieves spiritual fulfilment.

The gnostic manner of interpreting God and the world, with God unattainably removed and the world radically evil, absorbed into itself a good deal of Christian doctrine, above all that of the Trinity. This was notably the case of Valentinus with his extraordinarily complex, and, perhaps, still largely misunderstood, doctrine.[9] The main thrust of Irenaeus' effort was to disengage the trinitarian mystery from such mystifying entrapment and to present it in terms of God's self-involvement in a basically good, though fallen, world of divine creation. He keeps faith focused in the 'economy'. That, for him, is the safe ground, a world away from some extraneous and alien gnostic system. The Word and Spirit are simply the two hands of God in the work of salvation.[10] The differentiation of the three appears mainly in this operation 'ad extra', though some form of underlying Trinity is implied, at least inasmuch as God is eternally living with that Word and the Spirit through which he created and redeemed the world. Later theology will, in fact, employ some of the categories and vocabulary employed in gnostic thought, such as procession, some aspects of the 'psychological analogy', and even the word, *homoousios*. But this was certainly not the direction that Irenaeus took. He discouraged such speculation. Only God could reveal the manner in which the Word/Son originated within the divine mystery. It was not given to the human mind to have such knowledge. Irenaeus accented the 'givenness' of the divine gift in the fact of the 'economia'.

This temporary retreat from philosophical exploration of the data of faith into a more immediate sense of the data of the divine three occurring in the 'economia' of salvation eventually exacted its own price. Trinitarian faith continued to express itself in some intellectual form. The alternative was between doing this with precision or to let confusion grow, as theology fell victim to the unrecognized philo-

---

[9] See de Margerie, *op. cit.*, pgs. 102-105.
[10] *Adversus Haereses IV, Praef.*

sophical presuppositions of the language and culture that moulded it. The diagnosis of this situation characterized what we have termed 'the dogmatic phase' of trinitarian theology.

5. The Dogmatic Phase

By accenting the importance of the 'economia' in the face of gnostic speculation, Irenaeus and others like him were in fact holding to the ancient conviction of the 'Monarchia' of the One God: the one God was the sole ruling power, the one creator of the cosmos, the one sovereign presence guiding history. Such a God transcended the world of time and was intrinsically beyond human comprehension. In short, this was the inchoate philosophy common to both the Old and the New Testament. It struck at the heart of any dualistic or even polytheistic tendency. Problems arose when the attempt had to be made to bring the 'Monarchia' and the 'economia' of the three divine persons together. Were the 'three' of the economia merely modes of successive manifestations of the One? Or, if there was a genuine plurality in the One God, how was it to be conceived? Did the affirmation of God as Love imply a real self-giving?

Such questions could not be simply answered by referring to the prime authority of Scripture. For that only revealed the problems involved in interpreting the biblical word. Theological questions raised the hermeneutical considerations of exegesis. Indeed, it soon became evident that there were four types of biblical texts relevant to the emerging questions of trinitarian theology: those of 'adoptionist' tone, e.g., the baptismal pericopes of the Synoptics; those expressing Jesus' oneness with the Father, an especially Johannine emphasis; those stating some clear distinction between Jesus and the Father, especially when Jesus is 'sent' by the Father; and finally, those texts of John's Gospel and Proverbs 8 which imply that Jesus derives from the being of the Father as his Word and Wisdom.[11] With dogmatic hindsight we understand now that the last type of text would be fundamental to the trinitarian definitions and the theology out of which they arose. But in the discussion of that time, appeal to

---

[11] Pelikan, *op. cit.*, pgs. 175-200.

the word of Scripture proved no simple solution—just as it would not be in any later age.

One way of escaping such impending complexity was to occupy the firm ground of the 'Monarchia', and make that the organizing principle of theology. This would mean stressing the identity of the Father and the Son, and mitigating any implication of distinction between them. Compared to the 'low and mean views' of mere adoptionism, as with Paul of Samosata, this was a superficially attractive position. Not only did it conserve the inheritance of Israel and the New Testament on the oneness of God, not only did it retain the divine status of Jesus, but it could nourish itself on the profound obscurity of such theological statements as 'God was born', 'God became man', 'God suffered', 'God died'. Such statements as these were readily found in the tradition and could always be supported by the New Testament passages that implied or stated Jesus' oneness with the Father. In such a context, it was easy to move to a position where the Father, Son and Spirit were merely successive appearances of the One transcendent God. This timid theological beginning was pungently described by an early author in the following words:

> There exists one and the same being called Father and Son, not one deriving from the other, but himself from himself, nominally called Father and Son according to the changing of times; and that this one is he who appeared to the Patriarchs, submitted to birth from a virgin, and conversed among men. On account of his birth ... he confessed himself to be the Son to those who saw him; while to those who could receive him, he did not hide the fact that he was the Father.[12]

This naive 'modalism' was in some measure refined by Sabellius. He developed the notion of the one God, the Son-Father, with one essence but three energies. To explain this, he proposed the analogy of the sun with its three kinds of influence, as it gave light, caused warmth, and affected the stars. Tertullian and Hippolytus of Rome energetically refuted this kind of position since it made nonsense of

---

[12] Hippolytus of Rome, *Haereses* 9.10.11 (*CGS* 26, 244f).

the realism of Christian faith as it found expression in the 'economia'; indeed, it seemed to be "driving out the paraclete and crucifying the Father". A later theology might well say that the dialogical realism of the divine three in the events of the history of salvation is undermined if it is reduced to a monologue, in which the only speaker, God, remains radically unknown behind the masks of his appearances. Love would not in this case mean a real self-disclosure. In fact, in the early part of the third century, the reaction of Christian realism consisted mainly in stressing the biblical passages where distinction is expressed or implied within the divine reality, especially when some kind of 'dialogue' is implied between the divine *dramatis personae,* e.g., Gen 18:1-7; Ps 110:1; Hb 1:5-13.

There is no doubt a sound instinct in this form of doctrinal or 'economic' realism. For Modalism tended to subvert the real sense of God's self-involvement as Father, Son, and Spirit, as though these three were not really the divine agents of our salvation. In countering this sense of unreality, concerned Christian thinkers had to do more than cite a series of biblical texts stressing distinction in the Godhead, or merely point to the threefold name of God in baptismal liturgy. They had to come up with a better way of affirming the threefold reality of the God of their faith if the weak statements of Modalism were to be dealt with.

Both Tertullian (+223) in the West and Origen (+254) in the East addressed themselves to the problem. The former saw the problem clearly, and in his attempt at a solution decisively influenced the Latin vocabulary of trinitarian theology, e.g., *tres personae, una substantia.* When it came to giving a realist expression of how the One God could be really one and yet be compatible with the really distinguishable divine persons, Tertullian's answer was itself limited. Despite his realist instinct, his solution remained in the domain of metaphor working within the tradition of Stoic physics. The naive supposition was that all reality was necessarily corporeal, and that the cosmos was a vast material organism. Within such a world-view, Tertullian could do no better than present the divine reality as a great organism, undivided in itself, and alive with one divine power. Hence the three had to be organically related parts of the one divine substance. There are distinctions in the divinity which underlie the 'economia', a kind of concentration or 'distribution' of the divine reality in distinct, inter-related manners. His metaphors for the distinction between Father, Son, and Spirit are given variously as the root, stem and fruit; as the sun with its light and warmth; the source, the river and the stream. However evocative such metaphors might be, they in fact offer no critical solution to the problem that had been identified. Whilst such metaphors focused the real intent of faith, they still awaited the intellectual unfolding of Christian faith.[13]

By contrast, the great Origen contributed a specifically philosophical solution to the trinitarian problem of unity and distinction. The metaphorical materialism of Tertullian was succeeded by the philosophical idealism of Origen: the real was what could be philosophically conceived and distinguished. He used the conceptual system of Middle Platonism, which asserted that the One and the Good was the Divine. Origen identified this with the Father, *the God*. The Logos emanated from this One, and by participating in its goodness, imaged it forth and derived from its being. When Origen identified this Logos with the Son, the implication was that the Son is divine, but only in a secondary and derivative manner. A derivatively divine status was assigned also to the Holy Spirit.

Within the framework of such a philosophy, the Son and Spirit are necessarily understood as less divine than the Father. Though a certain conceptual harmony can be established between Christian belief in the Son and Spirit coming forth from the Father and this kind of emanationist thought, a dissonance occurs in the realm of Christian realism: for Christ, too, is Lord, to be adored without qualification. His "coming from the Father" does not imply he is less divine. Still, he is divine in a diminished sense because he is Son. True, Origen was using the best philosophical instrument available; but the new wine, once more, could not be contained in the old bottles. Christianity was looking for something more than a subordinationist expression of the Son's coming forth from the Father.

Although such an unwitting reduction of Christian faith provoked the necessity for Christian faith to define its own real terms, subsequent theology would owe a great deal to the great genius of Alexandria. In contrast to the more primitive speculation of Tertullian, Origen upheld the spiritual nature of the divine reality and

---

[13] J.C. Murray, *The Problem of God* (Yale University Press: New Haven, 1962), pg. 36.

the eternal and spiritual mode of the Son's coming forth from the Father.[14] Yet, for Origen, the Son was distinguished from the Father because he derived from him, emanated from him, participated in the divinity in some secondary sense. Father and Son were not divine on the same level. If the Modalists could think of the divine three only as successive historical aspects of the one radically unknown God; if Tertullian, while rejecting this view, could think of the Trinity only as condensations or distributions of the one divine substance, Origen chose the more philosophical explanation. Certainly, the three were within the divine sphere; but within the sphere there were gradations. The three could be distinguished only after the model offered by the Platonism of the day. For one divine person to originate from another necessarily meant being divine in a derived, and consequently inferior sense.

How this fell short of expressing the full realism of the divine *Agape* was now exposed in the conflict that raged around Arius, the presbyter of Alexandria, in the early decades of the fourth century. Whether he was the ruthless dialectician submitting the Christian mysteries to an alien logic, or more simply, a clear-headed preacher who wanted to preserve the realism of the incarnation and redemption, can be left to historical investigation.[15] What does seem quite clear is that Arius presupposed an unbridgeable gap between creation and the transcendent, impassible God. For God cannot be affected by the world in any direct manner. But, for Arius, the Logos-Son can act as mediator between God and the world, thus assuring the reality of the incarnation, at least in some diminished sense—and most of all, that of salvation. Though Christ is the mediator, he must still be located on the side of the creature: he is begotten in contrast to the unoriginate God, for he suffers within this world in contrast to the deity who is unaffected by creaturely action. As one scholar writes, "Behind all expression of Arian thought lay the hard and glittering syllogism that God is impassible; Christ, being *gennetos* (begotten) was passible; therefore Christ was not God."[16]

---

[14]For a concise and insightful summary of these positions, see Bernard Lonergan, "The Origins of Christian Realism", *A Second Collection* (London: DLT, 1974) pgs. 248ff.

[15]For a new line of investigation, see R. Gregg and D. Groh *Early Arianism. A View of Salvation* (Philadelphia: Fortress Press, 1981).

[16]G.L. Prestige, *God in Patristic Thought* (London: SPCK, 1962), pg. 156.

What Arius did occasion, if not provoke, was the utterly radical question that lay dormant in the theological positions preceding him. He forced theology back to the biblical terms in which the precise question could be asked, not to be emasculated with either metaphor or Platonic speculation. For the question was this: assuming that the Son proceeded from the Father, does the Son belong to the level of the creature or to the realm of the divine?

The answer he gave was probably inspired by the much-cited Prov 8:22-31, "The Lord created me at the beginning of his work, the first of his acts of old" ... and such texts as Rom 8:29 and Jn 17:3. The Son comes forth from the Father as a perfect creature, made out of nothing along with all creation. Therefore, "there was a time when he was not". Thus the Son is begotten in that he is created directly by God, while the rest of creation is created through the Son.

There are two presuppositions to the Arian position. The first is that God is and must be unoriginate: the divine cannot have its origin in anything else. The second is that everything proceeding from God, including the Son begotten by the Father, must necessarily be created. The God that Arius presumed had to be absolutely one, without beginning—and certainly unbegotten. To be God meant to be alone.

It is true that such positions were compatible with worshiping Christ and baptising in his name. But such a practice had continually to contend with the objection that it was in effect an instance of polytheism and reducing Christ to a mythological entity. On the other hand, the presumed Arian position "helped keep church doctrine both honest and evangelical."[17] This radical controversy not only demanded a re-thinking of the whole Christian notion of divine reality, and of how the Logos-Son belonged to it, but it also brought into sharper focus the genuine, created humanity of Jesus, the Word made flesh.

Before considering the response of Nicaea to this problem, let us reflect briefly on the question as it was posed in the received Arian terms. First of all, it phrases the question in real terms: it is not enough to have a metaphorical explanation, nor is it enough to have a philosophical set of ideas. What is being required is a definite

---

[17]Pelikan, *op. cit.*, pg. 200.

answer to a definite question: Does the Son belong on the side of the Creator or on that of the creature? The old modalistic confusion could not be tolerated, just as Tertullian's metaphors offered no solution, whereas the loftly solution that Origen commended began to look dangerously similar to what Arius was propounding. No longer would a vivid metaphorical suggestion of the unity of the three be adequate, just as a philosophical interpretation on such matters would misplace the issue. The church had to say Yes or No to the stark question implicit in the terms of her faith: Was the Logos-Son created or not?

This was also a new question. Certainly, it was made possible because a more differentiated intellectual mentality coloured Christian faith through the achievement of Greek philosophy. The immediate conviction of faith is that, in Christ the saviour, definitive salvation is offered, expressive of the limitless Love of God. If the first questions of faith are, how can we be saved?, and, how can we live in union with this Son in whom all things find their fulfilment?, a second range of questions now begins to emerge: Why is it that the Son is such a unique saviour? Who is he to be worthy of such ultimate trust? What he does must flow from what and who he is. So, what and who is he? Thus, there emerges a new type of questioning going beyond the function to the being and identity of the saviour, from the phenomenon of the grace to the giver of such gifts, from the action of God in Christ, to the status of Christ in relation to the one God.[18]

This kind of questioning is, too, inevitable. To refuse then or now to pose this type of question is to settle for something less than the complete meaning of Christian faith. Such faith has its gifts, but it also makes its demands. And implicit in every demand is the seed of the question, am I surrendering myself to God or something far less? When the culture allows and even provokes such a clear formulation of these basic questions, it is inevitable that they will be both expressed and demand a fundamental answer. When the natural dynamic of intelligence finds support in the philosophical acumen of the culture, then faith must give an appropriate account of the realities it is living. What is the meaning, the *logos*, of the Logos

---

[18] J.C. Murray offers a lucid account of all this, *op. cit.*, pgs. 40-44.

itself? Is it a divine meaning or something less? What is the sufficient reason for the reality of our salvation? Is it founded on the inmost reality of God, or in something less? What is the ultimate value of everything we find distinctive and fulfilling in Christian faith, in the coming of the only-begotten Son? Is it a truly divine gift, a truly divine communication—or something created, some intermediary which leaves God finally uninvolved in the cause of our salvation, and the Love of God something less than the noblest of human loves?

The issue is always the reality of God's Love. The New Testament was quite aware of the distinction between truth and cunningly devised myths (2 Pt 1:16; 1 Tim 1:4; 4:7; 2 Tim 4:4; Tt 1:14). It knew, too, the difference between the "many and various ways in which God had spoken to the fathers by the prophets", and how these led to and found fulfilment in the advent of the Son (Hb 1:1). It knew the difference between the image and the reality (Hb 10:1), just as it knew the difference between relating to God in an attitude of fear and enslavement and the liberation of communing with the real God in loving familiarity, brought about by the infusion of the Spirit of the Son (Rom 8:14ff). It dealt in realities; and the earliest believers knew it. The one and only God had decisively entered human history through the incarnation of the Word. Only in this Christ was salvation possible. It was a question of truth, guaranteed, expressed and indeed embodied in the divine Word made flesh, and communicated in God's own Spirit: it was this, and all this—or it was nothing.

Step by step, in the dialectic that led to the Council of Nicaea, this realist conviction was clarified. Now the old Modalism was perceived to undermine the real economy of salvation, disclosed in the presence of Father, Son, and Spirit. Tertullian saw this; but though he sharpened the discussion with his terminological contributions, he could not express the truth of the matter, locked as he was in the language of metaphor and an unsophisticated philosophy. Origen had all the resources of Middle Platonism, and tried to interpret the basic reality of faith more adequately. But the philosophical models he used, however much they had become a classic resource for affirming the nature of the real, ended by constricting him to a view of the Son and the Spirit as divine only in a secondary and derived sense. It was the lot of Arius to express the question in its sharpest and most threatening sense: Is this Son on whom human salvation turned, properly and fully a divine being, or a created reality? Creator and creature were biblical terms. Employing them to clarify the real question was not to get lost in futile speculation. It was to confront the essential issue of Christian faith. There was no middle term between Creator and creation; so where did Christ belong?

The answer to this question would be hammered out over the century and a half following Arius' posing it. In the great christological Council of Chalcedon in 451, it would be asserted that the one and the same, our Lord Jesus Christ, was truly God and truly man. But that was the precise comprehensive statement that proved so elusive in the conflicts leading up to the Council of Nicaea in 325. Manifestly, the reality of salvation would have to include both the divine and the human aspects. Unless God were uniquely involved in the act of salvation, it would be no ultimate salvation. There was no salvation in the Arian Son. If the Son is not God, fully Pantokrator, fully possessing the divine power, and on the divine level of being, then he is not our saviour and we are not saved.[19] Later, similar arguments would be adduced for the true divinity of the Holy Spirit. The function of the Spirit is sanctification and divinization. Unless the Spirit is divine, such actions have no final meaning.

Then there is the human aspect. Unless Christ possessed a genuine humanity, then that humanity has not been definitively brought into union with God. What is not assumed is not healed. Through the whole of the Arian crisis, the attention of the church was focused on the divine dimension of Christ—with predictable risks as the Monophysite exaggeration sacrificed the genuineness of Christ's humanity to an overwhelming divine nature.

This conflict was intensely theological, for the Christian reality of God was at stake. How could faith affirm the uniqueness of the divine mystery revealed in Christ? When the Modalists compacted this essential uniqueness into a Monarchia with three modes or manifestations; when, with Tertullian, faith is left with a metaphorical threefoldness; or when, with Origen, it is reducible to a Middle Platonic scheme of emanations, Arius forced the church to say Yes or No on the essential issue.

The answer could not be given in terms of a more sophisticated

---

[19]Murray, pg. 44f.

metaphor or image. Such would indeed keep their proper place; but of themselves they are drawn from the created world. Nor was the answer to be given by a judicious application of philosophical notions. That, too, would have its place in the elaboration of the meaningfulness of faith. But the meaning must derive from the truth of the revealed mystery, not from a previously elaborated philosophical system. The answer had to be given in terms of a judgment on the divine reality as faith had come to know it. This judgment had to allow for the utter originality of what had been revealed. It is the special merit of Athanasius to have seen this. As he reflected on the data of revelation presented in the Scriptures, he saw that the issue was not an image, not an idea, but an openness to what God actually is. To put it simply, he refused to approach the divine mystery, as Arius did, with a preconceived idea of what God is supposed to be. It came down to this: Was a culturally presupposed notion of God to prevent Jesus from being adored as divine, or was Jesus Christ to define the true character of God?

Athanasius formulated his affirmation of the divine reality in a deceptively simple manner: all that is said of the Father is also to be said of the Son except that the Son is the Son and not the Father.[20] Murray sums up this point with his characteristic conciseness:

> ... this conviction of the realism of the Word of God—that it is a real word with a real meaning—... sustained Athanasius in working out the celebrated formula which explained the sense inherent in the dogma stated by the Council of Nicaea. His study of the Scripture disclosed to him, as to Basil later, a general proposition. All the affirmations made by the Scriptures about the Father are also made about the Son, with one exception. The Son is not the Father. In particular, the scriptures affirm about the Son what they affirm about the Father, that he has as his own the two powers that are uniquely divine and proper only to God—the power to give life and the power to judge the heart of man. If, then, everything that is true about the Father is likewise true about the Son, except that the Son is not the Father, it follows that the Son *is* all that the Father *is*, except for the name of the Father.[21]

---

[20] *Orationes contra Arianos 4* (PG 26, 330).
[21] Murray, *op. cit.*, pg. 42.

Mystery and Definition 79

The significance of Athanasius' rule was that it enabled Christian faith to affirm the reality of God without distorting such an affirmation with the limitations of metaphor or the preconceptions of philosophy. This rule was behind the formulation and the subsequent interpretation of the definition of Nicaea in 325:

> We believe in one God, the Father almighty, maker of all things, visible and invisible. And in one Lord Jesus Christ, the Son of God, begotten from the Father, only begotten, that is from the substance of the Father, God from God, light from light, true God from true God, begotten not made, of one substance with the Father, through whom all things came into being ... who because of us men and because of our salvation, came down and became incarnate, becoming man, suffered and rose again .... And in the Holy Spirit.[22]

In view of the later doctrinal formulations and theologies, it is worth noting that the conciliar definition begins with the Father, not with the more generalized, less biblical, notion of divine being. The unity of the Godhead is implicitly related to the origin of everything in the Father—though this was not the explicit question that Nicaea was facing. Admittedly, too, the person and function of the Holy Spirit seems to be an ungainly addendum. Note also that the metaphorical and symbolic expressions are not completely abandoned, despite the new mode of doctrinal discourse: the metaphor of "begetting" still figures large, given as it is a further figurative connotation with "light from light".

The precise concern was that of responding to the need to define and, thereby, affirm certain aspects of the Christian mystery. In this regard, the definition accomplished four things. First, it was asserted that the Son was not created but begotten. Secondly, this generation derived from the Father not as a contingent act of the will, but from the very substance or being of the Father. Thirdly, and consequently, the Son is true God from true God. How this was to alter the theological notion of God was not yet an explicit matter of reflection—the precise way in which God could be these 'three', yet be

---

[22] Taken from J.N.D. Kelly, *Early Christian Doctrines* (New York: Harper and Row, 1958) pg. 232.

still the One God. Fourthly, the technical term, *homoousios*, was introduced, "of one substance with" the Father. In a provisional way, it gave direction and focus to the Council's assertion. Its full implications remained to be worked out.[23]

This word, *homoousios,* 'consubstantial', became the emblem of Nicaea's accomplishment. It was neither a biblical word, nor even a technical philosophical term. True, it did have a quasi-technical place in previous Gnostic vocabulary, referring to emanations from the different orders of being. Indeed, because of such an association, it had incurred ecclesiastical disapproval in the Synod of Antioch in 268. Yet, as it stood, with its literal meaning being "of the same stuff", it served a new purpose. For the judgment that the Council had to make was not served by the ordinary categories of experience, nor even by the biblical terms referring to God's presence and power. It was an instance of a new use of language by which the divine is not described but affirmed, by which God's saving presence to us is referred back to what God is in and to himself, as the foundation of his being-for-us. More particularly, because of what the Son was for us and our salvation, Christian faith woke to the need of speaking about what the Son was in himself, in relationship to God the Father. Not to use such a new kind of language, not to employ this suspect new term, was, as the Council Fathers saw, to run the risk of being interpreted always in an Arian manner.

Significantly, this key term does not express any precise content. Metaphorically, it denotes "of the same stuff". Doctrinally, in the context of the judgment it served, it connotes an openness to the divine mystery and the refusal to define it in any preconceived philosophical or other terms. Whatever God the Father is, however Scripture, liturgy, theology, and doctrine might describe or define the divine, the Son is, except for what is meant by the divine name, Father. More simply still, the Son, in himself, in his being, in his origin, is on the divine side of the divide, and is not contained in the sphere of creation.

A rather insubstantial charge is often levelled at this point: Nicaea "hellenized" Christian faith. Sharp refutations of this abound in the

---

[23]See Alois Grillmeier, *Christ in Christian Tradition, Vol I* (Oxford: Mowbrays, 1975), pgs. 267-272.

works of representative authors.[24] Certainly, Christian faith did come to a mode of articulation made possible by Greek culture, and it did make its own the ability of Greek philosophy to transcend the material and purely phenomenological conceptions of reality. But it used what was so available only to liberate its essential mystery from subservience to the preconceptions of any philosophical system. It broke away from primitive biblicism, from Tertullian's implicit Stoicism, from Origen's Middle Platonism, from Arius' cultural theism. In all, it was a struggle to affirm the originality and objectivity of the revealed truth. This can be affirmed through human conceptions but not reduced to them: "The only place where we cannot find Hellenism is in the word *homoousios*. It would be impossible to find a conception more remote from and at odds with all the ontologies of the Greco-Roman world than the conception embodied in this word, which says that the Son is all that the Father is except for the name of Father."[25]

After Nicaea had made its judgment on the divinity of the Son, it was inevitable that the status of the Holy Spirit would begin to attract more explicit attention. For at Nicaea, the Holy Spirit was mentioned only in the most summary manner, "and in the Holy Spirit". But now after that Council's affirmation of the Son as consubstantial with the Father, the terms were there to ask precise questions about the divinity of the Spirit. Was the Holy Spirit to be affirmed as one in being with the Father and the Son? Or, as proceeding from the Son, did the Spirit belong to some lower order of reality?

These questions had their theological novelty. Indeed, there does not seem to have been a separate treatise on the Holy Spirit until the latter half of the fourth century.[26] Gregory of Nazianzen saw the late consideration of the Holy Spirit as inherent in the economy of revelation: "The Old Testament clearly announces the Father, but the Son obscurely. The New Testament has shown forth the Son, but given only an indication of the divinity of the Spirit. At present

---

[24] I have in mind the writings of Lonergan, Murray, Pelikan, O'Donnell . . . .
[25] Murray, *op. cit.*, pg. 55.
[26] Pelikan, *op. cit.*, pgs. 211-220.

the Spirit is among us, and shows himself in all his splendour . . . "[27] Gregory envisaged a gradual assimilation of the divine mystery, with a consequent development of doctrine about it.

On the other hand, the liturgy continued to celebrate the unity of the Spirit with the Father and the Son in a pre-problematic manner. The various doxologies, the eucharistic epiclesis, the baptismal formulae attest to this. Yet on the theological level, there was, as Gregory admits, considerable confusion, and the tolerance of a wide variety of opinions regarding the manner in which the Spirit pertained to the divine order.

The main arguments employed for the divinity of the Spirit were soteriological. If he caused holiness and gave divine life, the Spirit had to be a divine agent. There were pitfalls in relating the Spirit to the Father and the Son in the divine realm: Did the Spirit derive only from the Son? If so, was he a kind of 'grandson' of the Father? The great Cappadocians were alert, then, not only to problems associated with determining the precise status of the Spirit, but also to those pertaining to the Spirit's mode of origin within the divine mystery. Scriptural texts such as 1 Cor 2:11 were read as revealing the Spirit's place within the divine reality. But a precipitate solution could have tipped theology either in the direction of the old Modalism or toward that of the recent Arianism in the effort to determine the status and origin of the Spirit.

The arguments underpinning the eventual definition of the Council of Constantinople in 381 dealt with the significance of the functions and qualities that the Spirit exhibited according to the Scriptures. The Spirit was 'holy' in a unique way, not sanctified but sanctifying, not holy by participation but by nature. Because this Spirit performed divine works, in creating and giving life, in causing grace and effecting divinization, he had to be divine. Gregory of Nazianzen was the first to use the term *homoousios* in this regard. And in the terms of Constantinople (preserved in what we inaccurately call the 'Nicene' Creed) the divinity of the Spirit is affirmed in more religious terms:

> We believe in the Holy Spirit, the Lord and giver of life, who proceeds from the Father . . . with the Father and the Son he is worshipped and glorified. He has spoken through the prophets.

---

[27] *Or.* 31.26 (*PG* 36:161).

6. Theological Development

Thus the divine status of the Spirit was affirmed against those who, in a confused or explicit manner, had thought of him as less than divine. This definition provoked an effort to find a theological *language* to express the *content* of faith. Given the judgment of faith, that each of the three was truly divine, how was the divine unity to be thought of? How were the distinctions between the divine persons to be formulated? How could the distinctiveness of each be expressed, and the relations of each to the others be conceived? In short, how could the doctrinal data be brought to some systematic theological understanding?

First, there was the matter of terminology. Tertullian had been the theological wordsmith of the West and left the legacy of "tres personae et una substantia". In the East, there was a more abundant theological vocabulary and a more exuberant theological creativity. This defied any easy precision. The eventual formulation amounts to one *ousia* (= *substantia*) and three *hypostases* (= *personae*). The process of clarification was not without its delicacy. For in long periods of theological debate among the Greeks, these terms had been used interchangeably. The resultant confusion often produced allegations of Modalism or Tritheism. Nonetheless, to make a long story short, the standardization of terminology was achieved, especially due to the judicious efforts of the Cappadocians, Basil, Gregory Nazianzen, and Gregory of Nyssa. They adapted the logical notion of a universal nature in relation to the individuals that possess it. This brought about the needed clarification. The risk of abstraction was minimized by their stress on the original *hypostasis* of the Father, the source of all in God. The Son and Spirit proceeded from him, as true God from true God. Thus, in theological understanding, by stressing the originating role of the Father, the unity of Father, Son, and Spirit was both secured and concretized as a communion.

The theologians of the time had a keen sense of the ineffability of the divine mystery. As Gregory of Nyssa wrote,

> ... following the instructions of the Holy Scriptures, we have been taught that the nature of God is beyond names and human speech.

> We say that every divine name, be it invented by human custom or handed on to us by the tradition of the Scriptures, represents our conceptions of the divine nature, but does not convey the meaning of that nature itself.[28]

Two questions continued to inspire further effort. First, how does the Spirit proceed within God? The Cappadocians were convinced that the Spirit's mode of origin differed from that of the Son, which was generation. They found unutterable this second mode of origin. Certainly, in the terms of John's Gospel, the Spirit "proceeds" from the Father and "receives" from the Son, and is even given by the Son. How to say anything more on this matter remained, and remains, a perplexing question.

The second urgent question concerned the distinctions existing between the divine hypostases. How should such distinctions be conceived? The Cappadocians taught that the three were to be distinguished according to the particular properties of each: Fatherhood, Sonship, Sanctification (Basil); ingenerateness, being generated, and procession (Gregory Nazianzen). These properties in turn disclosed mutual relationships based in the mode of origin, e.g., begetting and being begotten. Thus theology began to see that the root of distinction between the divine persons was relationship; and this category gave both content to the notions by which the divine three were distinguished, and suggested some way of conceiving of the distinctions that existed between them. It also left intact the divine unity of being in which everything was common to the three save where this "opposition of relationship" occurred (as later conciliar definitions would express it).[29]

The theology of the three distinct but related "hypostases" communicating in the one divine "ousia" culminated in the notion of *perichoresis*. This term connoted a mutual co-inherence of the divine persons; it sought to express how each of the divine persons dynamically and necessarily indwells in the others in the communication

---

[28] *Quod non sunt tres dii, PG* 45, 115. For translation and comment see, Pelikan, *op. cit.*, pg. 222.

[29] e.g., the Council of Florence in 1439 (DS 1330). For valuable emphases and asides related to patristic trinitarian theology, cf. E.L. Mascall, *The Triune God. An Ecumenical Study* (Worthing: Churchman Publishing, 1986), especially pgs. 24-34.

of the one divine nature and activity.[30]

The real issue in this doctrinal development was that of Christian realism. What Christian faith found in common with Greek philosophy was a concentration on meaning, on *logos,* over against polytheistic imagination, *mythos,* with all its undifferentiated symbolisms. After making this option for critical meaning, faith could not rest here in a philosophy. It had to press on to its distinctive apprehension of reality as *Agape,* Love.[31] The human reality of the Son must be the point at which the reality of God is defined, not the point where the divinity of Christ is denied. The self-giving of the Son reveals the self-giving God of the Gospel, the Father, giving his only-begotten Son for our salvation, and sending his own Spirit on the world, and demanded the affirmation that God had such a self to give. With the definitions of Nicaea and Constantinople, such an affirmation of the divine reality occurred. How it was to be understood, how it was to be integrated into all the meanings of Christian faith, how it was to be communicated effectively—such were considerations for the continuing business of thelogy. They demanded then as now the ongoing effort to make sense of the judgments that faith had to make to preserve its essential integrity.

In aligning itself with the philosophical tradition and in so learning to formulate the precise issues of its faith, the Patristic era was initiating a far-reaching transformation of theological meaning. The divine reality was not unrelated to the world in a sublime unconcern for these lower levels of reality. God was no transcendent self-enclosed Monad, subsisting in the solitude of its own perfection. The faith that through this time had prayed, celebrated, and suffered, now demanded that God be conceived of in utterly un-Greek terms. The divine meaning was that of a mystery of self-giving Love. God was never ultimately alone. The divine perfection was to be communion, a divine 'three' inter-related in a mysterious vitality. The reality of Christian salvation rested on this conviction, that the real God has given what was truly and exclusively "his own", his Son and his Spirit, "for us and our salvation".

---

[30]For an informative note on this, see Michael O'Carroll, 'Circumincession', in *Trinitas,* pg. 68ff.

[31]See the excellent analysis of J. Ratzinger, *Introduction to Christianity,* trans. J.R.Foster (New York: Herder and Herder, 1969), pgs. 99-137.

What Christian thinking discovered in the process was the distinctiveness of its vision of the ultimately real. Though such a reality could and should be affirmed, the essential Christian mystery was always exposed, in the minds of those who thought about it even with great reverence, to a kind of reduction process. The categories available were always suspect: it became important to make the "via negativa" a matter of tradition.[32] God's Word and Spirit were not to be conceived of as 'angels' or 'appearances'; they were not 'modes' or inner 'distributions' of the divine substance; they were not extrusions out of the divine realm, nor derivations from it, nor participations in it; they were not created or part of creation. Nor was this God three substances, nor one divine hypostasis, not three gods excluding unity, not one divine reality excluding distinction and relationships. The Son was not created but begotten; the Spirit was not caused but mysteriously proceeds.

Such a movement indicated, step by step, the hopelessness of logical solutions, metaphorical elaborations and unreflecting biblicism. It was a movement into the unknowing of faith as much as into its definition. With this came a sense of fragility in all the modes of expression, and the delicate dialectical complementarity in which they must be employed. There is the absoluteness of the one God, but also the relational character of the divine life, a self-communication which is the divine reality in itself and for others. The eternal character of this life and the processions involved in it was the ground of God's dealings with creation in time. The unchanging character of God had to confront the paradox, still so challenging to theology, of how the begetting of the Son and the breathing of the Spirit was compatible with the incarnation of the same Son and his shameful execution in this human world. Nicaea had initiated the process of defining the divine reality from the reality of Jesus Christ. The uniqueness of the Christian conception of God had begun to appear.

There were, of course, some shortcomings to this achievement. I mentioned before the old-fashioned charge against the theology of this period, that it had "hellenized" Christian doctrine. This can be

---

[32]Cf. Murray, *op. cit.*, pgs. 62ff.

properly abandoned.[33] Talk about the hellenization of Christianity or the christianization of Hellenism gives the impression of an idealist bias, as though we were merely referring to 'meaning systems' somehow abstracted from those who employ them to mean something. The issues of this great Christian period did not turn on the creation of a new philosophical system to rival those already culturally available. The main issue was, rather, the affirmation of distinctively Christian reality. To do this, Christian faith used Greek concepts and procedures, but, if there is one thing clear, the whole intent of this early theology was to use such resources, not to be used by them.

Nonetheless, in this creative process, a number of issues were left adrift in the presuppositions of the culture. Certainly, Christianity had pressed on to affirm the divine reality in the terms demanded by an authentic faith. Nonetheless, involved in this enormous effort were a number of the quasi-theological presuppositions of the Greco-Roman culture. They came together in a generalized notion of the divine, of what God was and had to be like. This generalized conception was so taken for granted that those educated in the presuppositions of the Greek culture could not stand back from it. Though the reality of God was indeed affirmed as the Love that truly did give itself in the divine Son and the divine Spirit, in the incarnation and its full actuality in the cross, massive cultural convictions about God's eternal, unchanging, unsuffering character prevented a full appropriation of the mystery of God as Love. How could theology elucidate this Love's compassionate self-involvement in the drama of our human history?

For the moment, let us simply register the kind of problem inherent in the very success of the patristic formulations of the Trinity. On the one hand, they were intent on affirming the Christian reality of God. On the other hand, as they concentrated on the dominant issues of the genuine divinity of the Son and Spirit, there was so much in the philosophical cultural background that was accepted as unproblematical.

Today the situation is different. What was then regarded as un-

---

[33]For a nuanced statement on this issue, see O'Donnell, *op. cit.*, pgs. 44-52.

problematical, part of the way things were, is today the intensely problematical point: How is God truly, compassionately involved in the agony of the world? How is God truly affected by human suffering and the struggle to overcome it? How does a genuinely trinitarian theology throw light on such deeply-felt questions?

To conclude this long reflection, it is as well to return to the beginning. The classic Christian doctrines I have been referring to would have been impossible had they not been earthed in an ongoing experience. The experience had fundamentally to do with a definitive sense of the divine presence. God was here amongst us in an all-fulfilling way. The only words to describe it are those that specify that God himself had been given, revealed, communicated, in the divine Word and the divine Spirit.

The psychological transformation that had occurred in the Christian mind, could allow no rest until the questions implicit in the original experience and its biblical testimony had been formulated, faced and answered. The transformation of mind and heart that was the human correlative to the self-giving of God, provoked what can only be termed an intellectual conversion, that critical determination to affirm the way things are. If the grace of salvation is not only God's gift, but God's self-giving in his Son and in his own proceeding Spirit, how should the divine reality be affirmed? If the basic Christian conviction is that God has given us God, what does this reveal about such a giver and such a gift? If the divine gives itself in Word and Spirit, does this not mean that God has such a self to give?

Such questions express the fundamental demand for realism in Christian faith. Trinitarian theology takes up the task of tying God's communication in Christ back into the very being of God: if it is true, then it is very true. Love has ultimate meaning.

4

Connections

We now move into a more systematic exploration of trinitarian meaning. In the previous chapter, we sketched the main stages in the emergence of the doctrine of the Trinity. Before that, we looked at the scriptural foundation. In the first chapter, "Perspectives", we had emphasized that the mystery of the Trinity was implied as a given in the identity of the church, as the focus of its communion and as the openness of its mission to the real sense of the contemporary world.

From each and all of these points of view, the Trinity is an intensely meaningful matter: as the focus and momentum of the church's life, in the vivid convictions of the scriptural writers witnessing to the fulfilment of the ages, in the definitions of the Councils affirming the reality of the original faith. What concerns us now is how to appropriate these meaningful instances of the Trinity in a way that makes sense, critical and hopeful sense, in the contemporary context. Not to attempt this is either to leave the central mystery of faith wrapped up in the venerable expressions of another age, or to commit it to the usually benign mercy of a mysticism which, while declaring God to be unutterable, unwittingly legitimizes any uncritical attempt to speak of matters divine.

Nor is it enough to say that the Trinity is sufficiently implied in the ongoing life of the church, as we move forward "in the name of the Father and of the Son and of the Holy Spirit". To leave it there is to replace the possibilities of theological understanding with a mantra. Implicitly, repetition becomes the criterion of orthodoxy. If the Trinity is the centre and impulse of the life of the church, presumably that life need not be unintelligent in its wonder and praise and in its desire to communicate to all peoples the meaning of the mystery in whose name they are offered baptism.

1. A Systematic Understanding

A living faith needs to understand what it lives. What is so uncannily 'given' provokes questions. The gifts of God demand some kind of understanding if they are to be both appreciated and communicated. The life of the church, the teachings of scripture, and the doctrines of the Councils are data that are assimilated only by exploring their meaning. It is a liberation for faith to have a coherent sense of the whole. This is what systematic theology tries to do: to work the data into a reasonably comprehensible meaning.

The data here, the 'givens', have both a profuse and diffuse quality when we begin reflecting on what the Trinity means. It is *profuse*, in that we are dealing with the culminating and definitive character of God's self-giving in Christ. It is *diffuse* inasmuch as the experience and expression of such divine profusion occur in so many different contexts, be they existential or literary, with all the variety of different witnesses and writers, different cultures, mentalities, developments, needs and concerns.

To deal with such profusion of God's self-giving Love, and diffusion in all the ways in which it is experienced and understood, the three general theological techniques mentioned by Vatican I's *Dei Filius* are valuable: theological understanding is possible by means of analogies drawn from human experience, through the interconnection of the mysteries among themselves, and in their reference to our final destiny.[1]

In this present chapter, I will treat the 'interconnections' first. In later chapters, we will consider some key analogies; after that, the eschatological reference.

Beginning with 'interconnections' recommends itself for the following four reasons. First, in view of the extensive introductory sections, this manner of proceeding serves as a transition from the

---

[1] See section 11 of Chapter one.

scriptural and doctrinal sections and opens the way to theological investigation. Secondly, it not only orders and summarizes a lot of the previous data, but it creates a certain holographic image of the trinitarian reality, before we turn to more precise considerations. Thirdly, by developing this holographic outline, we open up the field of meaning in which the various analogies can do their work. Without such a centering and reference, each analogy (be it in terms of psychology, community, process, etc.) can lose its sense of proportion and slowly reduce the reality to the limits of the model. Thus it becomes a way of forgetting the original mystery of faith instead of being modestly creative in remembering it.

In short, we are teasing out to more explicit proportions the quiet little phrase, so often unnoticed, of St. Thomas Aquinas as he writes on the use of analogical reasons: 'Once the Trinity is given, analogical reason has its place'.[2] I take this to mean that unless theology keeps being aware of the givenness of the trinitarian mystery, it can easily become locked up in its own models; it begins confusing the model with the reality, the analogy with the mystery, the map with the countryside.

Fourthly, I believe that this manner of reflecting on the Trinity actually enriches the emancipatory concern of theology. It keeps our image of the Trinity related to the whole field of God's saving involvement in human history. It is true that we are not hurrying to the implications of social praxis. This does not mean that it is not a central concern: in the deepest meaning of the word, the Trinity is the agenda of Christian life. To follow Christ is to share his solidarity with the poor, to be possessed by the Spirit of the new humanity, to have an efficacious desire that "Our Father's" name will be hallowed, that the kingdom will come, the divine will be done on earth as in heaven. The manner in which Christian faith extends into a trinitarian agenda, the way in which such trinitarian agenda is socially transforming, are central concerns of this work.

We will now move to the large theme of trinitarian interconnections. Within the proportions of such a *Gestalt,* we shall be able in subsequent chapters to treat various analogies useful in the elaboration of trinitarian meaning.

---

[2] "... trinitate posita, congruunt huiusmodi rationes". *ST,* I, 32, 1 ad 2.

Now, from a variety of angles, we will try to build up a composite, 'interconnected' theological impression of the Trinity. We have already suggested some of the dimensions of this by relating the Trinity to the existence of the Church in the introductory chapter. We linked it into our contemporary sense of reality. Such a theological hologram will be made up of the following themes, though many more could be added: the trinitarian image in human existence, the Trinity and creation, the Trinity and revelation, the Trinity and grace, the Trinity and the Paschal Mystery, the Trinity and the Church.

2. The Image of God

We shall, in fact, be treating this point rather extensively when dealing with the 'psychological image' analogy. For the moment, a few brief remarks will suffice.

This first connection is between the Trinity and our human selves in action. By 'in action' I mean that we are not just simply established in self-possession. Each of us is an identity disclosed as the 'I' that sees and hears, thinks, judges, loves, believes, hopes .... In this sense, we catch up with ourselves as we act. We are conscious of this self and of the enrichment coming to this self in the measure that we surrender to the dynamics of self-transcendence. By being open to experience, by searching for meaning, by enquiring after truth, by giving generously in love, by adoring in faith, we are given to ourselves as meaning-making selves, as truth-seeking selves, as selves in love, as selves expanding in adoration and ultimate trust. In short, we are always selves interacting with a universe, never apart from the Other—or trying to be apart from it. We are enclosed in ourselves only at the peril of self-destruction.

This open, self-transcending, relating self disclosed in the consciousness of our selves-in-action is the first connection. God has meaning not as a puzzle to test the sophisticated mind, not as an idea that puts a good interpretation on everything, but as origin and fulfilment of the dynamic self that each one of us consciously is.[3]

How then do we formulate this connection of the Trinity with the

---

[3] See Lonergan, *Method,* pgs. 6-20.

self-transcending self? In the 'interconnection of mysteries' how is the ultimate mystery of self-transcendence, the trinitarian *Agape,* correlated to our selves, to the ever-elusive mystery of the whence and whither of our human self-transcendence? The Christian God is "not the God of the dead, but of the living" (Lk 20:38). How is the Trinity related to our consciousness of life as the healing and fulfilment of what we are as living beings? Jesus came that we "might have life, and have it to the full" (Jn 10:10). He himself is the life, the way to it, the truth about it (Jn 14:6). How can we begin to make the connection between the life human beings experience and the life that God, Jesus, the Holy Spirit are? "It has not yet appeared what we shall be, but, when he appears we shall be like him" (1 Jn 3:2). What is the reason for this eschatological correlation? In different ways, the scriptures speak of the mutual indwelling of God and ourselves: God dwells in us and we in God (1 Jn 4:16; Jn 17:20ff). How are these two indwellings correlated? What is the interconnection?

There are a number of steps in answering these questions. But each stage of explanation is expressing one basic point: the mystery of the Trinity occurs in revelation because it has been experienced. It is not the telling forth of arcane truths, but the coherent expression of what men and women of faith have found God to be. It is the God who has revealed himself within the horizon of what human beings have sought and loved, found beautiful and ultimately significant. God is confessed to be Trinity because the divine mystery meets the genuine aspirations of the self-transcending self. God appeals as the Word of ultimate meaning, as the Spirit of ultimate value against the horizon of our human search for what is true and worthwhile. Systematic theology, in its more theoretical phase, will insist that trinitarian theology is all about the reality of God, not just our impressions of it, or our experience of it, or the way it indwells human consciousness. But that objective phase is the result of a methodical detachment from the 'interface' stage in which the meaning of God/Trinity and human subjectivity are inter-related. We can suggest this connection, then, in the following manner.

The human self as a self-transcending self, looks to some final fulfilment in terms of life, meaning, value, relationship.[4] Related to

---

[4] Lonergan, *Method,* pgs. 101-105.

this is the trinitarian self, a divine self-communicating self. The divine self-giving takes place, in Word and Spirit, and in final union with the Father. The original reality, the Father, utters the fulness of meaning into the human world: the Logos, the Word, the meaning incarnate. In Christ, "all things hold together" (Col 1:17). The Word of ultimate meaning enters into the human conversation as a question, a summons, a judgment, a new commandment, a promise, a prayer, a story and a parable, a new covenant: the way, the truth and the life.

Related to the sending of the Son is the Father's sending of the Spirit. Inspired by this Spirit, our self-transcending existence is enabled to appreciate the divine meaning that is incarnate in Christ Jesus. It is enabled to break free of cosmic dread and servitude, to be free with the ultimate mystery of reality, and to find it a nurturing, self-giving Love: "You did not receive the spirit of slavery to fall back into fear, but you have received the Spirit of sonship, crying, 'Abba, Father!'" (Rom 8:14f). This Spirit opens human existence to a new world of self-transcending values: ". . . the fruit of the Spirit is love, joy, peace, patience, kindness, goodness, faithfulness, gentleness, self-control." (Gal 5:22))

The energy of God's own Loving "has been poured into our hearts through the Holy Spirit which has been given to us" (Rom 5:5). The gift of the Spirit enables self-transcendence to expand in a field of new relationships: to God as 'Father', to Jesus as Lord, to other human beings as brothers and sisters in Christ—indeed to the whole of creation as waiting for and bringing forth the total Christ (Rom 8:19-22).

The Christian mystery meets and fulfils our human capacities for self-transcendence. The self-transcendence of "asking, seeking, and knocking at the door" (Lk 11:9f) finds its fulfilment in the self-giving God. The divine mystery is the homecoming of the human spirit.

This much is sufficient to suggest the first interconnection, that between the Triune God and our self-transcending human selves.

3. The Trinity and Creation

The imaging forth of the Trinity in creation and the configuration of that creation to its trinitarian origin, form and goal is, of course, one of the oldest themes in theological reflection. The created world is seen to contain *vestigia trinitatis,* traces of the fundamental mystery giving it existence. Patristic and medieval reflection often saw such "traces" in terms of "being, form and tendency". The fact that there was something rather than nothing, that this particular entity existed, was a trace of the limitless, originating power of the Father. That this something was this rather than that, that it possessed this particular form of being, bespoke a characteristic of the Son, the divine Word and Image, through whom all things were made. The fact that all these particular existents were interrelated in a universe and tended toward the perfection of the whole indicated a conformity to the Holy Spirit, the divine Love as unitive and ecstatic.[5]

The tradition of this kind of reflective thinking has been notably continued by John Macquarrie.[6] He employs Heidegger's meditative philosophy in his account of the *vestigia*: the universe of all that is, is configured to Father as Primordial Being, to the Word/Son as Expressive Being, to the Holy Spirit as Unitive Being. The universe comes to be out of the mystery of Primordial Being, the *fons et origo* of all that is. In its manifold articulation and intelligibility, it evidences the character of Expressive Being: it is not a chaos, but a unified intelligibility. As a dynamic field of inter-connectedness and development it suggests the creative presence of Unitive Being. If scientific writers such as Capra can use the ancient doctrines of Taoism to confirm their sense of reality, there is no need for trinitarian theology to be excessively timid in trying to meet the demands of a 'new paradigm'.

In the first chapter we noted the current search for a new paradigm of reality. In contrast to the former mechanistic model prevailing in science, contemporary thinking accepts a hologrammic image of the universe. This emphasizes the relationality of everything within the whole. It looks to the integration of everything into a kind of cosmic 'intentionality', one aspect of which is the human mind. As this way of thinking matures into a paradigm, it will offer trinitarian theology a chance to express its traditional doctrine of the 'traces' and 'image' of the Trinity in creation.

---

[5] *ST* 1, 45, 7.

[6] *Principles of Christian Theology* (London: SCM 1966), pgs. 179-185.

In the configuration of creation to the trinitarian God, theology discerned one discontinuity that the new paradigm I referred to would probably not appreciate. Though the whole of creation was dynamically conformed to the Trinity as bearing 'traces' of the divine, only human existence is the *imago Dei,* 'made in the image and likeness of God'.[7] The substance of this trinitarian image-theology is maintained in what we have said above in correlating the Trinity with self-transcendence. Such theology, structured as it was by the categories and concerns of Greek metaphysics (Plato and Aristotle), isolated the spiritual nature of the human being as the point of disclosure of the divine original in us.[8] Thus, notably for Augustine and Thomas Aquinas, this spiritual image of God in human beings provided the leading analogy for a theology of the Trinity itself. This will receive extensive treatment in the next chapter.

For the moment we shall merely indicate a desirably larger setting for this image-theology in the context of the interconnections we are sketching. Two points occur to me: first, the 'cosmic-connection' of the spiritual self; and secondly, 'the communitarian structure' of our spiritual existence.

With regard to the first point, the tradition was largely concerned with developing a 'hylemorphic' theory of the human existent: the human spirit/soul is necessarily embodied in matter, just as matter necessarily seeks its fulfilment in spirit. Technically, matter is said to be 'transcendentally related to' the human spirit soul.[9] This profound metaphysics was concentrated on human existence. Not surprisingly, this was the paradigmatic instance of matter/spirit inter-relationship. The actual human self is embodied spirit, and animated matter. In elaborating the manner in which human existence is configured to the divine (from which it has come, and in whose image it was necessarily formed), it is the human spiritual component that is privileged. God cannot be like the material component in humanity; hence the divine image has to be sought in the spiritual. This was specified in the Augustinian-Thomistic tradition as the spiritual being's capacity to know and will. These spiritual acts and capacities

---

[7] *ST* 1, 93, 1-7.
[8] *ST* 1, 93, 6-7.
[9] For Aquinas, the human being is never just a soul (*ST* 1, 75, 4).

analogously evidenced the divine spiritual reality: The Word is the expression of divine understanding whence the Spirit is the love that proceeds from such understanding. The human being is a spiritual self because it originates from the trinitarian self of God.[10] It is through reflection on our own spiritual existence that we come to some inkling of how God is and must be a Trinity.

The contemporary paradigm of reality has changed. The rather statically conceived, hierarchically ordered cosmic order, ascending from matter to spirit, from spirit to God, has been set in a much larger and more processive context. For example, what strikes the modern scientific mind is the organic inter-relatedness of the universe as a whole. Within this universe human consciousness appears as one aspect of a more generally conceived self-transcendence and systemic field of relationships.[11] In and through human consciousness, the whole cosmos comes to a new level of self-directive awareness: nature is taken up into the history of freedom. It also comes to a new level of self-reflective awareness: the universe comes to appreciate itself as 'creation'. It is not the explanation of its own existence. It comes from and tends to that which cannot be explained in intra-mundane terms.

Here trinitarian theology must try to imagine a more cosmic configuration of the Trinity with the universe. We human beings are not just the image of the trinitarian God; we are the living experience of how the trinitarian mystery is enfolding the whole of creation into itself. In the logic of the traditional Christian mysteries of which the Trinity is the summary, that is, in the logic of the Incarnation and the sending of the Spirit, this wider view of things suggests more adventurous formulations. In the giving of the Word and Spirit into the world the trinitarian selfhood of God is enworlding itself; and from the other standpoint, the world is becoming trinified.

Admittedly, in this image of things, human existence is still the contact-point at which this communication and transformation occurs. But the more we imagine human existence as earthed in the whole of the material cosmos, the more this cosmos appears to waken to a freedom in human existence. The whole cosmos is the

---

[10]*ST* 1, 45, 7.

[11]E.G., Capra, *The Turning Point* ... , pgs. 309ff.

body nourishing the human spirit, and, in turn, transformed by it. In our earthed and embodied self-transcendence, all the evolutionary dynamics come to fruition.[12] This broader formulation of human existence in cosmic terms suggests a bolder image of how the Trinity and the world are configured.

For to be human, and self-transcendingly so, means to live within an horizon of limitless mystery of life and being. Even as the mystery attracts us into 'ex-istence' (literally, to be outside ourselves) as we are given our place in the real world, it resists any effort to possess or comprehend it. Still, it does illuminate a universe of meaning. In human consciousness, the universe becomes aware of itself as meaningful. It stands forth as a limitless realm of intelligibility. Questions can be answered; more questions can be asked; explanations can be given; but these give rise to further questions. Eventually, this entire universe appears as a great single question: What is the meaning of all that has been found meaningful? What is the sufficient reason for all that is? Why is there this something, rather than nothing?[13]

At this point Christian revelation has its own resources. The point where our consciousness intimates a mystery of universal meaning is the point where the divine communicates itself as that Meaning, the Logos, the Word Incarnate. The first chapter of John's Gospel hymns the Word who was God, who was in the beginning with God, through whom all things were made, in whom was life, the light of all, who became flesh and dwelt amongst us, full of grace and truth, who radiates the divine glory, and makes the unknown God visible in human history (Jn 1:1-18).

Similarly, Christ is for the writer of Colossians the goal, the coherence and the consistency of the universe of God's creation: he is the firstborn of all creation, and all things are made in him, through him and for him. In him all things hold together; and even a dismembered world with all its problem of evil finds its point of reconciliation and peace in him, as "all the fulness of God dwells in him" (Col 1:15-20).

Correlative to this coherent and redemptive meaning is that other

---

[12]The writings of Teilhard de Chardin are necessarily the key point point of reference here.

[13]See B. Lonergan, *Insight. A Study of Human Understanding* (DLT: London, 1957), especially Chapter XIX.

phase of the divine communication, the Spirit of Love. This Spirit is the source of a transcendent loving in human history. It brings forth its fruit of faith and hope and love in human lives. In this history of human freedom, the universe awakes to its character as a dynamic field of development, as 'nature' taken up into the freedom of history, into a movement of self-determination, as human agency is transformed by a principle of transcendent Loving. Those who receive this new energy of Love and relationship are enabled to appreciate the full meaning of the Word who is Christ (Jn 16:24); it enables us to be free with the ultimate mystery in a liberated intimacy (Rom 8:15f); it inspires both the community (1 Cor 12) and mission of the church (Ac 2). With "sighs too deep for words", this Spirit helps those who wait in hope in the midst of a creation groaning for its liberation (Rom 8:19-27).

To this degree, the Gift of the Spirit is related to the character of creation in its hidden yearning for fulfilment. It is an energy calling forth loving collaborative involvement. It is God's support for hope's "inward groaning" (Rom 8:23); the "first fruits" (v. 23) of this Spirit are the dynamic assurance of a positive answer to the questions implicit in all human freedom: what is the worthwhileness of all our search for the good, and what is our capacity to attain to it? The Spirit 'indwells' as the gift of an inexhaustible impulse to a new level of self-transcendence in human history. While the meaning that is given redemptively in Christ is offered to human freedom, the Spirit enables that freedom to accept Christ who both gives the Spirit and is possessed by it.

In this kind of interconnection, the Trinity and creation are configured in the following correlation: the goal of creation is to be 'trinified': through the incarnate Word and the indwelling Spirit, creation tends through faith, hope and love to its fulfilment in God.

4. The Trinity and Revelation

Amongst the classic themes of theology, revelation figures large. In the context of trinitarian theology, it is central. For the Trinity is a revealed mystery, "a strictly supernatural mystery", in scholastic terminology, coming into human knowledge only insofar as God has revealed it. Now, there are two ways of looking at this, the one defective because of its abstraction; the other, more properly theological in its relationship to Gospel event. The defective conception of the Trinity as a revealed mystery envisages God giving us some secret information about himself. What was formerly classified as 'top secret' is, in the Christian era, strangely de-classified. We are now let into the divine secret.

In religious wonderment, one must ask, why? The answer to this question can take a number of forms. God decides that it is time to tell us more about himself, thus to release further information about the divine mystery. This, of course, is a matter of love, as all self-disclosures are. Yet it is not without its puzzling character. The believer has something new to believe in which all but contradicts the common tenets of religious belief in one God, a unique, simple, absolute reality. Yet the test of Christian faith is the acceptance of this puzzling feature about the one God. It provides the framework, if not the explanation, for our acceptance of how one of the three divine persons could become man in the incarnation. Even St. Thomas accepted that any of the divine three could become incarnated;[14] but, in fact, it is the Word/Son that became incarnate, appropriately enough as revealer of what the Father is, and as model for human beings. There is the further difficulty of the Holy Spirit. Though the personal presence of the Spirit is very explicit in Scripture, in the Western tradition the Spirit is almost an embarrassment when one searches for a theological explanation. The grace and infused love of the Christian life can be appropriated to this Spirit, even though, in fact, all God's works are really done in common by the divine three, since because God is one, and each of the divine three is God, no one divine person can have more power or special power in regard to the others. Still, whatever tensions there are in this scheme of things, the massive doctrinal fact remains: God is one in nature and three in the distinct persons. That has been revealed. That is the form of the inner life of God. Whatever incompetence theology might feel or whatever contradiction faith might experience is bolstered by the incontrovertible revelation of the "strictly supernatural mystery" of the Trinity.

The trouble with this kind of approach (admittedly, caricatured

[14]*ST* 3, 3, 5-6.

here) is that it forgets how our knowledge of the mystery of the Trinity arises. Its starting point is an abstraction, the absolute unified nature of God. It is juxtaposed with the Trinitarian doctrine: despite this absolute unity, God is three, Father, Son and Holy Spirit. Congealing in this abstract dogmatic scheme, the Christian puzzle persists as irresolvable. For the Trinity has never been related to human existence. From beginning to end it has been a statement about the divine existence, known, defined, and partially understood without any reference to the reality of salvation. In such an approach the Trinity figures as exalted but somewhat speculative information about God which really makes little difference to the human condition, except for the fact that one of the divine persons was sent to save us. Are the other two not so involved? Revelation, disconnected from the trinitarian mystery, is very abstract.

It is the particular glory of Karl Barth[15] to have established an interconnection between the Trinity and the process of revelation. He places the Trinity in the deep structure of Christian faith, rather than leaving it as a revered but irrelevant piece of information. How then do we express this interconnection? How is the mystery of the Trinity configured to the notion of revelation?

The key to this correlation is that the Christian event is central to the matter of the self-revelation of God. In Christ, the divine is disclosing itself as absolute Love. The human mind can, of course, try to form various conceptions of God; and these can be evaluated either positively or negatively. Classical Catholic theology with its doctrine of analogy has always admitted the positive bearing of such affirmations grounded in human experience, even though the ultimate mode in which God is true, good, wise, loving, and so on, remains hidden in the supereminent way in which such realities exist in God. Classical Protestant theology is deeply suspicious of such 'natural analogies', in its special sensitivity to our human propensity to manipulate the divine and to project onto the all-free and gracious mystery our own conditions and categories. Such conceptions are too obviously drawn from the sin-infected world. Still, I do not

---

[15]*Church Dogmatics I: The Doctrine of the Word of God. Part I,* trans. G.T. Thompson (Edinburgh, 1936). For further comment and exposition, see William J. Hill, *The Three-Personed God. The Trinity as a Mystery of Salvation* (Washington: Catholic University Press, 1982).

think that this classical dialectic, the one stressing the goodness of creation and the fact of the incarnation, the other the absolute freedom of God and the world's cry for redemption, need obscure the fundamental interconnection between Trinity and God's self-revelation. For both approaches share the conviction that only God can reveal God in the mystery of divine, transcendent freedom and identity. This self-revelation must originate and terminate in the incomprehensible divine Mystery. It must utter itself in a Word that does not reduce the Mystery from which it comes and which it expresses. It must be communicated in such a way that there is a true hearing of this Word on the part of those to whom it is addressed. It is precisely here that the doctrine of the Trinity is an articulation of the divine self-revelation.

For as Father, Son, and Holy Spirit the Trinity articulates the fact of a truly divine self-disclosure. The Father, as original Love, is present as Revealer. The Son is the Revelation, the embodiment in human history of the Father's self-expressive Love. The Spirit, inspiring the faith, hope and love whereby we appreciate the Mystery of God-with-us is the divine Revealedness, the continuing creativity of Love in history. In this one unified act of self-disclosure, God is present as the Limitless, incomprehensible Beyond and Goal, God ever-beyond-and-ever-greater; the Son is God-with-us; and the Spirit is God-within-us. Thus, the trinitarian doctrine comprehensively presents the distinctively Christian character of the unsurpassable intimacy of God's self-communication in Christ. Far from being merely abstract information, it expresses the form and dynamism of the divine self-disclosure in the history of salvation.

The believer is not on the outside of the divine mystery, looking up at a transcendent object. Imagining the matter in that way is to expect that the human mind and heart would be unwittingly always reducing the divine to human proportions. Rather, the trinitarian form of revelation implies that God is not so much an object to be believed, but the divine reality enfolding human consciousness into a new sphere of experience and meaning. It is to be 'within' the being of God. This is no mere human apprehension leaving the divine mystery unknown in itself, known only in its relationship to us. Rather, the trinitarian self-revelation of God means that the divine is not reduced to human limitation, but is disclosed for what it is.

Further, questions arise at this point: What are the appropriate terms for the plurality so implied in the divine mystery? "Persons" is the traditional doctrinal term, as we know. Can and should such terms be replaced, given the development in the notion of 'person'? Are "modes of being" (Barth) or "modes of subsistence" (Rahner) more accurate? In this preliminary exercise of interconnection and configuration, we can comfortably let such questions rest for the moment. The point here is simply to correlate the notion of revelation with that of the Trinity. In so doing, the pervasiveness of the trinitarian form and dynamism is stressed without hurrying to the treatment of more technical questions. Suffice it to say here that the divine three are disclosed in this 'enfolding' notion of self-revelation as three addressable subjects, distinctly invocable in themselves in the liturgy and mysticism of the church. Further, each of the divine three invoked in prayer enters into the trinitarian structure of the mission, as a profoundly personalizing force: the Spirit inspires liberty and a true community of persons; the Son is the form of truly personal life; and the Father is the ultimate mystery in which all unity is achieved (Jn 17).

5. *The Trinity and Grace*

Grace is another classic theological notion demanding to be correlated to the trinitarian mystery. It denotes that divine gift which transforms human existence. The beneficiary, to use traditional terms, participates in the divine life. In Scholastic theology the reality of grace was not articulated in a notably trinitarian manner: participating in the divine nature through the elevation of human nature in sanctifying grace and the theological virtues was the major consideration. Certainly, the other themes of the divine indwelling and the 'missions' of the Word and Spirit existed, but in a subordinate manner, intelligible only in relation to the 'created grace' that was God's primary gift.

In a way that parallels Karl Barth's trinitarian treatment of revelation, Karl Rahner reformed the notion of grace by accenting the trinitarian dynamism implied in it.[16] He appreciates more positively than the great Protestant theologian the anthropological structure

---

[16] Karl Rahner, *The Trinity*, trans. J. Donceel (London: Burns and Oates, 1970), pgs. 80-120.

which is correlative to the divine self-giving. Nature is ordered to grace as the condition for its occurrence. From his emphasis on the reality of God communicated to the reality of human existence, the trinitarian form of grace is made to stand out. The sweep of such a profound theology might be conveniently indicated by hazarding the following brief points.

1. Human existence is essentially a capacity for God. Humanity exists in the concrete order of divine providence so that God can be involved in a personal self-communication for the sake of creation. Hence, human being is a "natural" for this divine self-gift. Indeed, to be human means to be open to the infinite: to be listening for the Word that makes it known, to be surrendered to the Spirit which can liberate our capacities to receive the mystery from which and for which we are destined to live.

2. The divine gift is not the gift of something created, but the self-bestowal of God himself. It is not the gift of something, but self-giving. Certainly, there are created gifts that prepare for and mediate this ultimate self-giving; but God's love is looking to its fulfilment in a personal self-communication to creation summed up and represented in humankind.

3. As a divine self-communication grace is offered to other personal selves. There can be nothing about this gift that suppresses or distorts the reality of the other, just as there can be nothing about it that reduces the infinite genuinely divine character of the gift that is offered. Hence in the dynamics of the giving it must allow for, affirm, and fulfil the human selves to which it is offered. It must, in a word, be offered to them in their freedom, their intelligence, and their history.

4. The divine self-bestowal reduces neither the divine character of the gift, nor the human character of the recipient. It has to be accessible to human beings in human history. This requires that it be genuinely expressed and made accessible as an offer addressed to humanity in its self-understanding, in its self-determination, in its authentic self-transcendence. The divine gift must be expressed as 'there' in human history, a divine Word of communication in the great conversation that constitutes our identity and articulates the search for fulfilment. It is not enough, however, for the divine self-gift to be inaccessibly 'there' without enabling us to appropriate it in

human freedom: to be genuine it must both find expression in the 'objective' world of human realities, and transform human capacities to identify, appreciate, and receive what is being offered in its infinite, gracious originality. In other words, it must be both 'there' as truly offered, and 'here' as enabling our acceptance.

5. On a technical level, theology must be free to speculate on the philosophical categories which most serve to explore the reality of this transcendent gift and the transformative fulfilment it brings about. No categories drawn from human experience can adequately express the totality and intimacy of the divine self-giving in question, e.g., those pertaining to efficient, formal, material causality, or even the terms of interpersonal relations. The transcendent reality that such a philosophical application is trying to serve demands that the following three conditions be respected:

   a. a truly divine self-communication is occurring;

   b. in a way that does not de-nature human existence; and

   c. transforms and fulfils it in its self-transcending orientation.

A special kind of total actuation of human capacity is implied which leaves the reality of the gift as gift intact, and its character as a full divine self-giving. The human reality, as recipient of the gift, is not compromised but enhanced in its native potential. The divine selfhood indwells in our selves, not as suppressing human selfhood but as fulfilling its radical capacity. To be enfolded in the divine mystery, to dwell in God, does not mean a loss of human identity but the liberation and fulfilment of our whole relational selfhood.

6. Whatever may be said about the more technically philosophical categories most appropriate to classify and explore these dynamics of divine self-giving to human beings, four types of existential polarities serve to bring out the completeness of the Gift that is being made.

First, the Gift comes as a new beginning or originating point in human history—a new 'creation'. Yet it looks to fulfilment in an absolute future in which "God will be everything to everyone". Hence, the Word, incarnate in human history as a new beginning, releases a new Spirit of eschatological self-realization.

Secondly, Grace occurs in human history, as a factor and agent in our historical self-determination: God-truly-with-us. But this presence inspires a new self-transcendence, which will find its final point of attainment only beyond history when, possessing and completely possessed by the Spirit, the human community is one as the Father and the Son are one.

Thirdly, as we mentioned above, Grace occurs as an offer and as an enablement, God incarnate in the Word and as the infused Spirit of faith, hope, and love.

Fourthly, the three above-mentioned polarities are merely ways of expressing how the divine self-bestowal is manifest in truth and in love. The ultimate Mystery truly discloses itself within the conditions of human history: "This is my beloved Son. Hear him." (Mk 9:7) The truth of limitless Love not only appears as offered, but as enabling human freedom to respond: "God's love has been poured out in our hearts through the Holy Spirit which has been given to us." (Rom 5:5)

7. The truth and the love which are the modes of God's self-giving presence in the world is founded in the divine self-presence: the divine is not present to itself in some other truth; nor does it breathe some other kind of love. The truth and the love that are manifest in the Incarnate Word and in the outpouring of the Spirit are the Word of God and the Spirit of God. They pertain to the divine selfhood. Consequently Word and Spirit are modes of the divine self-giving to the world. The self-communication of God *ad extra* is essentially grounded in the self-constitution of God *ad intra*. Or, as Rahner unceasingly repeated, the 'economic' Trinity is the 'immanent' Trinity, and *vice versa*.[17]

8. In short, the divine three exist in a way that relates to an original self-communication in truth and love. The character of the Father is the transcendent Origin of such self-communication, the Word/Son is the all-exhaustive Truthful self-expression of this divine character; while the Spirit is the inexhaustible active mode of God's self-giving. Again, we come up against the question of whether the term three 'persons' is the most appropriate. And, further, we are entitled to ask whether any more clarity can be brought to the systematic understanding of the divine 'processions', why they are such, how they are related, and so forth. The next chapter on trinitarian analogy deals with such questions.

So, however briefly, we have some indication of how the Trinity and the mystery of Grace are fruitfully interrelated.

---

[17] K. Rahner, *The Trinity*, pgs. 21-38; 101ff.

6. The Trinity and the Paschal Mystery

In this section we will be trying to give some expression to the interconnection existing between the self-revealing, self-giving Trinity and the Paschal Mystery of the cross and resurrection of Christ Jesus. The neglect of this interconnection makes the Trinity into an ethereal doctrine abstracted from the dark drama of human history. The events of the cross and resurrection become detached from the loving self-communication of God. Theology has, in more recent times, attempted to correlate these two mysteries of faith in a number of imaginative ways.[18]

To speak most simply, the cross and resurrection of Jesus represent God's involvement in our human problem of evil. In that darkness, God is revealed as compassion reaching into the depths of the God-forsakenness. The divine Love gives itself as grace even in the point of maximum 'disgrace', when the Son is condemned and crucified. In other words, the paschal mystery makes clear that God's revelation keeps on being revelation even at the darkest point of human history: for there the genuineness of Love appears as sheer gift. Grace keeps on being grace even when evil appears most triumphant: for the self-giving that grace denotes is manifest in its most unconditional form, that is the Father gives what is most intimate to himself for the sake of sinful human beings, just as the Son loves his own "unto the end" (Jn 13:1), unto death, even unto death upon a cross (Phil 2:8). The Trinity is the Love that keeps on being Love in a way that overcomes the power of death, undoing any evil that the human will can perpetrate. The Mystery of the Trinity is communicated in the self-giving, unconditional, compassionate and ultimately victorious Love which God is (1 Jn 4:9-13).

How can we best express both the trinitarian dimension of the paschal mystery and the paschal dimension of the trinitarian self-communication? If we keep in mind that what is happening is God's self-giving to a sinful world, the following necessarily abbreviated points might provoke a fruitful line of thought:

---

[18]See above all Hans Urs von Balthasar, *Le Mystère pascal* [*Mysterium Salutis 12*] Editions du Cerf: Paris, 1972);E. Juengel, *God as Mystery of the World. On the Foundation of the Theology of the Crucified One in the Dispute between Theism and Atheism* trans. D. Guder (Grand Rapids: Eerdmans, 1983); J. Moltmann, *The Trinity and the Kingdom of God* (SCM: London, 1981).

1. First, in the cross we see the results of Jesus' refusal of any identity other than that of being totally Son of the Father. His death is the outcome of his rejection of any version of reality save that of the Kingdom of God. His self-surrender to the Will of God brings him to this point of absolute 'Godwardness'. His life of being totally from and for the one he exclusively invoked as 'my Father' meant for him an existence of inclusive solidarity with the lost, the poor, the defenseless,—all who looked to God for an impossible forgiveness or as the ultimate legitimation of the justice for which they had hungered. His exclusive relationship to the Father meant his inclusive relationship to all in the realm of a universal Love. The cross, from this point of view, exposes the nakedness of Jesus' identity: "not my will but thine be done . . . " (Lk 26:42); "Father, forgive them, for they know not what they do." (Lk 23:34)

2. Secondly, just as the cross manifests in its darkness the identity of Jesus as Son, it also allows the true identity of God as 'Father' to appear. The absurdity of imagining God as somehow demanding the blood-sacrifice of his only-begotten Son is contradicted by an appreciation of the Mystery of Love at work. God refuses any self-revelation in the world at this supreme moment of disclosure other than that of being the limitless, unconditional self-giving Love enacted in the cross. Such a God does not send "twelve legions of angels" to vindicate his authority; for the divine authority is exercised in the manner he remains 'in character': he appears only in the vulnerable compassionate humanity of the One who is so intimately his own, as his 'only-begotten Son'. He appears in the world not as a vengeful power among the other powers of this world. His Word, disclosive of the One who utters it, is the crucified. "This is my beloved Son. Hear him." In refusing any identity other than that of the Mystery which gives what is most intimately its 'own' for the sake of the sinful world, God is revealed as Creator: he respects the full drama of created freedom; he will not crush it. Rather, he appeals to created freedom through the transcendent liberty of the Love he is. At the heart of this respect for created freedom is the divine affirmation of the human freedom of the Son. There is no miraculous solution to the suffering and death resulting from the self-offering of the Son. The Father is no escape into an infantile way of life. The whole of the pain and drama of the world's crisis has to be faced and felt, and suffered, in the full expansion of freedom:

"Abba, Father, all things are possible to thee; remove this cup from me; yet not what I will, but as thou wilt" (Mk 14:36).

Love, in its transcendent origin, is thus revealed not as power or pretense. In a God-resistant world, it is the mystery which provokes the Son's act of absolute faith and hope in the salvation that can come only in a God-given realm of justice and mercy.

3. Less visibly but very suggestively, the cross of the Son also reveals the character of the Spirit. Once more, there is that quality of refusal. The Cross evidences how the Holy Spirit rejects the manner in which the 'evil spirits' dwell in the world and possess human beings. If the evil spirits which infest human history are characterised by Satanic self-centeredness and demonic self-destructiveness, the Holy Spirit leads to the vulnerability of solidarity with the poor and the weak (Lk 4:18), service of one's neighbour and forgiveness of enemies. The crucified, conceived in the power of this Spirit, possessing and possessed by it, exorcised evil spirits in the authority of the Spirit of holiness which indwelt him (Mk 3:22-30). On the cross, he offers himself to the Father (Hb 9:14) for the sake of the world, in order to release this Spirit of Love into the world: " ... and bowing his head, he handed over the Spirit" (Jn 19:30). The cross reveals the Spirit as that divine Spirit of the Father who gives his Son, and as the Spirit of Christ who gives his life for the world's salvation.

4. In the resurrection, the Son is glorified in his identity of being from and for the Father, in his solidarity with the weak and the hopeless. The identity which he had lived, which had been mocked and condemned as a blasphemous pretention (Lk 22:70), is vindicated. The relationality of Jesus' identity is consummated: God exalts him and bestows on him a name which is above every name, setting him above all creation. Jesus is revealed as "Lord to the glory of God the Father" (Phil 3:9ff). The final era of human history has begun. In the power and radiance of glorified being, Jesus destroys every rule, authority and power inimical to the divine realm (1 Cor 15:24). Jesus brings everything into the self-surrender of his own filial relationship: "When all things are subjected to him, then the Son will also be subjected to him ... that God may be everything to everyone." (v. 28)

5. The resurrection reveals God as the one who glorifies the crucified Jesus, vindicating everything that he lived and died for. It reveals God as the one who is not defeated by evil and death, but as

a Love that keeps on being Love even at the most intensely Loveless, Godless and Graceless juncture of world history. God, as Father, is manifest as the One who is 'for Jesus', as the one who has identified his cause with the destiny of the Son. The Word of God comes to complete utterance in Jesus' risen existence. The Father is revealed as the transcendent origin and goal of the whole being of the Son.

6. The Spirit, in the resurrection, is revealed as "the Spirit of him who raised Jesus from the dead" (Rom 8:11) and the one who will glorify Jesus and declare the whole meaning of his life and death (Jn 16:13f). This Spirit is the Spirit of the heart of flesh replacing the hopeless, loveless character of the "heart of stone": both Father and Son are present in the world through this ultimately irresistible Spirit which is the last breath of the Crucified (Jn 19:30) and the first breath of the Risen One (Jn 20:22). As the agent of the Resurrection, the Spirit leads to intimacy and freedom with the Father (Rom 8:15f) and to the recognition of Jesus as Lord (1 Cor 12:3). It inspires a new community of life in Christ (1 Cor 12:12) and groans with sighs too deep for words in the hopes of all believers as they experience the travail of all creation awaiting liberation (Rom 8:19-27).

7. The Trinity is revealed, then, in the paschal mystery, as God's self-communication to an alienated world. God enters into the consciousness of faith as the transcendent compassionate Love which gives what is most intimate to itself, the Son and the Spirit, into the darkness and self-destructiveness of the world. To this degree, the mystery of God 'enworlds' itself, incarnate in the self-giving Son, indwelling and 'enheartened' in the Spirit as this divine Gift transforms human subjectivity: the self-enclosed domain of the "heart of stone" yields to the Spirit-given faith, hope, and love of the "heart of flesh". As conformed to the Son and indwelt by the Spirit, the Christian community finds that the ultimate mystery of God is intimated as 'Love', as the 'Our Father' into whose presence we escape from the oppression of fear in all its forms. From this ultimate mystery so intimated, " ... neither death nor life, nor angels nor principalities, nor things present, nor things to come, nor powers, nor height nor depth, nor anything else in all creation will be able to separate us ... " .(Rom 8:38)

Thus, to a world afflicted by the excess of the problem of evil, the Trinity communicates itself in another excess: that of a Mystery of self-giving Love. The mystery is enacted in the incarnate Son, through the indwelling, originated and fulfilled in the Father. The cross reveals the unconditional character of the Love at work, while the resurrection of the Crucified points to the transformation of the universe that has begun.

8. The divine missions are the eschatological enfolding of all creation in the life of God. In this ultimate perspective, the Trinity connotes the scope of God's transforming Love. In Christ, the Son, the "first born of all creation", "the first born from the dead", creation is set free from its bondage to decay: the world comes home to God and reaches its full coherence and consistency in him, through whom, for whom, and in whom it was created. A finally reconciled humanity emerges, brought about by the compassion of the cross. The Spirit, poured out on all creation animates the whole, to become the principle of ultimate communion and unity: "that they may be one . . . ". (Jn 17) The Father, as the origin and goal of the universe, enfolds all to himself through the Son and the Spirit, to become "everything to everyone" (1 Cor 15:28). For "God was in Christ reconciling the world to himself" (2 Cor 5:19). The evils of sin and death are vanquished by a victorious Love. It triumphs on its own terms. It is never to be reduced to the power-play of the unredeemed world where violence and self-justifying pride make the values of the kingdom so vulnerable. But in the resurrection of the Crucified, self-sacrificing love is manifest as true life.

Thus, the Trinity is the form of the Kingdom to come. The divine three are personal articulations of the realm of God's culminating presence: God's dwelling in creation for the sake of the world existing in God.

9. As the Trinity manifests itself in the cross and resurrection of Jesus, the mysterious intersubjectivity of the divine persons in the one 'Love-life' of God is expressed. Jesus, as Son, exists "from and for the Father": his death is the result and sign of his total self-offering to the Father, just as the resurrection constitutes him "Son of God in power" (Rom 1:4) and "Lord to the glory of God the Father" (Phil 2:11). In the end, "he delivers the kingdom to God the Father" (1 Cor 15:24). The Father, on his part, 'highly exalted him,

and bestowed on him the name which is above every name, that at the name of Jesus every knee should bow, in heaven, on earth and under the earth ... " (Phil 2:10). The Father's glorification of his Son and the Son's glorification of the Father take place in the sending of the Spirit. Jesus' going means the Spirit's coming, sent by the Father at the request of Jesus and in the name of Jesus (Jn 14:16, 26). This Spirit, whose sending has been the object of Jesus' life, comes both to glorify Jesus (Jn 16:14) and to liberate all believers for an unheard-of freedom with God, as children and heirs (Rom 8:14-17). The whole meaning of the mystery of Christ can be thought of as opening the relational life of God to include the whole redeemed world:

> The glory which thou has given to me I have given to them, that they may be one, even as we are one, I in them, and thou in me, that they may be perfectly one ... that the love with which thou hast loved me may be in them and I in them. (Jn 17:22-26)

In short, the paschal mystery brings to light that reciprocal co-inherence of the divine persons which is called *perichoresis* (literally, a dancing around together) in Greek theology, the circulation of divine interpersonal life, and *circumincessio* (a communion of mutual yielding), or *circuminsessio* (a communion of mutual indwelling) by the Latins.[19] The Father 'passes over' into the mystery of the Son: "This is my beloved Son. Hear him" (Mk 9:7). The son 'passes over' into the Mystery of the Father: he lives to do the will of the one who sent him (Jn 6:39), as he says, "The Father is greater than I" (Jn 14:28). Both Father and Son yield themselves to the witnessing presence of the Spirit. This Spirit inspires faith in Jesus as Lord, and gives the freedom to relate to God as 'Abba'.

10. In the resurrection of the Crucified, the intersubjective reality of God is made invocable. As the cross subverts the reality of the false gods of self-serving power, it makes room for the truth of God as self-giving Love. It is a kind of 'black hole' where the ordinary ego-centered laws of worldly survival and domination are reversed, and the reality of Love's universe is glimpsed:

---

[19] See M. O'Carroll, "Circumincession" in *Trinitas*, pg. 68ff.

> If the Spirit of him who raised Jesus from the dead dwells in you, he who raised Jesus from the dead will give life to your mortal bodies also through his Spirit who dwells in you. (Rom 8:11)

11. This eternal Love which is "from the beginning" enters the time of human history in the duration of the 'three holy days', the *sacrum triduum*. This period unfolds a trinitarian narrative. Good Friday enacts the self-giving of the Father in the gift of his only-begotten Son; Holy Saturday depicts the Son's entry in the depths of human defeat and the God-forsaken world. His self-giving for others is "unto the end". Easter Sunday is the day for the surprise of the Spirit. Divine Love transforms. It is a Love stronger than death, a self-giving more powerful than any self-centeredness resisting it.

7. *The Trinity and the Church*

The very first chapter stressed how the mystery of the Trinity was bound up with the meaning of the Church, in its community and its mission. To that degree, in its essential constitution, the Church is a living icon of the Trinity. This reaches a special intensity in the celebration of the eucharist. There is no need to repeat that material here, especially as, in the later context of the church's mission in the world, we will have occasion to stress some aspects of it again. In the present context of 'interconnections', suffice it to note how the Trinitarian mystery structures the church's self-understanding. The following references are valuable. First, Vatican II's *Ad Gentes no. 2*:

> The pilgrim church is missionary by her very nature. For it is from the mission of the Son and the mission of the Holy Spirit that she takes her origin, in accordance with the decree of God, the Father.

Then, regarding the unity of the church, the Council's decree on Ecumenism, *Unitatis redintegratio,* specifically emphasizes the Trinity as the form and source of ecclesial communion:

> This is the sacred mystery of the unity of the church, in Christ and through Christ, with the Holy Spirit energizing a variety of func-

tions. The highest exemplar and source of this mystery is the unity, in the Trinity of persons, of One God, the Father and the Son and the Holy Spirit. (no. 2)

The Trinity is at once the principle of the unity of the People of God and of the whole human race.[20]

Obviously the various connections suggested so far imply an eschatological dimension to the meaning of the Trinity. Later, we will have a special chapter on this "reference to human destiny".[21] Further, these instances of correlation imply a variety of analogical links between the trinitarian mystery and human experience as it is transformed in grace. In the next chapter we will turn to the analogies implicit in the inter-relationships here outlined.

In this chapter, we have been trying to suggest a hologrammic impression of the Trinitarian mystery. We examined, in a preliminary manner, the various connections suggested in the themes of human existence, creation, revelation, grace, paschal mystery, church, and eucharist. These configurations are by no means exhaustive. Nonetheless, a more or less broad sense of the rich field of trinitarian meaning has, I hope, been evoked. Through such a multi-dimensional *Gestalt,* or theological hologram, the ground is prepared for the more precise elaboration of the various analogical models, in a way that keeps before us both an appreciative sense of the data and the relative usefulness of theological analogies.

---

[20]*Lumen Gentium* no. 4; *Gaudium et Spes* no. 24. See, too, B. de Margerie, *La Trinité chrétienne* ... , pgs. 303-318.

[21]For a good treatment of recent trinitarian theology in this regard, see Roger Olson, "Trinity and Eschatology: the Historical Being of God in Jurgen Moltmann and Wolfhart Pannenberg", *Scot. Journ. of Theol.* 36 (1986), pgs. 213-227.

5
Analogies

In the last chapter, we were rather busy treating of 'interconnections'. I suggested how the meaning of the Trinity was 'configured' to a variety of theological themes: the self, creation, revelation, grace, the paschal mystery, the church ... We were trying to imagine the Trinity less as a mathematical diagram and more as a hologram. This was largely a preliminary imaginative representation of the data. In such suggested connections, a trinitarian *Gestalt* pervading the whole of Christian theology makes its presence felt.

1. "Analogical Imagination"

We come now to the point of attempting a deeper penetration of the trinitarian data. If the preceding chapter was more contemplative in its procedure, more holistic in its presentation, this present chapter is more systematic and limited to certain historical instances of the "analogical imagination".[1] In the tradition of such analogical imagining and the reflection it inspires, we ask with Thomas Aquinas, and Augustine before him, what elements of our experience provide the best analogy for coming to a theological, though, admittedly, radically imperfect, understanding of the Trinitarian mystery.

---

[1]David Tracy's *The Analogical Imagination* (New York: Seabury, 1981) is the best modern resource for a sympathetic presentation of analogy in Catholic theological tradition.

116   *Analogies*

There is, of course, a long and rich history of this kind of trinitarian exploration. Its roots are clearly discernible in the Scriptures themselves, in the very use of such symbols as 'word', 'spirit', 'Father', 'Son'. Early in the development of Christian communication with the surrounding culture, the apologists such as Justin suggested that the Logos/Son should be understood after the manner of a spiritual emanation. Gregory of Nyssa developed, at a later date, the beginnings of a 'social analogy'. Augustine laid the foundations of a full-fledged development of what became known as 'the psychological analogy': our human activities of knowing and willing were used as an analogy of the trinitarian processions. In a later monastic theology, Richard of St. Victor elaborated a beautiful analogy of love and community as the privileged insight into how and why God must be one and three.[2] St. Thomas Aquinas developed and systematized the tradition sketched out by Augustine. This enabled him to ask and answer a whole series of theological questions provoked by the biblical and dogmatic data. Bernard Lonergan has initiated an effort to transpose such a mode of analogical reflection into the contemporary methodological context, where meaning is no longer elaborated in terms of metaphysical theory, but is grounded in the experience of the existential subject.[3] At the same time, there are contemporary attempts to re-conceive trinitarian doctrine in terms of analogies suggested by process philosophy[4], communications theory,[5] interpersonal relations,[6] and the psychology of love,[7] to mention just a few.[8]

---

[2] For these key historical examples see William J. Hill, *The Three-Personed God. The Trinity as a Mystery of Salvation* (Washington: Catholic University Press), pgs. 53-78.

[3] *De Deo Trino I-II* (Rome: Gregorian Press, 1959). The next chapter deals with this more at length.

[4] Joseph Bracken, *The Triune Symbol* (New York: the University Press, 1985).

[5] George Tavard, *The Vision of the Trinity* (Washington: University Press of America, 1980).

[6] Heribert Muehlen, *Der Heilige Geist als Person* (Paderborn: Schoningh, 1963).

[7] Eberhard Juengel, *God as the Mystery of the World,* trans. D.L. Guder (Grand Rapids: Eerdmans, 1983).

[8] Both Hill, *op. cit.* and de Margerie, *La Trinité chrétienne* provide rich documentation of many other trinitarian analogies, ancient and modern.

2. Theological Terms

Before proceeding to present at some length the main points of the Thomistic trinitarian analogy, a brief aside on some of the often problematical terms employed in modern theology. Admittedly, it is all an effort to 'imagine' the meaning of the Trinity in a way that makes the best intellectual and existential sense. The perduring challenge is to allow the original experience of God to speak to us today, first as a statement, then as a question, and then, we would hope, as provoking a new formulation. This complex process involves description of the experience, a coherent formulation of what it means, and further exploration of what is implied. To that purpose, writers will speak of symbols, metaphors, analogies, and models of the Trinity.

To speak generally, symbols are affectively-charged compact presentations of the mystery, be they deeds, gestures, events, words, or persons. Here we refer back to what has been said on the trinitarian symbolism in the biblical witness. Metaphor, on the other hand, is a verbal play of linguistic expression as it stretches the available language to evoke a sense of what is symbolically present, of what is incarnate, inspired, intimated in the basic symbolic structure. Metaphor is still on the descriptive level, and its aim is to engage the whole person in the immediacy of living faith and love.

Analogy is a way that looks to theological explanation. For example, and this point may appear controversial to some, the symbolic structure of the experience of God is obviously communitarian and dialogical: God is not something other than this One who is communicating with us human beings through his own Son and Spirit, just as our relation to such a God is in terms of the dialogue of faith, hope, and love. This basic symbolism blooms into complex metaphorical expressions of 'sending', sacrifice, friendship, and so forth. Analogical exploration works within this rich symbolic reality and the metaphorical expression it provokes. What is described in the symbolism of community, what is expressed in the metaphors of interpersonal relationships demands some form of theological explanation which both seeks to order the data and to offer some form of theological penetration of it which respects the mystery both hidden and revealed in the Christian experience. Thus, we might explore, through the use of analogy, what biblically-expressed communion of Father, Son, and Spirit in the one divine mystery might really mean.

The comparative newcomer to theological discourse is the 'model'. Its use in theology is analogically related to its use in the physical sciences.[9] As such, it strikes me that it is not employed with the realist commitment characterising the theological use of analogy. In some degree, at least, it abstracts from the complexity of the hermeneutics of faith. Nor is it tied to any particular theological method. Its use is pragmatic, constructed to respect an expected pluralism in interpretation and judgment. It is more a map allowing for many entries into a particular terrain. In short, a model is a provisional, practically orientated way of exploring the data, in order to conduct significant experiments. Like a map it does not aim to express everything, for it aims at some practical outcome. It operates within the speculatively modest and pragmatic concerns of modern scientific method.

To catch the emphasis of these four ways of approaching trinitarian theology—and all theology—, I would suggest something like this: symbolism pertains to the primary givenness of the experience of God; metaphor to the way this is creatively elaborated in language; analogy points the way to theological exploration of the mystery itself; models look to praxis, the significance of the mystery 'for us'. Needless to say, to collapse all these four into any one category causes immense confusion. For each one has its own point to make: symbolism deals with experience of the data; metaphor with the creativity of language; analogy with the systematic intelligence of theology; models look to praxis and agenda.

What I propose to do in the following pages is to concentrate on the analogical type of reflection. Previous and later chapters set it in the larger context of symbol, metaphor and model. Further, not only will we treat of analogical thinking here, but because of its special relevance to what follows, we will concentrate on the 'psychological analogy'.

---

[9] I. Ramsey, *Models and Mystery* (London: SCM, 1964).

3. The Psychological Analogy

Augustine introduced this type of thinking into Western theology.[10] In his refined psychological awareness, he adverted to five types of experience potentially relevant to the disclosure of the trinitarian reality. These can be specified as

a. the experience of a lover, the beloved, and the love uniting them;

b. being, knowing, and willing;

c. the mind's consciousness of itself, and the self-knowing and self-loving deriving from such;

d. the experience of memory, understanding, and willing;

e. the spiritual person's memory of God, and the consequent understanding of God and the love for God that takes place in the mind and heart.

We can catch the spirit of Augustine's exploration in the following lines:

> ... anyone who intelligently perceives that these three things are by nature divinely established in his mind, and what a great thing it is when an eternal and unchangeable nature can be recalled, beheld and desired—and remembers it by memory, contemplates it by understanding, and embraces it by his love, certainly such a one discovers the image of the highest Trinity. Man ought to direct all that is within him to remember, to see and to love this highest Trinity, in order that he might recall it, contemplate it and find his delight in it. But lest anyone should so compare this image, made by the Trinity but changed for the worse by his own fault, as to think it like the Trinity in every respect, I have warned him ... that he should behold in this likeness, of whatever sort it might be, the great unlikeness that is there also.[11]

There are three things to note here. First, human existence is marked with a trinitarian likeness because it is created by the Trinity.

---

[10]For a clear and enthusiastic presentation of Augustine's trinitarian theology, see Edmund Hill, *The Mystery of the Trinity* (London: Geoffrey Chapman, 1985).

[11]*De Trinitate*, XV, 20.

Secondly, an understanding of the Trinity results from a conscious participation in the divine mystery through the activities of faith and love. Thirdly, the knowledge of the Trinity that results from such dynamic participation has its limits and distortions. To adapt the words of Lateran IV, the likeness between God and ourselves must be set in the context of a greater unlikeness.[12]

Over eight centuries later, Augustine's experientially rich and subtle analyses called forth an impressive systematic elaboration in the trinitarian theology of Thomas Aquinas.

4. Aquinas' Trinitarian Theology

Thomas' trinitarian theology is marked with such rigorous coherence that its very success can give the impression that it is all an elaborate metaphysical deduction in terms of the then new-found Aristolelian metaphysics and psychology. Does this result from a forgetfulness of the theological enterprise as an exploration of the data of faith, as "faith seeking understanding"? The fact that Thomas chose to treat of the divine unity before addressing himself to the specific question of the Trinity has often given this impression. Whilst it is true that, in accord with his thoroughly systematic purposes, Thomas treats of the unity of God before moving on to the divine Trinity, this does not mean that his reflections are somehow transformed from philosophy into theology when he begins treating of the Trinity. Throughout his treatment of the Mystery of God, it is the one divine mystery that engages his attention, considered now under the aspect of unity, attributes, and so forth, now under the aspect of Trinity. Arguably, in contrast to a more Greek approach, this traditionally Augustinian mode is less apt theologically to emphasize the trinitarian mystery of God. Nonetheless, Thomas' aims are systematic, and the order he chooses powerfully serves them. At no stage is he not intending to explore the one concrete revealed reality of Father, Son, and Spirit. He knows he cannot say everything at once and opts for an order of exposition which in his judgment makes for the most coherent statement.[13]

---

[12]DS no. 806.
[13]See William Hill, *The Three-Personed God*, pgs. 62-69.

Having considered those things which belong to the divine unity we now pass on to what pertains to the trinity of persons with in the Godhead. Because the divine persons are distinct through their relations or origin, in the order of our exposition we shall consider first the origin or procession, then the relationships connected with this origin, and then the divine persons.[14]

Thomas is not trying to prove the Trinity. His aim is theological wisdom: an overall intelligible coherence in the data of faith:

That God is threefold and one is solely an article of faith and can in no way be demonstrated, although some arguments can be given that are not necessarily convincing or even probable except to a believer.[15]

Manifestly, Aquinas knows what he is about: Christian theology. There is too much faith in his exposition for a non-believing philosopher and too much philosophy in his theology for anyone content, for whatever reason, to be a simple believer. But for the specifically theological enterprise, the exploration of the meaning of God, in which faith subsumes into itself the techniques and categories of a philosophical search after wisdom, Thomas is a theologian at work: a Christian believer seeking to appropriate and expound the central mystery of faith in an ordered and illuminating manner. "Trinitate posita, congruunt huiusmodi rationes . . . " ("given the revelation of the Trinity, this kind of clarification is appropriate").[16]

Needless to say, we cannot go into the intricacies of Thomas' exposition. What is more manageable is to highlight the basic questions he is asking, and the main moves in his employment of the 'psychological analogy'.

5. Divine Be-ing

The notion of God which the first part of the *Summa* elaborates is that God is the sheer act of Be-ing, *Ipsum Esse Subsistens,* a mystery

---
[14] *S. Theol* 1, q. 27 (introd).
[15] *In Boet. de Trin.* 1, 4.
[16] *S. Theol.* 1, 32, 1 ad 1.

of pure 'Be-ing' beyond any finite determination and comprehension.[17] How God 'is' transcends any concept or category.[18] Our knowledge of the divine reality is necessarily analogical: created reality can, indeed, positively direct our minds toward the divine reality, even though such knowing must live from negation. The human mind can truly intend the divine reality by conceiving of goodness, wisdom, love and so on; but the divine mode of being in which these 'perfections' are actually realized in God is utterly beyond human comprehension. As Thomas succinctly puts it, we know "that God is" in terms of existence and the various attributes, but not "what God is". This darkness remains always a feature of theological knowledge. Though Aquinas' theology lives consistently in this darkness, it is a profoundly positive theology in its movement. God has disclosed himself in a communion and self-giving of Love. For this reason, Thomas distances himself from the excessively apophatic utterances of the pseudo-Denis. That kind of "negative theology" insists that we are united to God as to one who is altogether unknown (omnino ignoto). Thomas' carefully nuanced words are most interesting:

> ... although through the revelation of grace we do not know in this life the 'what is' of God, and thus are united to him as to someone unknown, still we know him more fully in that more, and more outstanding, of his effects are disclosed; and inasmuch as we attribute some things from divine revelation to him which human reason cannot attain, such as his being three and one.[19]

The mind of the believer is positively oriented to the transcendent, and therefore dark, mystery of God. But this dynamic of knowing lives in a context of communion and the religious fact that God has communicated with believers through grace and revelation. As a later idiom would have it, God remains the mystery even in the

---

[17] Aquinas' naming of God as 'sheer being' is allied to the biblical name of Ex 3, 14. His ontological understanding of God in this sense is, of course, not directly biblical. On the other hand, it contradicts no possible biblical exegesis. See Hill, *op. cit.,* pg. 63, n. 30.

[18] *S. Theol.* 1, 12, 12. For a good note see, Hill, *op. cit.,* pg. 64, n. 31. I am following Hill in his translation of *esse* as 'Be-ing'.

[19] *S. Theol.* 1, 12, 13 ad 1.

moment of his self-communication and self-revelation.

It is within this horizon of mystery and communication to us in the "more, and more outstanding effects" of grace and revelation that Aquinas proceeds to explore the mystery of the Trinity. It is not as though he is compressing the divine mystery into the limits of a human analogue. The opposite is the case. The creativity of analogical thinking unfolds in presence of the mystery. And this happens with the awareness of the primacy of that mystery and the limitations of our human knowledge. It is a knowledge that is intending the Mystery of God as something present, drawing the believer into communion. For the revelation of the Father's originating love, the saving presence of the Son, and the fellowship of the Spirit are not something that has to be proved. These "more outstanding effects" are there to be explored with the resources of human experience, thought, and speech. Such 'givens' in the life and prayer of the church are not somehow put on hold or bracketed out until theology can make sense of them. Because they are so radically given in the life of Christian faith, such beliefs call forth theological understanding.

The data of faith concerning Father, Son, and Spirit provoke many questions. The originality of Thomas' treatment resides in the order in which he treats such questions.

6. *Divine Processions*

The first question he addresses is how to understand, in the provisional analogical manner of human knowing, 'processions' within the divine reality. The scriptures, especially the Johannine writings, imply, and church doctrines affirm, a mysterious divine vitality, a life of differentiated communication within God. How can there be such a 'process' within the all-exhaustive actuality of the divine 'Be-ing' so that the Son can truly be said to come forth from the Father, and so that this original vitality can further manifest itself in the 'coming forth' of the Spirit?

The analogy that Thomas commends is one that seeks to respect the utter transcendence of the divine and to keep well away from any Arian implications. The following lines take us to the heart of Aquinas' analogical approach:

> As God is above all things, what is said of God is not to be understood in terms of the lowest type of creation, that is bodily things, but rather in terms of the highest creatures which are intellectual realities, even though these too fall short of representing the divine reality. So procession in God is not thought of as it occurs in bodily entities, or through local motion, or through the action of some cause in the production of some effect outside it ... but according to an intellectual emanation, as, for instance, an intelligible word proceeds from the speaker but remains within him. This is the way Catholic Faith understands procession in the divine case.[20]

Thomas invites one to understand the processive reality of God in spiritual terms. It is, first of all, an exercise in negative theology. For there is no question of God producing a creature (Arius). There is no question of acting in some external effect by dynamically identifying with it, or impressing his likeness on it (Sabellius and the Modalists). Needless to say the procession concerned is not an instance of purely physical movement either. These errors, according to Thomas, result from conceiving of the reality of procession in an external way ("*ad extra*"), not "*ad intra*", in a manner that pertains to the inner reality of God.[21]

Thus, the way is cleared for a positive understanding of divine procession in terms of an inner process, an activity immanent to the divine act. An instance of this is the activity of the intellect. The act of intelligence remains within the knower. Whoever understands finds that something comes forth within the mind. This is a conception of the thing understood. It derives both from intellectual faculty and its act of knowledge. Such a conception is manifest in speaking, for the interior word is manifest in the spoken word ("*verbum cordis*" ... "*verbum vocis*").

By using the resources of Aristotelian psychology, Aquinas begins to elaborate the psychological analogy. It suggests some understanding of how there can be a processive activity in God. The highest spiritual activity of intelligence produces something within the human

---

[20] *S. Theol.* 1, 27, 1.
[21] *Ibid.*

mind when it conceives of reality in the act of knowing. He takes this further: what the intellect conceives, the will can proceed to love. This leads to a fuller statement:

> Within God there are two processions, namely, the procession of the word, and also another kind of procession. In evidence of this, we observe that there can be no procession within God which actively tends to something extrinsic to the divine reality: it must remain within the divine agent. This kind of activity in an intellectual nature is the action of the intellect and the action of the will. The procession of the word is understandable by way of the act of the intellect. Then, according to the act of the will, we find another kind of procession within us, namely, the procession of love. Through this the object loved is within the lover, just as by conception of the word, the reality expressed or understood is in the one who understands ...[22]

Thomas intensifies this analogy by applying it to the case of the self as known and loved:

> When someone understands and loves himself he is within himself not only through a real identity, but also as a reality which is understood is within the one who understands, and as a reality which is loved is within the one who loves.[23]

Thus, Aquinas understands that the plenitude of divine Be-ing means a divine reality luminously and affectively present to itself in an absolute self-expression and self-possession. Sheer divine actuality is unlimited light and love: the divine reality comprehends and delights in itself (and all else, whether actually existent or not) in an all-exhaustive knowing and in an unrestricted ecstasy of loving.

This insight releases a further sequence of questions. So I will now sketch the main points of Thomas' unfolding of the analogy he has established, even though for reasons of brevity the actual sequence of the *Summa* will not be followed.

---

[22] *S. Theol.* 1, 27, 3.
[23] *S. Theol.* 1, 37, 1.

7. Twelve Questions

1. To recapitulate, how is 'procession' to be understood within God? Any answer depends on our readiness to form analogies of the divine being in terms of the highest created realities we know. This is the specifically spiritual being with its faculties of knowing and willing. In the act of understanding and in the activity of loving, such spiritual being is interiorly enriched by conceiving within itself reality as truth, and as a consequence, by going out of itself to reality as loved, as the good. In finite realities, there are the limitations of ignorance and evil, as well as deficiencies inherent in always being 'in potentia' for something more. In contrast, in the fulness of God's Being, these limitations and deficiencies do not exist: in the divine act are contained God's all-exhaustive conception of himself and all reality and a perfect loving of himself and all else.

2. Why are there only two processions within God? The New Testament and the later conciliar statements speak of only two processions, that of the Son and that of the Holy Spirit. Is there anything about the psychological analogy that might indicate why only these two processions are to be found in God? Thomas' answer is simple enough: the inner activity of a spiritual nature is complete in the two operations of knowing and willing. All other activity is reducible to these. What is more, they occur in that order; for love always presupposes a knowledge of the reality it possesses or desires. Thus the analogy provides a further insight into the data of revelation: the communication of the divine Word precedes that of the Spirit.

3. How is divine generation to be understood, in the case of the only-begotten Son? Thomas gives his answer here by connecting the meaning of generation with the intellectual conception of the Word. In such an intellectual conception all the requirements for the meaning of generation are found: the origin of one living entity from another joined to it as a living principle and resulting in the likeness of nature. The precise point here is that the divine intellectual conception can be called 'generation' not just because it is a vital communication, for this pertains also to the activity of loving; but because it intrinsically connotes a likeness in nature (which love does not). For to conceive of something in knowledge is to express its

precise nature. Loving is more a "breath" (*spiritus*), implying "a certain vital movement and impulse",[23a] engaging the lover in the doing of something, an outgoing dynamism rather than an interior expression. So, for Thomas, the procession by way of intelligent conception can be termed 'generation', whereas that by way of loving is not—even though, of course, in God, such love follows on the generation of the Word/Son and unites Father and Son.

4. How can there be distinctions within God? Thomas knows that there cannot be any distinction in God in terms of the utter simplicity and unicity of the divine reality.[24] The only way distinction can occur is through relationships. These must flow from the processive activities already described. Aquinas hones the analogy he is developing by addressing the following question:

5. How can there be real relationships within God? Since the two processions are real, there results real relationships: that which proceeds (Word, Spirit of love) is related to that from which it proceeds. Real processions necessarily imply real relationships, even within the mystery of God.[25] Thomas is once more working from the data of faith in elaborating his analogy. In the *Sed contra* of the article mentioned, he is clearly presuming, against any Sabellian or Modalist tendency, that God is really Father, Son and Spirit: the presumed Christian realism demands that there be real relationships within the divine, not just logical ones pertaining to our mode of speaking about God. The logic of his exposition seems to end in a certain embarrassment in that he has to allow for four real relationships: that is to say, there are two sets of symmetrical relationships. These are based on the two processions associated with knowing and loving which occur within the divine reality: paternity, filiation, 'active' and 'passive' spiration.

The purpose of deploying this analogy is to explore the trinitarian mystery of these three invocable divine persons, Father, Son and Spirit,—as faith discloses them. So, after indicating the processive actuality of the divine mystery in knowledge and love, and noting that this alone can be the source of any relational distinctions within

---

[23a] *S. Theol.* 1, 27, 4.
[24] *S. Theol.* 1, 28, 3.
[25] *S. Theol.* 1, 28, 1.

God, Thomas proceeds to the matter of the persons. This leads him to the question of the person; hence, the following question:

6. How can we speak of persons within God? What are the conditions justifying the attribution of personhood to 'these three'? The received Boethian notion of person was that of "an individual existing in a rational nature". How is this applicable in the divine case? That this highest of all perfections must be affirmed of God is clear. The meaning of such an affirmation is, however, problematical, given the transcendent unique divine reality. What cannot be allowed is three distinct intellectual natures in God, since God is one. This refines the conception of the divine persons as three distinctly subsisting relationships. Each one of these is, in its own manner, identical with the divine nature, though 'relationally opposed' to the others. The general notion of person as a distinct individual with its own separate nature is refined to allow for the uniqueness of the divine case. There, the meaning of person is based on the distinctly subsisting relationship within the new divine nature, and, in a distinct manner, identified with it. The general notion of person as a distinct individual is found to be too general for trinitarian theology. In this case, person means more "the distinctly subsistent reality".

7. But how are there only three divine persons? This question has to be answered since the two processions yield four real relationships. How can the number of persons be restricted to three? The answer lies in the way the 'opposition' existing between such relationships is understood: clearly there is a real polar opposition between Fatherhood and Sonship, and the loved that is breathed forth (Spirit) and the Loving principle that breathes it. But the 'loving principle', the Father and the Son are one: though distinct as Father and Son, they are one as the source of love. At the risk of pushing Thomas' terminology too far, we could say that the Loving Father generates the Loving Son, and as one principle they breathe forth the Spirit. This means that each is related to the proceeding Spirit as the one principle. Or as Thomas succinctly puts it,

> ... though there are four relationships in the divine reality, one of these, namely the activity of breathing the Spirit, is not separated from (either) the person of the Father (or) the Son, but belongs to each of them. And so, while it is a relationship it is not called a (distinct) property, since it does not belong to one divine person

exclusively. Neither is it a personal relationship, that is, constituting a person. But these three relationships, Fatherhood, Sonship and 'procession' are called personal properties as constituting the divine persons: for Fatherhood is the person of the Father, Sonship the person of the Son, and 'procession' is the person of the proceeding Spirit.[26]

Thus, the divine persons are pure relationships, distinctly subsisting within the divine mystery, and each distinctly identified with the divine nature. For God to be Trinity means that the one divine reality is on this personal level, utterly relational: the Father is a relationship of pure 'Son-and-Spirit-wardness'; the Son is unrestricted 'Father-and-Spirit-wardness'; and the Spirit is ecstatic 'Father-and-Son-wardness'.[27]

Let me stress once more that this use of analogy is not proving the Trinity: "It is used to manifest the Trinity, because, once the Trinity is given, this kind of clarification has its place, not however in a way that sufficiently proves the Trinity of the persons . . . "[28]

8. How is the distinctiveness of each of the three divine persons expressed? Once the divine reality has been opened up in trinitarian terms, five 'notions' are employed to further specify the trinitarian Mystery as a vitally communicative and relational reality. These 'notions' come into use to illumine the reality of the divine three, as each of the three divine subjects is divine, is God, in the distinctive manner and order which these notions suggest. They are listed as Unoriginateness, Fatherhood, Common Spiration, Sonship, and procession: the first three apply to the Father; the third and fourth to the Son, and the last to the Holy Spirit.

Through these 'notions' faith places the distinctiveness of each of the divine three in the trinitarian reality of God. These notional designations promote an understanding of the divine persons in their distinctiveness. As such, they contrast with what is essential in God, the common divine nature. Each of the divine persons is God, knowing, willing, acting in a divine way. But each divine person

---

[26]*S. Theol.* 1, 30, 2 ad 1.
[27]For a thorough exposition of these points, see W. Hill, *op. cit.,* pgs. 69-73.
[28]*S. Theol.* 1, 32, 1 ad 2.

possesses or receives the divine nature in the order and manner which the notions disclose: the Father by being the unoriginated source of the Son and the Spirit, the Son by being begotten of the Father, and with the Father, breathing forth the Spirit; the Spirit by being breathed forth in love.

9. What is the meaning of 'procession' as the 'notion' of the Holy Spirit? In terms of the five trinitarian notions, it would seem that the person of the Holy Spirit is the least disclosed of the divine three. On the other hand, the notion of 'procession', which is distinctively applied to the Spirit, is arguably the richest of the five. Thomas elaborates the basic notion in terms of the names traditionally attributed to the Spirit, 'Love' and 'Gift'.[29] A brief word here.

Speaking in terms of the one essential reality of God, we have to say that the divine nature is the only sufficient principle for the eternal divine act of love. The Divine Being would be unintelligible unless it were conceived of as loveable and loving. In this respect, the Father and the Son, both possessing the divine nature, are one principle of divine love, and of the Spirit associated with it. Yet speaking from within the interpersonal concreteness of our Christian communion with the Trinity, the Holy Spirit is the mutual love existing between the Father and the Son, the Spirit by which they love both themselves and us. Christian theology, even at its most metaphysical, cannot but privilege the interpersonal and self-communicative actuality of the divine mystery it explores.[30]

Linked to this personal name of the Spirit as 'Love' is the designation, 'Gift'. In reference to the Augustinian tradition on this point, Thomas writes:

---

[29]Concerning the historically vexed issue of the Spirit's relationship to the Son as it emerges in the *Filioque* controversies with the East, the Thomistic presentation stresses two points: first, we must think of the Spirit proceeding from the Son in some way, otherwise there is no foundation for a distinction between the Son and the Spirit. For the divine persons are distinct from one another on the basis of real relationships. The only basis for such relationships are the processions within the divine reality. So, in this scheme, the Spirit must proceed not only from the Father but also from the Son—as love proceeds from the conception of the reality loved. Secondly, a right emphasis is secured by allowing that the Spirit proceeds from the Father 'through the Son'. Everything the Son had is communicated to him by the Father in the act of generation: that is to say he receives the divine nature from the Father, and with it the capacity to be a joint breather of the Spirit. (*S. Theol.* 1, 36, 3).

[30]Cf. *S. Theol.* 1, 36, 4 ad 1; 1, 37, 2.

> ... the basis of gracious giving is love: to give something freely to another means that we have good will towards him. And so what we give first of all to someone is the love itself by which we desire his well-being. Clearly, then, love has the meaning of being the first gift, through which all other free gifts are given. Since ... the Holy Spirit proceeds as love, this procession has the meaning of being the first gift. As Augustine says, "through the gift that is the Holy Spirit, the many individual gifts are given out to the members of Christ".[31]

Thus the traditional designations of the Spirit as 'Love' and 'Gift' enrich the seemingly meager notional knowledge of the third divine person.

10. What is the meaning of 'appropriating' certain essential divine attributes or activities to one of the three in a special manner? Whilst Thomas' framework is obviously metaphysical in the Aristotelian manner, he continually tries to focus his theology in the concreteness of faith's disclosure of God as 'these three'. One of the most interesting indications of this is the technique of appropriation. This focuses the general philosophical and theological affirmations of the whole system on the tri-personal reality of the God of Christian revelation. A later theology, unburdened by the metaphysical ambition of Aquinas, will not feel this problem. But for Thomas, intent on a thoroughly systematic elaboration of the data of faith, there is the need to keep grounding speculation in the experience of faith, lest the systematic aims end by being a distraction from faith. Whatever be the analogy employed, it must not come between faith and the mysteries it adores:

> The appropriation of essential attributes to the persons served to bring out the meaning of faith. For even though ... the mystery of the Trinity is beyond the range of philosophical proof, it is nonetheless right to try to clarify it through the things we understand. God's essential attributes rather than what is proper to the persons are among the matters known on the rational grounds: from

---

[31] *S. Theol.* 1, 38, 2.

creatures, the source of our knowledge, we are able to come with certitude to the knowledge of the essential attributes, but not of the personal properties.... Therefore, just as we show forth the persons by making use of the vestigial or imaged likenesses of the Trinity in creatures, so too we use the essential attributes. Appropriation means making known the divine persons by means of the essential attributes.[32]

For example, each of the three divine persons, if truly divine, must be all-powerful, all-wise, all-loving, and so on: such affirmations flow from any metaphysical or theological consideration of Divine Being. Nonetheless, both in the experience of faith's communion with these three divine persons in the economy of salvation, and through the clarifying role of the psychological analogy, a more personal theological affirmation is justified. We are entitled to associate power, and the attributes associated with it, with the Father; wisdom, and similar attributes to the Son; love, joy, peace, and unity with the Holy Spirit. Appropriation is indeed a kind of word-game, a play of theological terms and symbols designed to evoke the tripersonal, communicated reality of the Divine. The great systematic cathedral of Thomas' system houses a living, personal presence of *these three divine persons,* Father, Son, and Holy Spirit.

11. How are the Three united? One of the benefits of the psychological analogy is that it leads to a beautiful understanding of the reality of the Trinity as communion, in the strongest sense of the word (*perichoresis, circumincessio*). The Trinity is a vital divine communication in which each of the divine persons is related to the others in an active state of mutual indwelling. Thomas, having in mind the Johannine passages on this point, e.g., Jn 14:10, gives three reasons for this. First, in terms of the divine nature itself: the Father, identical with the divine nature, communicates this to the Son (and Spirit), and hence dwells in the other. Conversely, the Son and Spirit are in the Father, because both are one with the divine essence which the Father originatively possesses. Secondly, in terms of the distinct relationships, each is in the other, since the meaning of the other is intrinsically implied in the identity of each, e.g., Sonship means

[32] *S. Theol.* 1, 39, 7.

'Father-wardness'. Thirdly, in terms of the origins: the processions within God do not terminate outside the divine reality, but pertain to the eternal activity of the divine Being possessing itself as the infinite truth and the infinite good. The Word is conceived in the divine mind and expresses everything that God is; just as the Spirit of love follows on such an expression and is God's joy in the divine goodness. Note, too, that, in this divine self-knowledge and love, creation is included, e.g., in the Holy Spirit, the Father and Son love both one another and us, "diligentes et se et nos".

12. The Divine Missions: In a final consideration, Thomas brings us back to the initial point of contact with the persons of the Trinity which, up till now, according to his order of exposition, he had been treating in terms expressive of God's eternal mode of being. He now brings his theology expressly back to the experience of salvation and grace. This, though the first in our experience, is the last matter to be treated, to allow for the maximum understanding of the way God acts as grounded in the what and how of the trinitarian Be-ing. The exposition passes from the consideration of the processions and relationships of the divine persons *ad intra* to their presence and relationships *ad extra*.

This communication of the Trinity *ad extra* is treated under the heading of the 'missions' of the divine persons. The 'sendings' of the Son and the Spirit are, of course, a clearly biblical category. In both the Johannine and Pauline writings references abound regarding God's sending both his Son for the world's salvation, and the Spirit as actualizing the redemption that has occurred in Christ.

Thomas' treatment of such communications begins with an analysis of the notion of 'mission', and how this can be meaningfully applied to God. How can a divine person be 'sent', without implying either inequality in the co-equal Trinity, or some primitive form of spatial movement rather fantastically conceived as added to God's presence to creation? In the notion of divine mission, Aquinas isolates two relevant points: first, the divine person is sent inasmuch as the eternal procession of the Son/Spirit is prolonged into time and history. To this degree, the divine mission manifests what the divine person concerned personally is within the divine mystery. Secondly, whilst the mission is an extension into time of the eternal procession, it occurs inasmuch as it means that the divine persons begin to exist in the world in a new way: "Thus, the Son is said to have been sent by the Father into the world, even though he was already in the world, because he began to be in the world in a visible way by taking flesh."[33]

Thus the divine missions are the Trinity's dynamic openness to the world and to history, at once communicating the divine Word and Spirit to the finite personal world, and at the same time gathering creation into the trinitarian communion. Thomas allows for two dimensions of these missions, the 'invisible' and the visible'. God is present to everything and everyone through the limitless divine Being, power and goodness. But in the realm of grace, God becomes present in a new and intimate manner. Through the gift of grace, the human person knows and loves God in a special experiential immediacy. This is the basis for speaking of the divine 'indwelling' in the 'temple' of the soul of the sanctified person. Similarly, we can speak of the graced person's 'possession' of the divine persons: through the gift of grace, the believer can enjoy this new intimate presence of the self-giving God: " . . . as grace is given, the Holy Spirit himself is possessed, and dwells in a person; so it is he himself who is given and sent."

In an 'invisible mission', the Son likewise is given in this experiential manner by a grace which enlightens the mind with the truth of the divine Word. Thomas will also speak of the Father as given and indwelling through grace, but not as 'sent'. That would contradict the divine character of the Father as the origin of the processions. So the Father is present as source and origin of the Word and Spirit.

The transformation of grace means that God indwells the soul, as the self-giving Father, Son, and Spirit. The 'invisible missions' of Word and Spirit cause the human soul to be conformed to the reality of God by participating in the character of the persons who are sent. It is dynamically conformed to the Spirit through the gift of charity, and marked with the character of the Son through the gift of loving wisdom: the finite mind is given a new love-nourishing knowledge, "For the Word is not any kind of word, but the Word breathing love."[34]

The divine missions are not only invisible in a spiritual indwelling.

---

[33] *S. Theol.* 1, 43, 1.
[34] *S. Theol.* 1, 43, 5, ad 2.

They are also 'visible'. The reality of God's self-giving makes itself connatural to the human mode of being:

> Now it is connatural for a human being to be guided by the visible to the invisible. Through the evidence of creatures, God has in some way manifested himself and the eternal processions of the persons. Likewise, it is right that the invisible missions of the divine persons be made manifest through visible creation. Now this occurs in one way with the Son, and in another way with the Holy Spirit: the Son, in assuming human nature in his outward visible mission, is manifested as the author of holiness. The Spirit, however, in his outward manifestation, is manifested as gift and sign of the presence of salvation.[35]

8. *Evaluation*

Such, then, is some indication of the main points in Aquinas' elaboration of trinitarian theology. He has employed his psychological analogy in the light of his understanding of the divine mystery as the unlimited act of sheer Be-ing, *Ipsum Esse Subsistens*. Since 'be-ing', *esse*, is the fulness and actuality of all perfections, the psychological analogy is grounded in the conviction that God is unlimited life, infinitely actualized in knowing and loving. The analogy, applied to this context, gives a systematic answer to the various questions arising from the data of scripture and tradition: How can there be processions in God? How can there be distinct divine persons? What is the distinctive character of each of the divine three? How are they communicated in time, in the economy of grace and salvation? Thomas' systematic treatment of the Trinity leaves us with an ordered understanding of the revealed God as the infinite Actuality of Be-ing, 'en-acted', as it were, in the dynamic communion of Father, Son, and Spirit. As such it communicates itself to the created spiritual order and enfolds the human personal world into that relational existence which is specifically divine.

---

[35] *S. Theol.* 1, 43, 2. The question of the 'missions' is well treated in N. Molloy, 'The Trinitarian Mysticism of St. Thomas', *Angelicum* 57, (1980), pgs. 373-388.

Thus, as it unfolds in the Thomistic synthesis, the psychological analogy is a uniquely suggestive way of exploring and ordering the dogmatic and scriptural data pertaining to the Trinity. It is not an image drawn from the material world, but from the specifically human sphere where the created person exists, acting through the spiritual faculties of intelligence and will. Of course, the very success of such analogical thinking can be its undoing. The analogy appears to be so coherent, so probative, that it takes on a life of its own. It can cause a kind of forgetfulness of the context in which it is first employed. For Aquinas, such a context always included the radically unknowable, 'eminent' order of the divine reality, and the simple acceptance of the Trinity as 'given' to the realm of faith, prior to any speculation.

Still, it is the fundamental analogy. As an hypothesis, it demonstrates its unique capability in responding to the questions implied in the data, and leads to a level of theological probability. Negatively, it excludes the errors of Sabellianism, Arianism, Tritheism, anthropomorphism. Positively, it orientates theological intelligence to the uniquely transcendent and communicative reality of God as Christian faith has experienced it. Indeed, it is not easy to reject the psychological analogy without re-introducing it in another guise.

Aquinas' achievement is an elegant and metaphysically austere exercise in classical analogical thinking. As such, it is productive of a striking systematic coherence. Even at this historical and cultural remove, it recommends itself as an undoubted classic in the area of trinitarian theology—at least to anyone refusing to be content with all too prevalent caricatures of Thomist theology. Perhaps the caricatures are to some extent pardonable in that the presuppositions, style, even the sense of reality of the medieval Thomas are so different from our own today. For his world was appreciated as participating in the divine reality and imaging it forth in various ways, in a manner that is barely comprehensible to a culture in which the 'absence of God' is a deeply determining feature.[36]

But in that medieval, deeply theological, world, Thomas works out his analogical exposition of the Trinity. He chooses the highest instance of imaging and participation, the human spirit, with its

---

[36]See N. Max Wildiers, *The Theologian and his Universe*, pgs. 161-265.

knowing and loving, as the focal analogy. Through a deft use of this, he brings into an ordered, intelligent exposition the various trinitarian data as he receives them from the Scriptures, the Councils, and the Fathers of the Church. We have indicated, all too briefly, how his basic analogy enabled him to make an intelligent statement about a twofold procession within the divine Be-ing, that of knowing and loving; how these real processions established distinct relationships; how these relationships grounded the reality of the divine persons; how the meaning and dynamics of these processions and relationships indicated the proper number, character and 'position' of the each of the divine persons in the Trinity, in their distinction from, and union with, one another; how each is given in grace when the Father 'sends' his Son and Spirit in the invisible and visible missions.

On the other hand, the usefulness of all this depends on a metaphysics of being, soul, faculties, and so forth, which is no longer generally accepted or understood. More deeply, one can experience today an uneasiness with a systematic approach that seems to proceed in such austere removal from the vitally experiential field of faith, hope and love, and the scriptural data which both expresses and nourishes such experience. The system appears also to some as too complete: to put it crudely, Thomas is admirably successful in getting the divine persons into his notion of 'Being-itself', but is not so successful in getting them out again in the ways that scripture discloses: for him the economic Trinity is not the immanent Trinity as contemporary theology would understand it. For Thomas, any one or all of the divine persons could have become incarnate.[37] The result is that the missions are not as disclosive of the distinct persons as the realism of the scriptural data imply. The question necessarily arises: Has the psychological image ended by having a life of its own, constricting the scriptural data into its own proportions—rather than serving such data as the absolutely privileged point of faith's contact with the self-giving God? Do we see here a clear point at which a "questioning back" must take place to "overcome metaphysics in the Christian Tradition"?[38]

[37] *S. Theol.* 3, 3, 5.

[38] See J. O'Leary, *Questioning Back. The Overcoming of Metaphysics in the Christian Tradition,* pgs. 165-201.

There is a deeper possibility of distortion. From beginning to end, Thomas does not mention that the Trinity is known and experienced as the divine self-involvement in our problem of evil, as the redeeming and liberating presence of God to human history. Scripturally speaking, the meaning of the missions is focused in the event of the suffering, death, and resurrection of Christ. Grace is sharing in the liberating victory of Love over evil in all its manifestations: the sending of the Son and the gift of the Spirit evidence the divine compassion. This aspect of trinitarian meaning is not present in Thomas' exposition. A systematic exposition does not permit any theologian to say everything at once; and anyone appreciative of Thomas' theology would point out that the motive of the incarnation is clearly understood by him to be redemptive.[39] Still, it remains true that the flight from understanding into absurdity, and self-destructive rejection of transcendent values do not expressly figure in Aquinas calm metaphysical analogy based in human intelligence and will. The mission of the Word and Spirit do not enter obviously into the need for redemption.

All this points to the necessity of retrieving this classic Thomist tradition in a contemporary context. In the next section, we will try to sketch a way in which this might be done.

---

[39] *S. Theol.* 3, 1, 3.

6

Transpositions

How is the Trinity a source of transformative meaning in human affairs? How is such a mystery the source of redemptive meaning in the context of our contemporary struggle with evil in all its dehumanizing forms?

Such questions are the most incisive way of initiating the process of transposing the Thomistic systematically elaborated meaning of the Trinity into a contemporary context. Such a transposition would require, of course, a thoroughly reconstructed theology. All we can do, in this brief sketch, is contribute to a major task. It will mean taking a bit further what others have done, as they have pushed forward the 'deconstructive' and reconstructive phases.[1]

1. An Experiential Foundation

To some degree, we suffer from an excess of classical meaning in trinitarian theology. Aquinas' great cathedral of thought was alive with a living divine presence. For us today, no longer sharing his cultural universe, the vast, intricate edifice no longer houses a 'real presence'. In so far as we inhabit a much bleaker theological universe,

---

[1] See the provocative suggestions of Joseph O'Leary, *Questioning Back, Overcoming Metaphysics in the Christian Tradition* (Seabury: New York, 1985), especially pgs 203-221. On the constructive side, an excellent example is still *Trinification of the World. A Festschift in honour of F. E. Crowe,* eds. T.A. Dunne and J.M. Laporte (Regis College Press: Toronto, 1978). The articles by Peter Beer, W.F.J. Ryan point in a good direction.

our problem is to ground theological terms in some fundamental experience. Otherwise, it will be one more instance of "having the meaning, but missing the experience".

It is not only a problem of emphasizing the experiential ground of theological thought. For that ground is itself developing and expanding.[2] In the opening chapter, I mentioned the desirability of relating trinitarian theology to the experience of the church in the crisis of its community and the challenge of its contemporary mission. We stressed, too, that the articulation of such a focal theological theme must ideally be related to the paradigmatic way in which we experience the cosmos itself. This is so different from the hierarchically ordered theological universe of the medievals, and the flatly atomistic and mechanistic worldview of the early modern period.[3] Even here, it is not just a matter of interpreting the trinitarian mystery in terms of our present ecclesial, cultural and cosmic experience. There is an even more demanding challenge: that of discerning how the Trinity involves us in a transformative or 'world-forming' field of meaning. This affects the contemporary sense of human identity as it stimulates, in turn, new ways of social belonging to inspire new hopeful programmes of political action, even on a global scale.[4]

To speak more precisely, the return to experience provokes not only the fresh questions of cognitive meaning concerning the ultimate character of reality. It also produces new questions affecting the constitutive meanings informing human identity: how does it liberate us to be free and hopeful agents in solidarity with all who struggle for human fullness? Similarly, it raises questions in the area of communicative meaning: How does it enable us to belong to one another as a global humanity, to cross former boundaries, and communicate in richer, more genuine dialogue? Finally, how does human experience provoke questions as to how the Trinity is a

---

[2] How the changes in one's worldview necessarily affect one's theology is well documented in N. Max Wildiers, *The Theologian and his Universe. Theology and Cosmology from the Middle Ages to the Present* (Seabury: New York, 1982) The 'his universe' of the title unwittingly substantiates the thesis of this excellent book.

[3] See Wildiers, *op. cit.*, pages 79-130.

[4] A valuable, though general, reference here is Helmut Peukert's *Science, Action and Fundamental Theology. Toward a Theology of Communicative Action* trans. J. Bohman (MIT Press: Cambridge, 1986).

comprehensive effective meaning, an 'agenda'? How does it inspire, challenge, command, and call to transforming activity in the social, political, and global arenas?[5]

2. From Doctrine to the Phenomenon of Christian Experience

Let us begin with a first move in transposing the inherited systematic meaning of the Trinity. To express this as concisely as possible, I would suggest that the need is to move from the doctrinal system to the phenomenality of religious and Christian experience.[6]

This is neither to demean trinitarian doctrine nor to deny its importance. It is simply to relocate it. One might observe that, if a doctrinal system is no longer living from some form of accessible religious experience, it quickly becomes an agglomeration of free-floating concepts. Trinitarian theology is teased out into a tissue of definitions which end up by defining nothing but purely logical entities. These congeal oddly in certain contexts as tests for orthodoxy. Without a vivid sense of the 'Love-life' manifested to faith through the self-giving Three, invocable as Father, Son and Spirit, what are believers left with? A catalogue of abstruse technical terms about person and nature, processions, relationships, and properties which may, at best, have a certain twilight-life in an ideology of orthodox adherence. But the possibilities of transformation are reduced to becoming ever more practiced in the recitation of dogmatic formulae. Such may be sufficient to ward off heresy; but too easily we forget the Love which these terms were originally meant to confess.

In a previous chapter, dealing with the biblical witness to the trinitarian mystery, I indicated the varied, complex ways in which the Scriptures are a record of the People of God's transforming

---

[5]See Bernard Lonergan "The Functions of Meaning", *Method in Theology* (DLT: London, 1971), pgs. 76-81.

[6]I am sympathetic with O'Leary's aims here even though I am less negative about metaphysics. I cannot see what is wrong with asking, is it real?—once the data are clearly perceived. In a more limited context, I attempted one aspect of this tranposition in "The Gifts of the Spirit: Aquinas and the Modern Context", *The Thomist* 38 (1974), pgs. 193-231. Further, I accept that Aquinas's analogical approach to the Trinity was far more experientially grounded than is commonly understood, even if his basic concern was systematic. The best modern study here is Bernard Lonergan, *Verbum: Word and Idea in Aquinas* (London: DLT, 1967).

experience of 'God', invoked and confessed as Father, Son, and Spirit. I will simply recall the headings of the previous rather extensive, even though schematic, treatment.

First of all, the New Testament writings are a fascinating expression of creative rhetoric: the definitive self-involvement of God is 'worded' in all the variety of genres which biblical scholarship notes— parable, hymn, prayer, doxology, teaching, exhortation, command, and so on. Secondly, and fundamental to this rhetoric, is the narrative structure and direction of the biblical data. The formula, 'Father, Son and Spirit', is a compressed narrative. These three names are the most telling terms of the Gospel story. Thirdly, the story of God is told in different ways insofar as it allows for different patterns of interplay between these master-symbols of the divine involvement in human history. Fourthly, this rhetoric, the narrative it discloses andthe symbols it employs, arise out of and return to inter-related experiences of the definitive presence of God in Christ. It is celebrated in the church which lives from the fundamental 'first hand' experience of the disciples, just as this lives from the unique personal experience of Jesus himself.

Obviously, all we have attempted is merely a schematic approach to the New Testament's experience of the self-involving God. I would now like to sharpen this phenomenological focus a little more. I will restrict myself to the Johannine writings, not only for brevity's sake, but also because they provide the best opportunity for articulating the Christian community's living experience of God as self-giving Love.[7]

3. The Johannine Experience

There is an obvious sense in which the whole of the Johannine writings are a record of the phenomenon of the 'measureless' gift of the Spirit (Jn 3:34). This Spirit is given, sent by the Father in Jesus' name. Thus, the Christian community comes to know God and

---

[7] Here I am indebted to O'Leary, *Questioning Back,* pgs. 221-225; E. Juengel, *God as the Mystery of the World,* trans. D.L. Guder (Eerdmans: Grand Rapids, 1983); and D. Stanley, "The Purpose of the Fourth Evangelist and the 'Trinification' of the Christian", in *Trinification . . .* pgs. 259-278.

Jesus as the Son, in the realm of "eternal life" (Jn 17:3). Here, the presence of the Spirit is implied as the medium in which, or better, the mediator through whom, God is disclosed as truth and light. Through this "other counsellor"[8] believers are drawn into a loving familiarity with the otherwise invisible God, and with the once unrecognized, and now-absent, Jesus

The Spirit is the one through whom the signs are deciphered,[9] and the glory of the mystery revealed. Pre-eminently, such a Spirit is "the Spirit of truth"(Jn 14:17; 15:26; 16:13; 1Jn 4:6; 5:7). But the truth is of a special kind: the glory of the God "who so loved the world that he gave his only Son" (Jn 3:16). It appreciates the advantage of Jesus departure (Jn 16:7); of his completion of the work the Father had given him to do (Jn 17:4f); and of his return to the glory of the Father which he had from the beginning. The "other counsellor" brings to mind everything that the disciples could not hear before, "the things that are to come", in a way that discloses the full significance of the presence of Jesus even though he is absent in earthly form (Jn 16:12).

All this occurs in a community which knows the tensions of still being "in the world": the witness of the Spirit, though it reveals the glory of Jesus as Son and Word, as the only Son of the Father, reveals also the sinfulness of the world in rejecting what is present. The Spirit of truth is one of judgment, in which light and darkness are seen for what they are. The Spirit witnesses to this complete truth. As such he convicts the world of untruth in all its forms, while enabling the believer to see the signs and works of Jesus as truly manifesting the glory of God. For this lacked its full evidence when "the Spirit was not yet"(Jn 7:39). Through this Spirit, Jesus is appreciated as the Word made flesh (Jn 1:14), the focal manifestation of the invisible God. What the evangelist expresses in the prologue, the believer confesses at the end of the Gospel: "My Lord and my God" (Jn 20:28f). This confession occasions praise for those whose

---

[8]See Gary M. Burge, *The Anointed Community* (Grand Rapids: Eerdmans, 1987) pgs. 204-220.

[9]D. Stanley's essay, "*The Purpose of the Fourth Evangelist* . . ." illuminates this point: "In the Book of Signs, John twice denominated this Christian understanding (of the earthly life of Jesus) as "remembering" (2:22, 12:16); in the Book of Glory he points to the Paraclete as the author of this remembering (16:8-11)," pgs. 271-273.

only access to God is faith as it is inspired by the Spirit: "Blessed are those who do not see but believe."

The Spirit is not some kind of independent irruption from on high. He is certainly from the 'invisible Father', but, at the same time, is intimately connected with the significance and presence of Jesus. For the Spirit is discerned in the faith of those who confess that Jesus has truly come in the flesh (I Jn 4:1-6). Likewise the gift of the Spirit is associated with Jesus' death and resurrection, indeed as the last breath of the Crucified and the first breath of the risen one (Jn 19:30; 20:22). The Spirit adds nothing to what Jesus is or has said as God's definitive Word in the world. Rather, he brings to mind the full significance of this in the historical life of the believing community (Jn 16:12-15). The Spirit of truth illuminates the world as the universe of God's self-giving presence. The truth of which the Spirit is the witness is that "God is Love". In the language of the Johannine 'signs', blindness is replaced by sight (Jn 9); and even death itself is transformed by the life manifest in Jesus (Jn 11:25).

In the light of the Spirit, Jesus is grasped as the bearer of grace and truth, in fulfillment of the previous dispensation (Jn 1:17). The glory is manifest, and the signs and works appear in their full manifestative power.

In one sense, the Father is always the invisible, unknown one: "no one has ever seen God" (Jn 1:18; 6:46; I Jn 4:12). But, the only Son, Jesus, has seen him and manifested him. "The phenomenality of Jesus Christ is one with the phenomenality of God."[10] The truth of the invisible God appears in and through Jesus, the Word Incarnate, the embodiment of the glory, life, truth, spirit, light.

Jesus as the incarnation of the divine meaning cannot be named in any terms other than those of divinity (Jn 20:28). To fail to confess his identity in this way is a wilful resistance to the truth, a preference for the darkness, or a stage somehow preliminary to the full knowledge of faith and the witnessing Spirit. The double *theologia negativa,*—that of the invisibility of God and that of the departure of the earthly Jesus—is the condition of the *via eminentiae* of the Spirit's witness to the revelation of the Father in the Son.

The 'fullness' of life and glory is expressed in the complex sym-

---

[10] J. O'Leary, *Questioning Back,* pg. 221ff.

bolism of Jesus as the only Son, descending from and ascending to the Father, pre-existing in a glory which precedes his earthly appearance and to which he returns. The communion of the Father and the Son is further described in terms of mutual indwelling. This provides the model for the mutual indwelling existing between the Father and the Son and those who love him (Jn 14:23; 17:20-26), between the Spirit and those who receive him (Jn 14:17), between the God who is Love and those who love (I Jn 4:16).

To sum up, the theology of John is uniquely an expression of the truth which the Spirit witnesses to. It focuses *on* Jesus as Son and revealer of the Father. It is focused, however, *in* the light of the Spirit's witness. But the source of the light and the truth it discloses is the Father. From him Jesus comes, as does the Spirit; to him, the Son returns: that original and final mystery, the realm of light, truth, love, spirit, welcoming us into the house of many rooms. Through the light of the Spirit, the invisible space of the divine mystery is filled with the incarnate reality of Jesus Christ. The only Son is God's self-definition in the conflict-ridden world of light and darkness, Spirit and flesh, life and death, being in the world but not of it, truth and the lie, love and division....

4. *'God is Love'*

In the Johannine letters, the majestic theology of the Gospel achieves a kind of existential concreteness in the affirmation of God as Love (I Jn 4:8, 16). It is clear that God is so confessed in the problematical context of spiritual discernment.The given indwelling Spirit is the assurance that we dwell in Christ despite the conflicts, limitations, and ambiguities of this present existence (I Jn 3:2f; 19ff). But our experience of the Spirit must be tested (I Jn 4:1-6). The unique test by which the "beloved", that is those who have received God's favour and perceived his glory in Christ, is the realism they accord to Jesus Christ as God's unsurpassably unique manifestation "in the flesh" (v.2). The Spirit of truth enables the "beloved" to see this. Such a witness necessarily invites to a deeper involvement in the 'Love-life' that God is. For as "beloved", Christians already participate in the original Love as it enables them to love. Thus, they manifest the life and the truth that God is. The command and exhortation to love are part of the logic of 'Love-life' in which the Christian community is already enfolded: "as he is, so are we in this world" (v.17). Christian existence is a dynamic image of the divine reality of self-giving Love. It looks to an eschatological realization (I Jn 3:2).

At the heart of such a perception and summons is the energizing reality of the "God who is Love" (I Jn 4:8). Not to realize that in Jesus God has given the world what is most intimate to himself, his only and beloved, Son, is to be ignorant of both the reality of God and of love. All Christian loving flows from the primordial self-giving of God in the sending of the Son: in this way, the mystery of the invisible God is enacted in sending the Son and in the self-sacrifice of the Son for the loveless world: " . . . he is the expiation for our sin . . . for the sins of the whole world" (I Jn 2:2; 4:10]. The new commandment is merely an expression of the actual reality at work: "Beloved, if God so loved us, we ought to love one another." (I Jn 4:11).

Again, the *via negativa* intrudes: "No man has ever seen God" (Jn 1:18; I Jn 4:12). But the mystery of the truly divinecomes into human experience by participating in the Love that God is: "If we love one another, God abides in us, and his love is perfected in us." (I Jn 4:12). To act out of this Love is to be aware of the gift of communion with the Ultimate: "Beloved, let us love one another; for love is of God, and he who loves is born of God and knows God." (I Jn 4:7). The *via eminentiae* of this knowledge of God is connected to the believer's participation in the 'Love-life' that God is. In turn, this is nourished by an experience described as the witness of the Spirit: "By this we know we abide in him and he in us, because he has given us of his own Spirit"(I Jn 4:13). As coming from the Father, as revealing Jesus as the Son, as abiding in the believer, this Spirit is "truth": "And the Spirit is the witness, because the Spirit is the truth" (I Jn 5:7).

The Love that God is, is not simply that God loves the Son, as Lover and Beloved, though John clearly presupposes this as an essential condition of what he is expressing. Rather, it is God revealed as Love in the concreteness of Christian experience.[11] For

---

[11]It seems to me that any distinction between ontological and functional Christology or Trinitarianism, as well as any distinction between the 'immanent' and the 'economic' is utterly

Christian existence is living in, and from, the Love that God is. God is now involved with the world in an unsurpassably climactic manner. For Christians to know God means that they acknowledge the divine mystery as it is enacted and embodied in an event of unconditional Love for the world. For God gives the world, seemingly incurably ignorant and hostile to both love and God, what he most loves, what is most intimate to his own identity, the Son. In giving the Son, God is manifested as Loving self-involvement in history. In communicating the Spirit, such Love establishes the Christian in the ultimate dimension of life and truth: the divine "Being-in-Love". The "beloved" themselves become the lovers. In that lies their witnessing power in "overcoming the world" (I Jn 5:5).

All the other Johannine affirmations of God in terms of light, life, spirit, truth, oneness, and glory seem to function as determinants of the confession that God is Love. The originating Love which God is, enacted as it is in the sending of the Son, is brought to expanding awareness in the gift of the Spirit.

5. From Divine "Be-ing" to "Being-in-Love"

The Be-ing of God is manifested not only as communion, but as communion in self-giving. The divine reality is not the philosophically affirmed *actus purus* of all perfection but the enactment of unrestricted self-giving. The life of God is not a life of impervious transcendence from the world, but of actual self-transcendence toward the world. To sum up, the divine mystery, as incarnate in Jesus Christ and manifest in the gift of the Spirit, is "Being-in-Love". As such, it draws believers into its own dynamics.

In contrast to the Thomistic exposition of the psychological analogy offered in the preceding chapter, here we are dealing with a psychological reality of a quite different order. It is the experience of life as originally, radically, and ultimately Love. This is the burden of the literally "in-spired" expression of the Johannine writings. The Spirit is here the principle of a new consciousness. This Spirit causes

---

foreign to Johannine theology. The later theological use of such distinctions have a limited role and, perhaps, a very provisional one against the day of a critical Christian realism able to distinguish between data, understanding, and judgment.

the reality of God and the meaning of Jesus to be experienced and understood in their climactic significance. Thomas, in his systematic theology, knew all about the Johannine writings, as his great commentary on John makes quite clear.[12] But here we are deliberately transposing his metaphysical psychological analogy into a more phenomenologically-oriented description.[13] We are thus giving more weight to the fundamental experience of faith in the elaboration of trinitarian theology.

I would now like to attempt a sketch of this first transposition. It is a transposition from a systematic principle of doctrinal theology to the phenomenology of faith's experience. It means starting, not from a philosophical meaning of the psychological image, but from the scripturally given psychological experience. This has a number of elements.

The first concerns the definition of God. The notion of God as "Be-ing", metaphysically conceived as "pure act", must be made to serve the biblical affirmation of God as *Agape,* the enactment of the divine reality in human history as Love. We pass from the notion of God as sheer, unlimited Be-ing, to the biblically grounded notion of God as Being-in-Love, incarnate in Christ and communicated in the Spirit.

Secondly, the philosophical account of the psychological image yields to a psychological account of faith's experience. The psychological image is now founded in a sense of being enfolded in the Love-life of Father, Son, and Spirit: "As he is, so are we in this world" (I Jn 4:17). "Beloved, we are God's children now. It does not yet appear what we shall be, but we know that when he appears we shall be like him, for we shall see him as he is." (I Jn 3:2). Just as the notion of God as sheer Be-ing must be made to serve the biblical confession of God as Love, so the philosophical or doctrinal exposition of the psychological image must be grounded once more in the paradigmatic Christian experience of God as the scriptures disclose it. The former use of the psychological analogy looks to a

---

[12]See the *Aquinas Scripture Series 4-5: Commentary on the Gospel of St. John,* ed., James Weisheipland trans. Fabian Larcher (Albany: Magi Books, 1980-).

[13]This is what Lonergan calls "generalized empirical method". For an outstanding description of this, see his essay," Religious Knowledge" in *A Third Collection. Papers by Bernard J. F. Lonergan,* ed. F. Crowe (Paulist Press: New York, 1985), especially pgs. 140-144.

systematic ordering of scriptural and doctrinal data. The proposed phenomenology of Christian consciousness attempts to disclose what is implied in the praxis of the Christian community.

Thirdly, this does not mean that the former psychological analogy is of no value. It is simply relocated. To accent self-giving presupposes self-possession. For we are dealing with the way the divine *expressiveness* itself is Love and it is true that Love is unlimited loving. Certainly one thing is clear: John, as every other scriptural writer, was not speaking about appearances of God in a way that leaves the reality of God uninvolved. Throughout all the biblical witness, the issues are first, truth, even if with the special biblical emphasis of God being true to himself; and, secondly, our way of getting to it. The Johannine accent however stresses that the final truth is Love, and that the way to get to it is through love, Love enacted in the unique self-giving in Christ and opened to human consciousness through the Spirit.

This preliminary move in the transposition of trinitarian theology accents the phenomenological character of the biblical data. It grounds reflection not immediately on dogmatic formulae, but in the experience of communion with the self-giving God manifested in 'these three'. This transposition can be succinctly indicated as a passage, first, from doctrines to the phenomenology of Christian experience of communion; secondly, from the metaphysical mode of analysis to a more experientially and scripturally grounded reflection.

In doing this, the psychological image is not summarily dismissed, but allowed to work in a new concreteness. It cannot be summarily rejected, since Scripture provides ample testimony to the fact that God is communicating himself, through the Word and Spirit. This surely pertains to the divine consciousness. The Word is God's unique self-utterance, just as the Son is the Father's climactic self-communication—as, too, the Spirit is God's self-investment in our appropriation of what he has expressed and done for the sake of the world.

6. *The Psychological Analogy and Self-Transcendence*

This return to Scripture and the experience of the self-communicating God has to be appropriated in the contemporary categories that best serve it. We cannot make it depend on a metaphysics which would win only a dubious acceptance in today's pluralist world of thought. What we do have is the experience of ourselves and of that essential openness to truth and value that unites us prior to any ideological differences or religious conflicts. It would be difficult to imagine some individual or some group that did not prize such orientations. This experience of self and its journey to fulfillment offers a special opportunity to transpose the elements of the metaphysically elaborated psychological analogy into something more experientially accessible.

The most elegant account of this is to be found in the works of Bernard Lonergan.[14] In the following pages, my dependence on his achievements, and those whose work he has inspired, will be clear. In place of the older metaphysical method account of the spiritual faculties of intellect and will, this approach is termed "intentionality analysis". It seems to me that treating the scriptural data in terms of a phenomenology of God's self-communication as Love demands such an account of existential experience if such a mystery is to be properly appreciated.

In the first place, intentionality analysis deals with the acting, conscious, human subject. It does not start with any prior theory about the soul and its spiritual faculties of intellect and will. It starts with the living subject, not as a theory, but as the conscious 'I' present in the actions of any one of us, the shared 'we' in the performance of any of our group or community decisions. In other words, we are not talking about some 'thing', however spiritual, nor about some philosophical theory, but clarifying the dynamic experience of being ourselves. The concrete, dynamically acting subjects that we are, individually and communally, provide the primary and immediate data. Intentionality analysis catches us "in action", in our self-transcending performance. It investigates how human consciousness expands through all its inter-related levels. These are empirical (sensations and consciousness), intellectual (acts of understanding), rational (judgments), responsible (making and taking decisions), and religious (questions and answers about the ultimate in meaning and

---

[14]Especially in *Method,* pgs. 3-25; 104ff; and in "Religious Knowledge" in *A Third Collecion. . . .,* pgs. 131-135.

value). All this is implied in our performance as human beings: we experience, feel, think, ask questions, reflect further, judge, decide, commit ourselves to these others or this or that course of action, give ourselves to religious faith, hope and love. In this sense it is all 'here' as we act, as we experience all the push from within and pull from without in the complex momentum of human existence as we love, feel the stirrings of conscience, find the sense of self-fulfillment, or are unsettled by our lack of such a dynamic peace.

Secondly, the 'self' present in our living performance is a 'self in action'. To be a self is to be constitutionally involved in a movement which is probably best named "self-transcendence". To struggle with questions, responsibilities or commitments, trying to love others, trying to discern the will of God, is to be present to ourselves as self-transcending selves: in our questioning and weighing the evidence, in the decisive action or loving commitment bound up with being what we are, we are caught up in a process of becoming. To that degree, our real self is always ahead of us. Not to decide, is to settle for a self less than what we feel we are meant to be; not to love more generously is to fall back into an unloving existence; not to seek further is to become ideologically defensive; not to be open to the great challenges of the day is to bury one's head in the sand; not to discipline our perceptions into a more discriminating sense of beauty in word and form, in movement and sound, is to be a barbarian in regard to all the beauty that human beings appreciate and create.

On the other hand, to give ourselves to this ongoing challenge to transcend our present selves in the direction of a more attentive, intelligent, responsible, faithful, loving, creative self is to enter into a 'real world' and its expanding mystery. For it is a world understood, explored, and even transformed, by the creativities of self-transcending agents. They are the ones who continually strive to replace absurdity, error, evil, and ugliness with meaning, truth, love, and beauty. They respond to the questions that life poses with all the meaningful works of science, art, philosophy, religion, politics. Further, it is a world that is not only analyzed or interpreted, but a world that is being increasingly directed in its histories, great and small, by human agents. For these characteristically ask not only, what is the way things are?, but, what is to be done?; not only what can be done? but, what should be done in accord with everything we value in ourselves, in others, in the world, in the universe itself?

Such a real world is a 'free world' at least in the sense of facing every human person with his or her personal conscience: reality is so complex, and the dimensions of human responsibility so daunting, that the temptation to allow oneself to become a drifter, a conformist, or even an automaton is quite real. To be more is to break out of the closed circle of private satisfactions and fears into a solidarity with others in the pursuit of values. Only in this way can an elemental justice be possible, in the family, city, society, nation, and, in our day, in the increasingly polarized world.

7. Self-Transcendence and Religious Experience

This world which we meaning-makers and value-seekers find and form is one which is continually taking us to the 'limits': limits to human life in death, failure, guilt; all the limitations of time and space and energy. To find these limits in our consciousness, is to live, even if not to formulate, a whole series of questions: is our self-transcendence into death, into ultimate defeat, into simply being at the mercy of a history and universe ultimately indifferent to what we have found to be the driving force of authentic human life, in the meanings we have expressed and the values we have sought?

There are, too, inextricably tied up with all the experience of negativity all the positive experiences of limits, when we are taken out of ourselves in the direction of what the dull eye of routine, the deaf ear of preoccupation, the numbed heart of too much calculation has failed to notice before : wonder, joy, the experience of great loves, the strange grandeur of moral achievement. In such moments, there is an uncanny 'more' in the experience of the mystic, the artist, the martyr, the prophet, the great thinker. Such people dramatize in their lives what all of us experience more dimly or admiringly in our own. Questions stir about the nature of the universe itself: We seem to be made for such love, and beauty and truth, to transcend ourselves into such a fullness of life. Is the 'world' of our varied and problematic experience the ultimately real world? Our self-transcendence faces us with negative and positive limits.[15] These continu-

---

[15] No one has treated this experience more evocatively than Sebastian Moore in such books as *The Fire and the Rose are One* (DLT: London, 1980), *The Inner Loneliness* (DLT: London, 1982), and *Let This Mind be in You. The Quest for Identity through Oedipus to Christ* (DLT: London, 1985).

ously fuel the dynamics of ultimate questions: to refuse to acknowledge them is to settle for a meaningful world that is lost in an ultimately meaningless universe; a moral world which is ultimately pointless in an indifferent universe; a world of dramatic human history finally insignificant as a minor moment in the unfolding of an impersonal universe....

The dynamic of the self-transcending subject is powered by the quest for meaning and value, by the search for the fullest self-realization in the ultimately real world. To deny such ultimacy is to accept, in the end, that the whole human quest is meaningless, worthless and forever frustrated, to settle for a human existence as a promise that will never be kept.

We are speaking here about the anticipation of an ultimate self-realization. We spoke, too, in more objective terms, of a promise of fulfillment in a universe, congruent with what we are as persons and the meanings and values we live by. It is here especially that the religious faith operates in human consciousness. For it is a kind of ultimate fulfillment in the self-transcending movement of our existence: in adoration and prayer, we discern the meaning of all meaning in the Divine Word. In an unconditional love, we give ourselves to the Will manifested in and intensifying all the values human beings pursue. With such a Will we collaborate, as loving God with all our minds and hearts leads us to love what God loves, and thus to love our neighbour as ourselves, and this world as God's creation.

The horizon of life and our human history is no longer a blank signifying nothingness, not a mere screen on which human beings project futile desires in a doomed search for meaning and worth, not a black hole swallowing up the whole human endeavour into some final, unwitnessed extinction. Rather, such an horizon of life, even though it can never be fully expressed, is experienced as filled with the all-fulfilling presence we commonly name, 'God', the ultimate reality in which we live and move and have our being.

How this experience of radical self-fulfillment occurs is puzzling enough to express. That it occurs seems clear, in the faith and hope and love of millions of people who inhabit this planet. They live in a field of new ultimate awareness: it brings a sense of loving familiarity with the mystery of the universe; it brings courage in self-sacrifice, in the face of suffering and even death. It opens out new hopeful patterns of belonging to the human community, of participating in human history, of facing all the ills bedeviling the world. True, this religious realm has its perversions. Very human things have been ascribed an ultimacy they obviously do not possess, when religious energies no longer inspire genuine self-transcendence but are diverted into self-justification and even self-destruction.[16]

Still, the witness of countless good lives goes on, productive of hope and love and adoring faith. Lonergan, impressive intellectual though he was, finally described this religious dimension in terms of an ultimate form of "being-in-love".[17] He was thereby relating it to what others had termed "being grasped by ultimate concern" (Tillich), "consolation without cause" (Ignatius of Loyola, Karl Rahner), "the experience of the Holy" (Rudolf Otto). But however it is named, this dynamic state actualizes the capacity for self-transcendence as it is revealed in the questions embodied in the implicit thrust of our existence. In Lonergan's terms, the self-unfolding of the authentic subject is energized by certain "transcendental notions", the thrust in our consciousness as it intends meaning, truth, value. His words express this neatly:

> The transcendental notions, that is, our questions for intelligence, for reflection, for deliberation, constitute our capacity for self-transcendence. This capacity becomes an actuality when one falls in love. Then one's being becomes being-in-love. Such being-in-love has its antecedents, its causes, its conditions, its occasions. But once it has blossomed forth, and as long as it lasts, it takes over. It is the first principle. From it flows one's desires and fears, one's joys and sorrows, one's discernment of values, one's decisions and deeds.[18]

This dynamic state of self-transcendence has all the intimacy of personal communion, and all the global concern of dedication to a

---

[16] As Lonergan would say, "religious development is dialectical ... human authenticity is never some pure and serene and secure possession ... Genuine religion is discovered and realized by redemption from the many traps of religious aberration...." See *Method*, pgs. 110f.

[17] See his treatment of this in *Method*, pgs. 105ff, and the remarkable essay, "Religious Experience" in *A Third Collection*.... pgs. 115-122.

[18] *Method*, pg. 105. If this category, 'falling in love' strikes one as excessively sentimental, see Walter E. Conn, "Affective Conversion: the Transformation of Desire", *Religion and Culture. Essays in Honor of Bernard Lonergan, S.J.* eds. Timothy Fallon and Phillip Bo Riley (Albany: University Press, 1987) pgs. 78-93, for a very informed remark.

great cause. There are different ways of loving, different levels of self-transcending love. In the fullest possible realization, the highest form of loving subsumes all conditional and finite forms:

> Being-in-love is of different kinds. There is the love of intimacy, of husband and wife, of parents and children. There is the love of one's fellow men with its fruit in the achievement of human welfare. There is the love of God with one's whole heart and whole soul, with all one's mind and with all one's strength (Mk 12:30). It is God's love flooding our hearts with the Holy Spirit given to us (Rom 5:5). It grounds the conviction of St.Paul that "there is nothing in death or life ... nothing in all creation that can separate us from the love of God in Christ Jesus Our Lord" (Rom 8:38f).[19]

In this account, God occurs as a question in all the questions we ask and live. What is the meaning of all our meanings? What is the sufficient reason for all the sufficient reasons we have? What is the worthwhileness of all our values and commitments? But being-in-love with God is the fulfillment of all such searching, all such questioning, all such loving, all such 'intending'. Or, as Lonergan says, "being in love with God is the basic fulfillment of our conscious intentionality".[20]

8. The Features of Religious Experience

We would have to return to the scriptures and supplement them with the writings of the great mystics and prophets of all religions (or even of those of no recognized religion!) to give an adequate phenomenology of what this ultimate "being-in-love" implies. Lonergan's concise account presents it as a love without limits or qualifications, without conditions or reservations.[21] Precisely because it is unre-

---

[19] *Method*, pg. 105.
[20] *Method, pg. 105.*

[21] *Method*, pgs. 106f. His treatment here is rounded out in his essays, "Religious Experience" and "A Post-Hegelian Philosophy of Religion" both in *A Third Collection*, pgs 115-122; 202-215.

stricted it is the fulfillment, the full unfolding of trajectory to self-transcendence. It is not something that the religious think or will themselves into; rather, it occurs as a dynamic state, a field of new awareness drawing all our previous perceptions and commitments into it, opening up a new horizon in which our previous meanings and values are transfigured and transvalued. As such it is a new principle of action. For it modifies human consciousness and inspires us to take all kinds of virtuous action .... The fruit of the Spirit is love, joy, peace, patience, kindness, goodness ... self-control (Gal 5:22). Whilst it is a radical alteration of consciousness, and therefore experienced, this does not mean that it is known fully, or even adverted to. Other elements in consciousness can work to obscure or repress what is at work in the heart. What is more, we may lack the religious tradition or the theology to articulate the meaning of what is happening. Still, there is a basic awareness of mystery. This implies a kind of deep sense of attraction to something or someone ultimately meaningful and valuable, and present as loving us. We are claimed and possessed by this mystery. Yet it remains beyond anything in our experience or understanding, hence it is awe-inspiring, provoking at once surrender and adoration.[22]

The presence of this being-in-love does not occur in those kinds of consciousness that are proper to sense-experience, or even to thinking and judging or deciding in mundane terms. It happens at the centre, the point where we are most self-determining, the point at which we are turned out of ourselves to make some ultimate kind of self-surrender. This may be "broadened and deepened, heightened and enriched but not superseded ..."[23] It occurs at that high point of consciousness where we are not just sensing, or thinking, or judging, or deciding, but self-surrendering lovers in the presence of what is ultimately loveable and ultimately loving.[24]

---

[22] *Method*, pg. 106.

[23] *Method*, pg. 107.

[24] Lonergan, *Op. cit.*, "To be in love is to be in love with someone. To be in love without qualifications or conditions or reservations or limits is to be in love with someone transcendent. When someone transcendent is my beloved, he is in my heart, real to me from within me. When that love is the fulfilment of my unrestricted thrust to self-transcendence through intelligence and truth and responsiblity, the one that fulfils that thrust must be supreme intelligence, truth, goodness. Since he chooses to come to me by a gift of love for him, he himself must be love...." (pg. 109)

This "being-in-love" draws all our other conscious states and activities into itself—other loves, intimate and social; all our capacities for experiencing, knowing judging and deciding. It extends their range and significance by setting all such actions and experience in a universe of religious love, giving the flow of conscious life new direction, new energies, new sensitivities, new passion.[25]

This is what Lonergan calls "sublation": being-in-love subsumes all our feeling and sensing, our knowing and willing, not to destroy such conscious activities but to allow them a "fuller realization in a richer context."[26] This richer context is the world transfigured and transvalued as the theatre of God's loving action and as the sacrament of the divine presence.

9. Correlating Divine and Human "Being in Love"

In this account, the fulfillment of human existence is understood as a kind of transcendent "being-in-love". Given the fact that the scriptures disclose God as Love in the foundational experience of the early Christian communities, a correlation suggests itself between God's Being-in-Love and human being-in-love.[27] Human love is a supremely personal value, and as such looks to an ultimate confirmation.[28]

It is, therefore, a matter of transposing the tradition of the psychological analogy into the modern context. As we have stressed, this

---

[25] For Lonergan, self-transcendence "reaches its term not in righteousness, but in love, and when we fall in love, then life begins anew. A new principle takes over, and as long as it lasts, we are lifted above ourselves and carried along as parts within an ever more intimate yet ever more liberating dynamic whole." See "Natural Right and Historical Mindedness", *A Third Collection* ... pg. 175.

[26] *Method*, pgs. 241ff.

[27] This will be understood in terms of "sublation" mentioned above. As the older terminology had it, grace does not destroy nature, nor is grace the same as nature; rather, grace transforms nature, healing, perfecting, elevating it. For an application of these categories to love, see M.C.D'Arcy, *The Mind and Heart of Love* (New York: Meridian, 1956); R.O. Johann, *The Meaning of Love. An Essay towards the Metaphysics of Intersubjectivity* (New York: Paulist, 1966); George Tavard, *A Way of Love* (Maryknoll: Orbis, 1977); Fred. E. Crowe, "Complacency and Concern in the Thought of St. Thomas", *Theological Studies* 20 (1959), pgs. 1-39; 198-230; 343-395.

[28] "Personal value is the person in his self-transcendence, as loving and being loved, as originator of values in himself and in his milieu, as an inspiration and invitation to others to do likewise." (*Method...* pg. 32).

requires both a return to the Scriptures and a contemporary appropriation of the experience they record.

A certain correlation is already implicit in what we have been describing in terms of divine and human loving. First, God is the original Lover, loving in a way that supposes no human merit. Hence, the gift of Love is experienced as something 'infused', a mysterious event occurring within human consciousness, whether this be a dramatic conversion or a slow change of heart.

Secondly, in giving the only Son, Love is manifest as a climactic self-involvement. God's love is self-giving in the Son, self-uttering in the Word. This occurs within human consciousness as the luminous affirmation of our human worth: for the Word became "flesh", and the Son is like us in all things but sin; our self-transcending selves unfold in the presence of the self-giving God.

Thirdly, Love is unconditional. It keeps on being Love to the limit of allowing the Son to be crucified for the sins of the world. To respond to such Love is to be conformed to the Crucified, in a self-sacrificing struggle against all evils.

Fourthly, Love is not defeated, but is manifest in a victory consonant with its character: the resurrection of the Crucified. To live in the energies of such transformative Love is to experience the "peace the world cannot give" (Jn 14:27f), the "joy that no one can take from you" (Jn 16:22-25), the Love "that nothing in all creation" can resist or diminish (Rom 8:37ff),—a life reaching beyond any death we know (Jn 6:35-40).

Fifthly, as the Spirit of the Father and the Son is sent, Love is abidingly communicative. The Spirit works in human consciousness to inspire faith, hope, and love, the true worship of the Father in Spirit and in truth.

Sixthly, the gift of Love is made into a world of unfolding history. It does not occur merely in a series of individual transformations. It forms the Body of Christ, the Church, the People of God. To collaborate with this Love is to be in communion with all those who receive it, to be a member of the Body, to belong to the Church, and to be part of its mission.

Seventhly, the unconditional self-giving of the Father in the Son and the Spirit looks to the eschatological transformation of "new heavens and a new earth", "a new creation", when all "shall be one", when "God will be everything to everyone", the consummation of the Kingdom of God. Relative to this eschatological point is our hope for the ultimate vision of God, in a world-transcending destiny.

10. The Trinity as Divine "Being in Love"

But this correlation of God's self-communication and human self-transcendence can be made more intelligible. Here intentionality analysis, as Lonergan has developed it, is a powerful tool. It provides the key for transposing the scriptural data into contemporary experiential terms. What then are the main points of such a transposition?

In one of his later essays, Lonergan gave a tantalising indication of how this might be done, as he concluded an essay on Christology. He is addressing himself to the question of the hypostatic union. For one of the divine persons to become incarnate opens up the further question of how to speak intelligibly of three distinct and conscious subjects of divine consciousness. To do this, Lonergan says we must take the analogy of consciousness seriously:

> The psychological analogy has its starting point in that higher synthesis of intellectual, rational and moral consciousness that is the dynamic state of being in love. Such love manifests itself in judgments of value. And the judgments are carried out in decisions that are acts of loving. Such is the analogy which is found in the creature.[29]

11. The Psychological Analogy of Love Applied

We have been outlining how this "analogy is found in the creature". The passion of human existence is to unfold into a fulfilled self-realization. But this can only happen through the unfolding dynamics of self-transcendence, as human beings resolutely intend meaning, truth, value, the beautiful, the holy, the supremely loveable. This comes to a special point of fulfillment in a transcendent being-

---

[29]"Christology Today: Methodological Reflections" in *A Third Collection....*, pgs. 93f.

in-love, with its analogies in the order of human relationships, be they intimate (lovers, friends, family), or social (society, nation, the world itself).

The fundamental self-transcendence enacted in these cases is not a transcendence into the meaningless, or the absurd, the imaginary, into something untrue or unwise or unreal. The fulfillment attained in all this, if it is truly to be a state of being-in-love, is neither mindless infatuation nor inactive insincerity.

Anyone in love is not going to accept the charge of infatuation: this can be levelled if the object I think I love is destructive to myself or others: an unworthy person, a hopeless ideal, an obsession that says more about my own unacknowledged needs than instancing the supreme attainment of becoming a self for the other. Rather, an authentic state of being-in-love holds within it a judgment of the genuine worth of the other. The initial falling in love has matured into a standing on one's feet, well founded on reality, which will remain rock-solid despite the tensions and the conflicts involved in trying to insert such love into the reality of the real lives of particular human beings in a complex real world. Similarly, the first fervour of commitment, to a group or a great cause, has to get beyond the easy enthusiasm and youthful idealism into a realistic judgment of what is being asked, and to what one is committing oneself. Otherwise the would-be lover or the enthusiastic activist will eventually be disillusioned, convinced he or she is 'taken in' by a world of unreality or manipulated by a self-serving ideology. In both cases, love can only be a state of fulfillment when it is nourished by truth, when it is not a flight from the real, but a dedication to it.[30]

Nor, to keep the analogy going, is such a being-in-love likely to tolerate the charge of insincerity, that it was 'all talk', or, for that matter, mere 'love-making' in the very restricted sense, as though the lover's heart was not really in it, and no real self-giving involved. Rather, authentic being-in-love must be marked by a sincerity which is continuously productive of acts of loving: it must show the creativity of continual loving activity.

Our familiar human world shows plenty of humour and cynicism on this point: familiar stereotypes, however inappropriate they might

---

[30]Cf. "The cognitive interpretation of affectivity" in W.E. Conn, *op. cit.,* pgs. 263f.

be in the modern cultural context, have at least the advantage of making a clear point in what we are discussing. For every woman that has reproached a man for being interested only in the physical side of loving, and to be notably dull and uninvolved in all the rest—uninterested in the development of the woman he alleges he loves, unconcerned for her feelings, untouched by the exhausting routines and worries of home and family—the implied charge is that of insincerity. Such deficient love is not moving forward into lovingness. It is not being true to itself. It is not moving forward into collaboration and in compassion, to carry through into the whole reality of life. Such defective loving is simply not committed to all the variety, patience and interaction which a genuine being-in-love would require. In similar ways, to set the balance right, a man might make similar complaints about the woman in his life—if she is uninterested or uninvolved in what he judges to be his 'real life', his work, his position, his achievement.

A sincere "being-in-love" is ever disposed to reach beyond itself into the 'more' of the other's world of experience. For it manifests itself not only in the ecstatic affirmations of love-making but also in the involvements of compassion and collaboration. Genuine loving implies a commitment continually to affirm what is the value in the relationship, and to struggle against the sufferings, one way or another, bound up with it. It seems to be a readiness to 'take time', to let such love have, and even make, its history.

This challenge to genuineness is routinely faced in all the social forms of being-in-love. The first fervour of being involved, say, in a group working for social justice is soon tested by the complexity and demands of the task. There is no quick solution: research, so much routine hard work, the massive agendas of meetings, the incompatibility of the group's members, the disedifying politics involved in deciding who is to be in charge of what ... If a conviction about the importance of the matters involved does not produce what is commonly felt to be a remarkable amount of patience and dedication, and a still greater sense of humour, enthusiasm soon wilts, and love fails.

These are rather pedestrian but, I think, instructive examples: for to ponder on what makes a couple's relationship work, or a group effective, is to find similar experiences in ourselves: to be truly 'in love', in whatever instance or degree, means that we have the evidence that the love is worthwhile, and that we are prepared to make it work, to 'make love' in all the ways demanded by what most defines who and what we are, as our best and loving selves.[31] All this is merely the supreme example of self-fulfillment being achieved only in self-giving. Love must keep on loving, if it is to be a state of "being-in-love".

Now that is the human case.[32] In the case of God, it is not so much that God has love but "is Love", is unrestricted pure Being-in-Love, the 'actus purus' of Loving, *Ipsum Amare subsistens.* God's Love is not determined by any prior existence of the good, as in the human case. In no sense is it the answer to a good or a love that is extrinsic to it. Biblically this is brought home in God's giving of the only Son for the salvation of the sinful human world: "in this is love, not that we loved God, but that he loved us and sent his Son to be the expiation for our sins" (I Jn 4:10). And in the lapidary words of St. Thomas, "God's love is infusing and creating the goodness in things"; ("amor Dei est infundens et creans bonitatem in rebus.").[33]

But the analogy from the human case has its application. The divine Being-in-Love is not irrational nor insincere. As Lonergan expresses it,

> Such love expresses itself in its Word, its Logos, its *verbum spirans amorem* (SThI,43,5 ad 2), which is a judgment of value. The judgment of value is sincere, and so it grounds the proceeding love that is identified with the Holy Spirit. [34]

God's Being-in-Love is fully conscious. It manifests itself in a judgment grounded on a divine evidence of the infinite value of the divine Love, and proceeds from that into all the activity of loving. Such Being-in-Love is then to be conceived as a state of utter self-transcendence. The divine Loving is an infinite affirmation of the worth

---

[31]Cf. "Affectivity as Constitutive of Identity" in Conn, *op. cit.,* pgs. 264-268.

[32]For further analysis and literature on "being in love" see the excellent article, Walter Conn, 'Affective Conversion: The Transformation of Desire', in *Religion and Culture. Essays in Honor of Bernard Lonergan, S.J.,* eds. Timothy P. Fallon and Philip Boo Riley (Albany: State University of New York Press), pgs. 261-275.

[33]*Summa Theol.* I,20,2. See too Juengel, *God as the Mystery of the World,* pgs. 329ff.

[34]"Christology Today....", pg. 93.

of such Love; and an unrestricted commitment to being Love in every conceivable instance. These 'processions' ground relationships within the divine Being-in-Love. The relational character implies a threefold subjectivity. Each of the divine three is identified with the divine Being-in-Love in a distinctive manner. Each is distinctively consciousness of being Love: "The Father as originating love, the Son as judgment of value expressing that love, and the Spirit as originated loving."[35]

We are conceiving of God, then, as an infinite self-realization in Love, where loving and self-transcendence are utterly identified. In God the stratified consciousness particular to the human case, (empirical, intellectual, rational, moral, religious) does not exist. That is where the analogy breaks down. For the divine consciousness does not expand to the peak state of loving. Rather, it is conceived of as being, totally, in such a state. Hence, the divine mystery is an eternally self-constituting activity of Being-in-love, one divine consciousness articulated into a communion of Father, Son and Spirit. It is Love without origin, uttering itself in truthful self-expression, and being always true to itself in self-giving. The point of similarity between the divine and the human case resides in the principle that affectivity most constitutes identity.

12. "Being in Love" as Gift

The biblical terms narrating the divine mystery of Love are Father, Son, and Holy Spirit. Christians thus invoke God as lovingly self-involved in the human struggle for self-transcendence. Such invocation constitutes the basis for any understanding of God in an interpersonal manner. The Father remains the original mystery to us who might 'have love' at least to the degree of realizing we are not Love in the divine manner. From such Love comes the initiative to give what is most intimate to itself, the Son, into the world of our questions and struggle for human meaning: the Word is made flesh. The Son reveals the character of self-giving Love as he gives his life for the life of the world.

---

[35]Lonergan, "Christology Today . . .", pg. 94.

In the world of self-justification, the Son as Word becomes the summons to a new kind of self-transcendence. As Son, he is the presence of the divine self-transcendence into, and in, such a world. Thus, in him is expressed the pattern of the self-transcendence to which we are summoned: "Beloved, if God has so loved us, we also ought to love one another" (1 Jn 4:11).

The Spirit, the gift of the God who is Love and of the Son who incarnates it as Love's self-utterance, is this Love's communication, its inexhaustible openness and creativity. For the Spirit brings the human person into a dynamic union with Christ, to present him as, "the way, the truth and the life". In this regard, the Spirit enables us to be hearers of the Word and followers of the Son, intimates of the Father (Rom 8:14ff). Through "the Spirit of truth", believers appropriate the meaning of Christ and are conformed to the Love he embodies.

The communion with Father, Son, and Spirit which believers enjoy, the divine indwelling which they experience, is an entry into the divine consciousness of Being-in-love. This is an ultimate field of life and all its relationships, a new way of meaning and valuing the universe. Its horizon envisages the culminating point at which God will be everything to everyone (I Cor 15:28). It contemplates a new creation in Christ in which the old order has gone, and something new has begun (2 Cor 5:17). It includes all creation which, while originating in a transcendent Love, now groans in one great act of giving birth, as the Spirit opens human consciousness to the mystery of Love at work (Rom 8:19-28).

So, we have taken the biblical confession of God as Love and, through an analysis of human consciousness, tried to develop the psychological analogy in more biblical and contemporary lines. Many applications remain to be made and implications to be drawn. So far, at least a beginning.

13. *God's Love Communicated in Global Experience*

There is, however, one further point to make. It consists in stressing the global rather than the individual experience of human subjectivity. Probably, given the limitations of expression, I have given the impression that the human subject is an isolated individual. It is time not only to emphasize the planetary dimension of consciousness, but also stress the main points made above in a larger context.

To speak of self-transcendence as the dynamic of authentic human existence is not to be engaged in some kind of isolated introspection. After all, experience is of something 'other', often to a disconcerting degree. Understanding always presupposes some kind of dialogue, or at least a common language; morality results from and leads to a high form of human collaboration; the transcendental questions and answers we live put us in the presence of a mysterious universe. All the forms of being-in-love one might experience are a passionate or matter-of-fact orientation to what is 'other', whether that other is a beloved individual, a group, a society, or the wider world. In other words, the psychological analogy does not imply a lonely or isolated individual. I think the most striking and topical expression of this analogy is in terms of the global historical human community. For at this juncture in human history, we are being clearly challenged to an immense act of global self-transcendence for the sake of a future in which human beings can survive and flourish.

To look at the emerging global scene as a spectator or analyst, or to commit oneself to it as an activist, is, of course, to be involved in a world of momentous tensions. Fresh energies, new aspirations, global visions are vividly in evidence as we attend to the efforts to structure a new economy, form international laws, secure a global peace, value the earth in a responsible ecological awareness, promote cultural exchanges, affirm and promote the rights of the poor and oppressed, and deal with the endemic diseases that have afflicted human beings for millennia. Some of these efforts combat directly the problem of evil with its self-destructive turn, characterised especially today in the arms race and the more dramatic examples of greed and oppression. Here the issue is to find a hope that is beyond all human hope. Other global movements are an appreciation of human ills, diagnosed for the first time: here I have in mind the issues of global ecology and economy. Others are largely a matter of pushing ahead with human realities as they have been developed through technology, e.g.,global communication, health care; or as they have developed through a whole series of enlightened political decisions,such as the issues of human rights.

Active resistance to the global threats, active promotion of the wonderful possibilities of human progress and welfare, imply an historical capacity for self-transcendence. Commitment, in any realistic sense, to the human future demands hard decisions with harsh demands in the present. For instance, what happens to those caught up in the economy of the arms race? What happens to prevailing consumer habits if the ecology of the earth is taken seriously? The beginnings of global self-transcendence are manifest in all individual, group, social, national, and international efforts to promote peace, justice, and all the global dimensions of human welfare. There is evidence of a new way of being-in-love and with the world of our fragmented and suffering humanity. Such love nourishes itself on new images of global belonging, as our vulnerable planet is photographed from outer space. It inspires a new passion for a now-possible unity and wholeness, along with a compassion for the millions brutalized by oppressive regimes or trapped in exploitative economies. All kinds of courage and creativity are in evidence, as evils are named, new visions expressed, and great hopes find embodiment in the martyrs of our time.

What are the dimensions of such a global being-in-love? As members of the agonized global community seek to extend their efforts into a more human future, what is demanded is a commitment beyond our individual, group, national, and historical biases to a human future somehow inclusive of us all. This is to experience what has been suggestively named "solidarity". Somehow, an as yet unknown, unrealized realm of human belonging has made its presence felt. We are participating in an inarticulate universal concern and vision. It makes a difference to how we think, feel, to how we understand ourselves and others; it inspires new images, new creativities, new courage in bold new decisions, new capacities to hope in the face of evils discovered now in overwhelming proportions. In short, a new horizon has occurred in human living. A mysterious conversion to the ultimately human, to its global proportions, is taking place.

The horizon is one thing, in which some new fullness of humanity is intimated. Yet it means something. It starts and promotes a new kind of conversation, even a new way of telling the human story as that of one human race, one species. The transformation that has to occur in our politics, legal institutions and economics, in our religious traditions and philosophies, that our sciences might implement and our arts image forth, must somehow be spoken. The "ideal speech situation" must become a reality in allowing for the whole and healing truth to be expressed. Are we moving into something meaningful or not? Is this global concern to be nourished by the best available evidence, to lead us to a transforming truth about ourselves, or is it not? Can all the traditions and symbols and sciences that have hitherto formed particular limited standpoints become truly dialogical? Can words be heard and spoken between speakers who previously were locked away from each other through distance, ignorance, prejudice, hatred? Somehow we have to be involved in making sense of the new situation. We are involved in the process of *meaning* the global situation of our humanity in a critical, realistic and inspiring way. To intend such a meaning is necessarily to be part of a global conversation in which absurdities are exposed and new possibilities are grasped; in which evils are named and confessed, failures diagnosed and identities affirmed; in which plans are made, policies formed, and a hopeful way forward is opened up.

As with all kinds of love, expressing such love and its worth, meaning it in the words we utter, looks to a history of continuous meaning and involvement. It is not enough to put a new construction on the world, to interpret and analyze our belonging to it in a new way: it demands participation, commitment, decisions to make the future happen as hope has envisaged it. For concern not to be mere sentiment, not mere idealism, demands the ongoing self-transcendence of immersing ourselves in the developing, struggling human reality . We must see ourselves as active principles of humanization in the emerging global world: it means peace-making, the ongoing collaboration of science and politics, the creativities of the arts, the forgiveness of enemies and the establishment of justice, all the things that only a self-sacrificing love can make possible.

What we have been attending to in this new global consciousness is the historical self-transcendence that is occurring: self-sacrificing decisions are being made; they are made out of an evidence that diagnoses past evils and understands new ways of communication, new forms of culture; they result from an intimation of what no human eye has seen nor ear heard against the horizon of the hoped-for future into which we are attracted and into which we move.

Christian faith discerns that the divine Being-in-Love, Father,

Son, and Spirit, is communicated to this global human history. If the divine three are 'God', Infinite Being-in-Love, by a self-constitution that is a continuing loving self-transcendence, then we human beings achieve our full global subjectivity by sharing in this Being-in-Love. The three divine subjects of the divine self-transcending Love are communicated to the global self-transcendence of humanity.

14. The Trinity 'En-Worlded' and the World 'Trinified'

God is intimated and 'enworlded' as the originating and finalizing reality in which we belong. The divine Word is incarnate as the meaning of human existence. The Love is irreversibly involved in our history. The indwelling Spirit is 'inspired', 'en-heartened' as the ever-creative enabler of the humanity intimated in the mystery of 'Our Father' and incarnate in the Son as 'our brother'. By inspiring intimacy with God, now invocable in this Spirit of freedom as 'Abba' (Rom 8:15f), by disclosing the ever fuller reality of Jesus Christ (Jn 16:12-15) and gifting the community of believers with all the graces of individual (Gal 5:22) and social self-transcendence (1 Cor 12:4-13), the Spirit leads us forward to "the things that are to come" (Jn 16:13).

The divine self-transcending Love is manifest as self-sacrifice. For God's self-giving in the Son and through the Spirit is directed to human beings locked in an apparently insuperable problem of evil. As the Son empties himself into the suffering human history as Jesus of Nazareth, the Father empties himself into the vulnerability of having no self-disclosure in this world other than Jesus, his only Son. Similarly the Spirit is exposed to human rejection by witnessing to no power and no truth other than the Love that is shown forth in the Crucified. At no point is it simply a matter of God being the gracious fulfillment of an untrammelled trajectory of self-transcendence. God's self-communication is revealed as compassionate self-involvement with our problem of evil. God acts within human history to heal the times from the destructive self-justification which barricades itself against the only Love that can give us hope.

The divine Being-in-Love, communicated as Father, Son, and Spirit, has to contend with all lesser forms of being-without-love. The accumulated absurdity of the "heart of stone" is dramatically documented by Paul[36], and described by John as a refusal of the light (Jn 3:19-21). The Word incarnate is uttered into a world of human conversation in which the new commandment appears as an absurdity. The Spirit has only the power of Love to counter "the principalities and powers" (Eph 6:12) of this world, all the familiar demons that infest the human condition and impel toward self-destruction. The presence of the Father, intimated in the unlimited horizon of grace and mercy embracing human existence, is obscured by the self-projections of existential idolatry.

Nonetheless, as we mentioned in a previous chapter, this divine Being-in-Love refuses to be anything other than itself. The Son, precisely in the moment of experiencing the demonic intensity of the world's evil, gives himself for the life of the world. The Spirit is not changed into one more worldly power, but empties himself into the vulnerability of Love. The Father is not set above the world as a patriarchal idol, thus legitimating worldly authorities. Rather, he is revealed as the subversive mystery of unconditional Love incarnate in the Crucified. This Being-in-Love comes to its own victory in the resurrection of the Crucified, and in the history of self-sacrificing love it energizes.

But, even here, this victory appeals to human freedom and does not suppress it. It is victory communicated to human beings in history. The immediate radiant evidence of the Risen Lord, and the vision of the 'invisible God' must wait to the end. Only by the witness of the Spirit of the Father and the Son, is Love's victory communicated. For this Spirit transforms human lives, individually and communally, into conscious participation in the universe of Being-in-Love. The excess of evil calls forth the "excesses" of the "never ending" Love that "bears all things, believes all things, hopes all things, endures all things" (1 Cor 13:7f).

15. Trinitarian Meaning

In this understanding of the trinitarian mystery, a globally-oriented Christian faith can 'mean' the Trinity in four ways, cognitively,

---

[36]Rom 1:18-32.

constitutively, communicatively, effectively.[37]

First, the Trinity is a cognitive meaning. It is the ultimate reality in the objectively known universe. It is not, of course, one object among many, but the reality which is originating and finalizing relative to everything else. It makes a difference to our apprehension of such a universe when the paradigmatic reality is self-giving Love, when ultimate reality is relational within itself and in regard to all else. To the degree a Christian understanding of the universe affirms this trinitarian mystery of reality, it will be at home in the world of meanings implied in the contemporary "turning point".[38]

Secondly, the affirmation of ultimate reality as Being-in-Love, as the divine self-constitution as Father, Son, and Holy Spirit, means something quite transformative for human identity and the institutions objectivizing it. Typically, Christian identity is expressed in terms of our being sons and daughters of the Father, members of Christ, and temples of the Spirit. As such, the human person is divinely 'meant' and valued in the Father's self-expression in the Word, and consequently loved in the creative, outgoing Spirit of that Love. To be a human person is to be drawn progressively into the Love-life that is God's Being: it is to be personal as God is personal, in self-transcending relationships, leading to a self-fulfillment in an other-directed existence. To understand trinitarian meaning as the foundation of the universe is not merely to affirm something about the ultimate character of the universe. It is to sense oneself as 'someone' within it, to dwell in the mystery and to be indwelt by it, to be intimately related to the whole, and drawn into its fundamental dynamism. To affirm the mystery of the Trinity in these terms means to celebrate an identity within the universe, to belong to it, and to participate in it with the energies of a transcendent love, faith, and hope.

Thirdly, such trinitarian meaning is communicative. Explicitly so, in the constitution of the church as the community made one in the

---

[37]See B. Lonergan, "Mission and the Spirit", *A Third Collection pgs. 23-31.*

[38]Fritjof Capra, *The Turning Point, Science, Society and the Rising Culture* (Flamingo: London, 1984).

unity of the Father, Son, and Spirit. But the church is involved in a wider solidarity than that of explicit Christian commitment. The Trinity is the mystery explicitating the meaning of the universe in terms of self-giving Love. The mission of the church reaches beyond itself to the eschatological realization of the fullness of our humanity and our world in God. In a later chapter, more will be said on how the Trinity is related to the social and political dimension of the struggle for life and justice, and how it nourishes the sense of solidarity, so notably in evidence today.

Fourthly, the trinitarian mystery, as we have implied above, necessarily becomes an agenda for Christian existence. In the energies of the universe of Love, Christians must contest all other ways of being in the world and all lesser versions of the human future. In faith's discernment of the trinitarian mystery, we can celebrate the ultimate form of existence as participating in the divine Being-in-Love. In the mission of the Church, the Love that has been disclosed inspires Christians to reach into the living heart of other faiths, there to find the same Love at work: there we can learn more of the mystery involved in human history. In the context of such learning, we can utter the healing and transforming word of explicit Christian evangelization. Further, this mystery of self-transcending Love inspires self-sacrificing commitment to our neighbor and our world. It is always a point of new beginning: the problems of evil don't go away, but the mystery of Love keeps on being itself, to enable the transformation of our human defeats into a deeper faith, love, and hope.

Conclusion

At the end of this long sketch of some of the fundamental moves in transposing classical trinitarian theology into more contemporary terms, let me accent and summarize the main points.

The traditional doctrinal terms were transposed into more biblically based categories. The Johannine confession of God as "Love" was given the pre-eminent place. This does not demean the conciliar doctrines. Rather, it places them in their proper hermeneutical context. The doctrines of Nicaea and Constantinople are only ways of affirming the Johannine confession: the true God has been manifest in the sending of the "consubtantial" Son and continues to be possessed in the experience of the church in the ongoing gift of the "consubstantial" Spirit. This particular emphasis accords well with the manifold experience of the Trinity expressed in many ways in the scriptures. It is a richer context than the necessarily more limited doctrinal one.

Transposing trinitarian meaning in this way affects our way of defining God. The definition of God as *Ipsum Esse subsistens*, sheer Be-ing, yields to the notion of God as "Being-in-Love". This is not a denial of the necessity of metaphysics. I think of it, rather, as pointing to the need for a more appropriate metaphysics to serve the special realism of Christian faith.

More specifically, we transposed the psychological analogy from its traditional expression in the categories of Aristotelian faculty psychology. Intentionality analysis grounds this analogy in terms founded in consciousness. Following Lonergan's lead, we analyzed the peak state of consciousness as a self-transcending "being-in-love". We examined this in terms of individual and global experience. Then we used this experience as an analogy for the divine Being-in-Love. Consequently this yielded an understanding of the Trinity. The Father is the original self-transcending Lover expressing what he is as Love in his Word, and giving this Love in the unlimited Loving in the Spirit.

This leads to an understanding of the Trinity as Divine Love 'en-worlded': the Word incarnate, the Spirit infused, the Father intimated. This 'en-worlding' looks to a world 'trinified'[39]. The world is being drawn into the universe of Love. Its form is Christ and its energy is the Spirit. Its all-englobing origin and goal is the Father.

Finally, we have been accenting the transformative meaning of the Trinity. In traditional terms, it is the central mystery of salvation. In the present frame of reference, it is the divine mystery made known as it communicates itself to human consciousness:

---

[39] This neologism seems to have been coined by a well-known Lonergan authority, Fred Crowe, S.J.: "we are accustomed to speak of the deification of man and his world, and I wish to stress the fact that the only God there is is a triune God, he communicates himself to us as triune, and therefore the deification of the human world is really its 'trinification." The statement is found in his lecture notes, *The Doctrine of the Most Holy Trinity*, (Willowdale, 1965) pg. 178.

> There is in the world, as it were, a charged field of love and meaning; here and there it reaches a notable intensity: but it is ever unobtrusive, hidden, inviting us to join. And join we must if we are to perceive it, for our perceiving is through our loving.[40]

This self-communication of God, as Father, Son, and Holy Spirit, inspires and fulfills the dynamics of human self-transcendence, as this occurs in the drama of history. Contemporary global aspirations find the Trinity not only as a theological point of synthesis, but also an agenda: the Word, the ultimate meaning legitimates a new dimension in global dialogue. The Spirit is experienced as a creativity in bringing about a truly global human community. The Father is invoked in the attractiveness of the ultimate mystery, the absolute Future in which all human beings belong together in God: "...the world, life and death, the present and the future, are all your servants; but you belong to Christ and Christ belongs to God." (I Cor 3:22-23)

---

[40]Method . . . . pg. 290.

7

Applications

We have been exploring at some length how the psychological analogy might be transposed into the modern context. This meant grounding such analogical thinking more firmly in religious experience. Such experience is historical. As such, it molds and motivates self-transcendence of the human subject, individually, socially, globally, ultimately.

1. The Trinity and the Dimensions of Experience

Our religious experience is structured by a history made up of a past, a present and a future. As influenced by the past, it is primarily *their* experience that concerns us—that sense of transformed life shown forth in the early Christian communities grounding the biblical witness. For these early believers celebrated the Love that had revealed itself as ultimate grace and truth in Christ, to involve them in the ongoing transformation of the Spirit.

As it is present, it looks to *our* experience. This occurs in the way we experience individual and social transformation through love. Through such loving, we realize what is best in ourselves and most valuable to others.

In its openness to the future, our experience is more an orientation to *what we need to experience* for the emergence of one global humanity to come into being. For now the human conversation has opened out to include the whole of history. Reacting against the suffering, oppression and fragmentation of the past, such a conversation intends the all-inclusive future of an emancipated humanity. Indeed, some political theorists do not hesitate to view this new solidarity *sub specie amoris*.[1]

The illuminating experience in each of these analogously related cases was the dynamic state of being-in-love. We are not fabricating a general univocal concept of love which is then somehow applied uncritically to what God is and what we are. For our procedure is analogical. The two cases are related in their likeness and unlikeness: God *is* Love; Christians 'love' by participating in such a divine mystery. Further, it is a properly theological use of analogy. The basic analogue is the divine case of Love, the self-giving God (I Jn 4:10). Yet we still have to try to make sense of "what no one has ever seen" (I Jn 4:12). It has to be appropriated, reverently and critically. This demands deliberate self-appropriation of our own experience of loving:". . .he who loves . . .knows God" (v.7).

An "intentionality analysis" of human loving makes possible a fuller appreciation of the divine mystery implicated in such experience. This is not to forget that there is a greater unlikeness in any equivalence the human mind might establish between the infinite and the finite (Lateran IV). Being-in-Love is 'supereminently' realized in God. On the other hand, God is not less being-in-love than human beings: the divine existence does not stop short at pure Be-ing or pure Intelligence! To be God is not to possess a diminished subjectivity.

Thus the mystery of Love resonates in human existence as a deeply, transformatively human Word. It is present to the human spirit as an all-enabling Spirit. God's self-giving is disclosed at the point where we human beings are most self-transcending.

The New Testament makes surprisingly 'agnostic' statements about our human capacity to know God (Jn 1:18;6:46; I Jn 4:12; I Tim 6:16). Such limitations serve precisely to underscore the only way of knowing God. This is through God's own self-communication as Love.[2] In "the cloud of unknowing" faith meets God in the reality of

---

[1] See Fred R. Dallmayr, *Polity and Praxis. Exercises in Contemporary Political Theory* (Cambridge, Mass: The MIT Press, 1984), pgs. 217-223.

[2] See Eberhard Juengel, *God as Mystery of the World,* pg. 366ff.

Love.³ This mysteriously occurring charged field of love and meaning invites our involvement. It is perceptible only through love.⁴

2. Experience and Christian Mystery

In the historical experience of Christian faith, the mystery of this Love is named and invoked in trinitarian terms. The Father is confessed as the Originating Lover before, above and beyond any of this world's conditions. The Son as the self-expression of that Love in truth contesting any other version of God and humanity. The Spirit as the inexhaustible activity or 'event' of this origin and meaning, drawing the created universe into itself. As Eberhard Juengel puts it:

> It is solely the Spirit of God as the relation of the relations who constitutes the being of God as event.... The constantly new event of love between the Father and the Son ... is the Spirit.... The trinitarian God who is love implies then the eternal newness according to which the eternal God is always his own future. God and love never grow old. Their being remains one that is coming.'⁵

In the traditional theological use of the psychological analogy, what was most perfect in human experience was applied to the divine case of the Trinity. This suggested a way of appropriating not only the meaning of God who is Love as Trinity, but also the experience of that Love as gift, as 'grace'⁶. The Trinity is the mystery which can have meaning only to those who are religiously converted, who live in a matrix of ultimate Love, receiving, adoring, surrendering. In this sense, the Trinity is the "mystical dogmatized"⁷.

---

³*The Cloud of Unknowing. A New Translation by Clifton Wolters* (Penguin Classics, 1961), pgs. 58-62.

⁴See Lonergan, *Method* p. 290 "... In the realm of religious experience Oliver Rabut has asked whether there exists an unassailable fact. He found such a fact in the existence of love. It is as though a room were filled with music though one can have no sure knowledge of its source. There is in the world, as it were, a charged field of love and meaning; here and there it reaches a notable intensity; but it is ever unobtrusive, hidden, inviting us to join. And join it we must if we are to perceive it, for our perceiving is through our loving."

⁵Cf. Juengel, op. cit., pg. 375.

⁶Cf. Lonergan, *Method*, pgs. 107; 120ff.

⁷Sebastian Moore, *The Inner Loneliness* (New York: Crossroad, 1982), pgs. 103f.

This makes for a more reverently engaged trinitarian theology. The Trinity does not occur to faith to puzzle the mind into submission, but to convert our loving into the ultimate proportions of Love.

We have not yet had recourse to the systematic notions of nature, person, relation, community, process. Our account has been more phenomenologically based in the concreteness of an inter-subjective communication. It is true that we are attending to that 'field of love and meaning' in a concrete way, somewhat different from the systematic Thomistic order of processions, missions, and the dynamic assimilation by which each graced person is conformed to the Word and the Spirit. What we are doing here is merely beginning the desired transposition of the classic trinitarian theology. Whilst it is wise to wait on greater competence to complete this task, there is no need for such patience in affirming the essence of the Christian mystery. Thus we described this as an ultimate 'Love-life' drawing believers into itself. The truth and value of this Love is expressed in the incarnate Word. It transforms freedom in the gift of the Spirit. It looks to the final communication of the Mystery, as origin, ground and goal of all, the Father.

In this familiar scheme of things, the original Mystery remains one of Love: God is eternally Love, turned toward the world of creation (Eph 1:4-6). It is at work throughout history in the Spirit. It appears for what it is in the incarnation of the Word. And this is not a surface-appearance: it occupies all the dimensions of human experience, the height and the depth, in the life, death and resurrection of Jesus.

3. The Mystery of Love

This original mystery of divine Love, communicated in time, is illumined by analogy with what we can find in ourselves. We are our best selves when we are 'in love', when we are most self-transcending to what is truly good and loveable. So too is God; but God does not arrive at this love or simply have it: God is this Love, in utter self-transcendence in the self-expressive Word, and as unrestricted self-giving in the gift of the Spirit. The Love that God eternally is, keeps on being Love according to the demands of history.

This is the uniqueness of the divine reality, to be Love. Has theology been too taken up with talking about the one divine nature common to the three divine persons, instead of affirming the uniqueness of the mystery articulated as Trinity? I think so. For God, 'to be' is to 'be-in-Love'; and 'to be-in-Love' is to be Trinity, as the one self-communicating mystery. Neither Love nor Trinity are superadded to the divine constitution, as it were. Love is not a quality that God has or an attitude that the divine three cultivate: it is what God *is*. This, of course, means that God does not depend on anything beyond the Godself to be Love. That is the significance of the classical trinitarian doctrine.[8] By equating "God is Love" with "God is Trinity", we escape the implication that Love is merely a mode of the divine being, that the reality of God could have been otherwise.

If we remain conscious of the limitations of an analogical way of speaking, it may be said that the Divine Mystery is constituted as Being-in-Love by being Father, Son, and Spirit. God is expressly and luminously Love through the self-utterance which is the Word, the divine 'Love-light'. Love is true to what it is in the inexhaustible event of the Spirit, as inclusive openness to all. To say that God is Father is to say that God is "from God": the Love that God is, comes from no where else, no one else. It is pure originality, pure self-giving. To say that God is Son and Word, is to say that Love is 'of God', infinite in its self-expression and self-communication: it is beyond the finite, and expresses itself as the divine meaning and value of God, and all else that might come into existence to receive it. To say that God is Spirit, is to say that Love is communicated 'as God': God's gifts and loving are not finite; they terminate in a perfect communion within God and with God, "in the unity of the Holy Spirit". The Father and Son are united in the Spirit, and with all else in the same Spirit. This is to say that the divine self-giving as Love is the outcome of the divine self-possession as Love: God's relationship with the universe does not originate out of need, but out of the most unconditioned autonomy.

The Love that is given from God, of God, as God is invoked as Father, Son, and Spirit.[9] It is unrestricted self-giving, infinite is its origin, infinite its object, infinite its communication, Or, as has been well said, "the being of God, the essence of his essence, is his giving

---

[8] Juengel, *op. cit.*, pg 316f.
[9] For a profound theological reflection in this context, see Juengel, *op. cit.*, pgs. 380-390.

away that which is particularly his own."[10] The Father puts himself completely into the Son; Father and Son put themselves completely into the Spirit.

The limited expression of theology, inevitably linked to a linear exposition of what it understands, predictably gives the impression that each of the divine three is just one aspect of God. The analogies used must continually come back to the divine mystery as one that is constituted in relationships: the meaning of each of the three necessarily implies the presence and activity of the other two, just as the meaning of the three is unintelligible save in the mystery of the unique reality of the One God.[11] The Father is Love as infinite self-giving, hence all that God is. The Son is the expression of this Love as infinite self-expression, hence all that God is. The Spirit is God, lovingly and truthfully given, hence all that God is. This is merely a restatement of the meaning of what the Greeks called *perichoresis* and what the Latins called *circumincessio*, that reciprocal co-inherence of the divine persons in the one divine reality.

The only God is this self-giving Love: the way it is with God, is the way God is with us; and the way God is for us is true to what Love is in itself. It is possible to raise a speculative doubt about this equation if one steps outside the Christian experience and its normative scriptural and doctrinal expression. But, from the inside, as participants, as communicants in the divine mystery, Love is the foundation of faith's realism: God is not only ever beyond us, as Father, as origin and goal, but with us as Son, and within and between us as Spirit. At each point, we have dealings with the divine Love-life.

The divine self-communication and our human self-transcendence meet in the context of the mystery of Love. In the experience of the reality of the self-giving God, the Love that alone loves our selfhood into being is revealed. Any separation of the immanent Trinity from the economy of God's self-giving fails to appreciate the real being of God as Love. Theology sounds such solemn nonsense if it talks about the reality of God 'in itself'—as though there were some other

---

[10]Heribert Muehlen, *Die Veraenderlichkeit Gottes als Horizonteiner zukuenftigen Christologie* (Muenster: Aschendorff, 1969), pg. 31.

[11]For more on the fundamentally relational character of divine reality, see Catherine M. La Cugna, "The Relational God: Aquinas and Beyond," *Theological Studies* 46(1985), pgs. 647-663.

way into the mystery of God's being other than the Love that has been revealed. In the same way, to confine oneself to a consideration of the supposedly 'economic' Trinity while speaking of Love and yet coyly abstaining from any ontological statement, strikes me as a supreme example of theological forgetfulness. Both of these extremes are equally pernicious to Christian realism. The *via negativa* operates not to undermine the being of God as Love: God is not less 'being in love' than the human case. Rather, God is Love in a supereminent degree. As such only God can fully 'self-communicate' with the other.

Time and history are God's way of letting Love happen in the universe. The Spirit respects, liberates and inspires human freedom so that history can come to bear what God is, so that God can come to be Love with us, in time, in history, in the visions and dreams of human hearts, in the experience of us who are not love, for whom love is no native language. In ways as ambiguous as they are episodic, we might 'have' love. But such loves, if they are to last, are always looking for some transcendent integration, an expansion to a fuller scope. But when God has us, when Love possesses our humanity completely, then time will reach its fulfillment, and the new heavens and new earth begin.

This adds up to saying that the universe is ultimately a 'uni-verse', that is, made into one relational reality through the mystery of Love: the creation of primordial Love defining itself in the comprehensive truth of expressive Love, looking to its fulfillment through unitive Love.[12]

4. The Community in Love

From everything we have been saying, it is clear we can speak of the divine three as a community of Love. Yet I realize the psychological analogy of being-in-love used here might be disappointing to those who prefer to use as the basic analogy, "a community of persons" as we find in the writings of eminent trinitarian thinkers.[13]

---

[12]Contrast this with the more ontological language of John Macquarrie's *Principles of Christian Theology* (New York: Charles Scribner's Sons, 1966), pgs. 180ff.

[13]I find the best treatment of this in Joseph Bracken, "The Holy Trinity as Community of Divine Persons", *Heythrop Journal* 2&3 (1974), pgs. 166-182; 257-270.

This present approach might seem to be too close to an antiquated essentialism, or, perhaps, irritatingly romantic. Apart from making the expected disclaimers that we are speaking in analogical terms of what human beings can find in themselves or admire in others, and that you can't say everything all at once, I would like to offer the following eight points:

1. No one can reasonably deny that the Scriptures describe a divine communion of Father, Son, and Spirit, as each is invoked in faith. The Spirit is represented as one who inspires unity and forms community. The Father and Son are represented as speaking to one another, especially in the prayer of Jesus. The oneness existing between the Father and the Son is paradigmatic for all Christian unity. There is a reality of community or at least communion implied, and a kind of dialogue. For that reason, it is hardly questionable that the realities of community, union, dialogue, and so forth, are analogically related to the trinitarian mystery. My reservations pertain to the degree these can be the basic analogy in exploring the meaning of the Trinity.

2. For it seems to me that the analogy of human community applied to the Trinity is of value only if it assumes and explicitates the psychological analogy of being-in-love; in this way it indicates what kind of communitarian reality is implied. Of itself it does not express sufficiently the essential uniqueness of the divine reality as the one mystery of Loving self-giving.[14] Not to look for an analogical understanding of the kind of communal Be-ing implied in the Trinity, strikes me as simply affirming a 'social Trinity' with inescapable tritheistic overtones. Such an un-analogical statement accents the divine inwardness in a way that diminishes our understanding of the Trinity as a gift transforming human history.[15] Most of all, to speak of the Trinity simply as a community of persons offers no understanding of why there are three and only three divine persons, and why they are to be invoked in their distinctions as Father, Son, and Spirit.

3. Further, if we construct generalized community analogies of the Trinity in terms other than being-in-love, we easily begin to downplay

---

[14]Cf. Juergen Moltmann, *The Trinity and the Kingdom of God*, pgs. 177ff.
[15]Cf., Tad Dunne, "Trinity and History", *Theological Studies* 45, (1984), pg. 142.

the uniqueness of the scriptural data. The prime analogue is not that of isolated, already constituted individuals searching for community, who grow into a state of "being-in-love;" or that of an already constituted community historically and socially preceding the individual whom it 'personalizes' in a nurturing psychological ambience. However valuable such an analogy might be for ecclesiology, and however prized the reality when it occurs, it is not radical enough to allow for the uniqueness of the divine reality as sheer Being-in-Love. God is originatively Love as Father, expressively Love as Son, communicatively Love as Spirit: three subjects in the one conscious infinite act of Being-in-Love. Each divine person has a distinct meaning in the self-constitution of Divine Mystery; each is Love in a distinctive manner. They are not an already constituted threesome which then begins, as it were, to exhibit the quality of love. Rather, the three are intelligible as Trinity only insofar as they manifest the Divine Mystery as sheer Being-in-Love. For this reason the tradition speaks of the *perichoresis, circumincessio, circuminsessio,* of the divine persons rather than of a community of three persons.

4. This by no means denies that dialogue, community, and so forth are essential analogies once the basic analogy of being-in-love is explored. Indeed, as I have implied, they are especially applicable as secondary analogies illuminating the relationships of the three divine subjects in the one conscious activity of Love. The interpersonal and communitarian models certainly illuminate our understanding of the consciousness of Jesus in his relationship to the Father; and most of all, the communitarian analogy throws light on the corporate consciousness of the Church as a "people made one in the unity of the Father, Son and Holy Spirit".

5. In other words, the Trinity is not a communitarian process, a social genesis, more or less conceived of in historical terms. Rather, the unique reality of God as trinitarian Loving makes history, and makes history communitarian, and even trinitarian. 'Our Father', eternally turned toward history as the originating and final Love, is the one in whom community is achieved, in whose presence humanity finally becomes 'we', when God will be "everything to everyone". The Word, as the self-expression of God as Love, bespeaks all the perfection of loving and interpersonal communication, everything which genuine dialogue makes possible between human individuals. It is this Word that is made flesh. It is uttered into the human

conversation, thus embodying all the modalities of loving expression that the incarnation reveals—address, prayer, parable, commandment, call, judgment, commitment, promise. The Word is the one in whom ultimate dialogue, *dia-Logos,* becomes possible, as it commands the forgiveness of enemies, love of one's neighbor, adoration of the Father, hope for all. Such a divine Word pertains to what social theorists have come to call "the ideal Speech Situation".[16] But the difference, for the Christian at least, is that such a situation is not an utopian aspiration but a response provoked by God's irreversible self-communication in history. The Spirit, as the fulfillment of the self-communication of God in limitless Loving, makes this Word audible, and inspires the implementation of the truth it expresses and the community it calls to.

6. In short, though not a community and dialogue in the human sense, God, as the Mystery of Love, is that in which community and dialogue become. For this unique self-giving Love originates, expresses, enables and redeems the human search for community in history and thus provokes the reality of hopeful dialogue.

7. Concretely, to the degree we present God as a field or matrix of community-forming Love involving the world in itself, the Spirit is the 'first divine person' in the realm of experience. In that shared Spirit of self-transcending Love, we identify the Jesus as Love's self-expressive Word uttered into our history; through the Word, and in the Spirit we relate to the Father as the original and final horizon within which the cosmos is revealed as a universe of Love.

8. Such a differentiation certainly implies a divine communion. Within the one divine consciousness, the one Being-in-Love, there are three divine subjects. It is a communion transcending any human analogy of community. Understandably, some will object that we are making Love into a substance and undermining the truly personal character of the Trinity. I would reply that we need to use all the analogies we can find; but the basic one, the one most illuminative of how the unique and one divine reality is Love, yet invocable as Father, Son, and Spirit, is to be found in that apex of human conscious self-transcendence that technically we designate as "being-in-love". It is this Love that constitutes the trinitarian communion.

---

[16] See the next chapter.

The Trinity is not a community that somehow begins to love. In the transposition of the Thomistic psychological image promoted here, the result has been that the Trinity is a way of expressing God as Love, as self-giving Lovingness. This contrasts with a theologically puzzling conception of the Trinity as a community of three persons which then goes on to explain why God "so loved the world". Given this conception, one still has to ask: only three persons and why precisely these three? In exploring the divine reality as Love, clearly Father, Son, and Spirit are distinct and relational terms in the divine realm of Being-in-Love. Those who think of God first of all in communitarian terms must be less than satisfied that we have respected the personal character of each of the three. Suitably, then, we pass on to the next point.

5. *The Language of "Three Persons"*

Because the three are not members of a community in any obvious human sense, does this mean that the word 'person' is no longer useful in trinitarian theology? The approach of the last section implied that the notion of person must be applied analogically when speaking of the Trinity. Not only is this use analogically related to human personhood, but also amongst the divine three themselves: in the one Being-in-Love, each is a personal subject in a distinctive sense.[17]

It would appear that 'person' is currently employed in at least nine linguistic contexts: dramatic, aesthetic, psychological, legal, philosophical, physical, zoological, grammatical, theological.[18] The average educated person can use this subtly connotative word confidently in most of these senses even if the common field of meaning is something of a philosophical puzzle.

Here I might make one simple remark. In theological and the

---

[17]Lawrence Porter, "On Keeping 'Persons' in the Trinity: A Linguistic Approach to Trinitarian Thought", *Theological Studies* 41/3(Sept. 1980), pgs. 530-548.

[18]*The Oxford English Dictionary*, vol. 7 (London, 1933), pgs. 724f. To these must be added the current inflated usage devised to avoid 'sexist language', e.g., salesperson. What is being attempted in purging English of sexist connotations by replacing 'man' with person, has the disadvantage of reducing the refined meaning of 'person' to a social role.

more meaningful and value-laden types of discourse, the context of 'person' language is that of real or possible love. Love in its most authentic experiences is between persons. To speak the language of love and not use the language of person would be linguistically and psychologically violent. That is why there is some special sensitivity in the retention of this word in trinitarian theology where what is most loving and what is most personal coincide. The use of the word 'person' in reference to oneself or the other (individual or communal) implies that love, in some sense, has occurred—at least as accepting such others into a shared world of rights and values.

Theologically speaking, the notion of person serves the language and experience of God as Love. On the one hand, God is certainly not three individuals univocally understood in terms of a human threesome. On the other hand, the "distinctly subsisting reality in an intellectual nature" (Aquinas) is an austerely philosophical formulation prerequisite to the affirmation of God as self-giving Love: the One who is "beyond us as gracious Origin and end of all" is a distinct subject; the One who is "with us" as the truth and revelation of the Giver is another; the One who is given "within and between us" is another, in the one mystery of Loving self-communication.

The community of faith turns to God in three modes of address, rhetorically, to celebrate the reality of such Love. This is the foundation of the affirmation of the three as 'persons' and the original reason for the theological use of this word. Thus, modalism is kept at bay: the self-differentiated reality of God as Love (Lover, the truth of Love, the gift of Love) is truly communicated. God is not acting the part of Lover but enacting in human history what the divine mystery is. The use of the word 'person' counters Arianism, for the three are invocable in the realm of the divine: the terms Father, Son, and Spirit are God as affirmed and invoked in divine self-giving, self-expression, self-gift. It is not tritheism, for that is not only a religious impossibility, but the failure to understand analogical predication.

The concrete realism of Love demands that its invocation of God in this way leads to and lives from an affirmation of God as truly invocable, relational, relatable. Any erosion of the force of personal language deeply disaffects Christian faith.

Already the doctrinal tradition and Thomistic theology have conceived the divine persons as its distinct relations subsisting in the one divine nature, grounded in the processions, which in turn are the efflorescence of the divine Act of Be-ing. This has always been a problem for human imagination. We have to imagine the reality of the persons somehow consequent on the divine Being, the divine processions, the various relationships, since the notional always comes after the essential and is somehow tacked on the divine essence in our picture of the Trinity.

Can our transposition of the scholastic categories into phenomenologically based experience, of *Esse Subsistens* into limitless self-transcendence, of the Act of sheer Be-ing into "Being in Love", better satisfy the religious imagination and better meet the demands of theological thinking? I think so, because it allows the systematic starting point to be personal, namely, the Father as infinite original self-giving Love, expressing himself in the Word and communicating himself in the Spirit. The Thomistically dominant notion of God as undifferentiated Be-ing is now more clearly contextualized in the concrete mystery of Love. The divine transcendence from the world is located in the horizon of God's self-transcendence toward the world. "Trinitate posita, congruunt huiusmodi rationes".[19]

To a large degree, the analogy of self-transcending love overcomes an excessive rift in the economic and immanent consideration of the Trinity. For by emphasizing the 'self' in the self-communication of God, it underscores the invocable self-involvement of God in history. Admittedly, it is still difficult to overcome the linear, temporal character of our thinking. No one can say everything all at once, but the choice does turn on what you say first and how you say it!

But how can God be truly tri-personal when we have been conceiving of the divine reality as one infinite act of "Being-in-Love", in the one conscious self-giving Love? Obviously, this is the psychological form of the question: how can there be real distinctions when there is only one divine nature? The answer is that each is Love in a distinct but related manner: The Father is the Origin of Love for the totality of God and all in God; the Word is the self-expression of Love for God and all in God; the Spirit is the ever-new communication of Love toward God and all in God. The identity of each of the divine persons is unintelligible without the other two. The divine

---

[19] *S. Theol.* 1,32,1 ad 1.

consciousness is possessed in three subjective manners which are necessarily inter-subjective. Each lives in the consciousness of the others; the particular self-consciousness of each must include the presence of the others. Once more, *perichoresis*. This is a greater instance of shared consciousness than the model of an 'I-Thou' relationship can express, even though, in the appropriate context, such an analogy is useful, as we said before.

In terms of existential imagination, the love-analogy indicates the personal character of the Trinity. For it shows how we human persons are radically 'personalized' by the divine three: the Spirit is the divine gift that stimulates a truly personal acceptance of the other, be this other divine or finite. Spirit-Love transforms human freedom, as a "subsisting relationship" opening the human person to a universe of ultimate relationships.

The Son is the expression of the relational character and self-transcending dynamism of true personhood. As Son, he is the divine expression in history of the transcendent origin and goal of the truly personal; and, as Word, he is God's irrevocable affirmation of the worth of the person.

The Father, the all-fulfilling mystery, finalizes the mystery of human personhood: its origin is 'from God' and its goal is 'in God'. In 'Our Father', the human person comes home to a universe of persons who live from and in the one ultimate mystery of Love.

Given the elasticity of the term 'person', the mystery of Love which it elucidates, the divine conscious subjects revealed in the divine self-communication which Christianity celebrates, I cannot see any compelling reason to qualify its usefulness.[20] There is some fear that it might give a tritheistic impression. On the other hand, to abandon it for some modalistic expression might leave the language of person at the mercy of a narcissistic interpretation, or at least of a non-relational understanding which would be of limited usefulness in an increasingly global world.

The classical question was how to understand the three distinct divine persons in the one divine nature. I am inclined to think the modern question is how these three are to be named in the dynamics

---

[20]For an especially illuminating treatment of this and so many other questions, see the insightful, though comparatively unrecognized, Ghislain Lafont, *Peut-on connaître Dieu en Jesus-Christ?* (Paris: Editions du Cerf, 1969), pgs. 229-289.

of the mystery of Love as it 'personalizes' the social and historical movement of our humanity. It is not our deeply conditioned and alienated human individualities that are the paradigm of personhood, but the divine three who give themselves in Love. It is the Trinity that is the source, form, and fulfillment of personal life and genuine progress.

The problem appears to be the modern psychological notion of person: an individual centre of interior, inviolable consciousness. Theology cannot pretend to control how such a term as 'person' is used in all contexts, even if Christian theology invented it! There is no Christian copyright in this matter. But what is the real problem? Are we in danger of conceding defeat here too easily in a world dramatically faced with the realization that the authentic person is one who realizes his or her identity in relationships, in increasingly social, planetary and even cosmic proportions? In other words, is the so-called modern understanding of person as an independent freedom, really, psychologically or socially defensible?

Perhaps at the heart of this problem is really a wrong theology: a deistic notion of God, a purely transcendent Being enclosed in a self-sufficient solitary indifference in regard to a creation that runs on its own laws? Has Christian theology baptized its imagination sufficiently to exorcise this projection of inner capitalism?

So, for all these reasons, I think we must support an analogous use of the term 'person' in trinitarian theology. Though it is not found in the scriptures, it does serve to clarify the meaning of the biblical experience of God while providing a challenge for our modern understanding of the personal. In short, the use of the term secures the Christian realism of God's invocability as Father, Son, and Spirit. It enables us to express the trinitarian reality as differentiated into three distinct subjects inter-related in the one divine consciousness of "Being-in-Love". It enables theology to express the meaning of this as it is realized in time, as this is communicated to human subjects for them to become temples of the Spirit, members of Christ, children of the Father. Further, it lives from the personalizing effect that the Trinity has on human existence: the person of the Father is adored as the ultimate Love grounding the personal universe; the Son is adored as the ultimate truth of our personal destiny; the Spirit is adored as the liberating expansion of our personal relationships.

So, what is there about the divine mystery that constitutes it as Being-in-Love? It is the tri-personal differentiation of God as Father, Son, and Spirit. God is self-communicating mystery, able to express and give itself totally, while always remaining the personal giver in the gift and in the giving. The use of the term 'personal' reminds theology that it is exploring a mystery of Love. God does not have love, but is Love.

6. *The Trinity and Process*

God's self-involvement with the world has been imaginatively depicted by the contemporary development known as "Process Thought". This kind of thinking evidences, first, a vivid appreciation of the evolving, processive nature of the universe and of human consciousness within it; secondly, a profound sense of God's immanence in this evolution; thirdly, and perhaps most impressively, a sense of the divine compassion: it stresses that God is not protected from creation by the divine attributes of omnipotence, immutability, omniscience. There is real *kenosis* of the divine into the finite. God is really related to the world and affected by it.

Basically, Process Thought stresses that all reality is developing, and that it develops in a field of universal interaction. Not to understand God in this way, is to exclude God from the world of human experience. Becoming is what is basic to every reality we know, including ourselves. Perfection consists in the ability to adapt in continuing creativity, to enter into a wider field of interaction. If all reality is characterized by such interaction and development, the reality of God must be understood in such dynamic terms. Such a line of reasoning is familiar to theological tradition. God must be conceived of in terms of the highest perfections found in creatures. Such is Aquinas' argument for applying the notion of 'person' to God.

Hence, God must be God-in-Process if God is to be affirmed as real. The divine achieves its identity through creative interaction with the rest of the universe. For God to be God means to be caught up in a continuing process of development, interacting with the world in time so that he is really affected in his divine being by the reality outside him. He risks his being in the world, is enriched by it, and creatively improvises its future from the possibilities that emerge.

The classic divine perfections of ontological transcendence, immutability, eternity, impassibility and omniscience have to be reconstructed so as to include a necessary relationality, change within God, a development through time, immersion in human suffering, and learning through experience.[21]

The process system of thought provokes some fundamental problems for the classical and more complex tradition of Christian doctrine. What Process Thinking tries to elaborate in the one term, process, the Thomist tradition, which we are here transposing, uses four: the Being of God, processions within God, missions as the temporal extension of the processions, and the transformation that results as grace, divinization, trinification. Even though this classic tradition holds to the realism of the incarnation in strict Chalcedonian terms, it rather bewilderingly states that God is not 'really related' to the world.

Now, the aim of this present exploration has been to transpose these classic elements into the phenomenality of Love. This has meant a certain reversal of the Thomistic order of exposition: divine Be-ing, processions, relationships, persons, missions, grace. For we treated first the occurrence of a transforming gift of being-in-love, then the divine gift intimated in the experience of this, then the divine Giver implied in the gift as an infinite, original, self-expressive and self-communicating Being-in-Love: Father, Son, and Spirit. Such a transposition demands a reformulation. This implies a new formulation of how God is related to the world.

In a general sense, our use of the psychological analogy is a 'process theology', even though not, of course, in the modern use of the term. More accurately, in keeping with the theological and doctrinal tradition in which we have been working, the better name would be a 'procession theology'. The self-constitution of God is not dependent on any reality outside the divine—which is the implication of process thought in general, as we shall soon mention. The processions of the Word and Spirit in the one dynamism of infinite Love articulate the meaning of God as "Being-in-Love" in the essential

---

[21] Representative works are Charles Harsthorne, *The Divine Relativity: A Social Conception of God* (New Haven: Yale University Press; 1948); John B. Cobb, Jr., *A Christian Natural Theology* (Philadelphia: Westminster Press, 1965); Lewis Ford, "Process Trinitarianism", *Journal of the American Academy of Religion* 43/2(1975) pgs. 45-57.

self-constitution of the divine: God is Lover as Love expressed in the Son, and given as Loveable and enabling Loving in the Spirit.

In this model, the universe is drawn into the realm of the divine through the incarnation, cross and resurrection, and through the sending of the Spirit. The missions are projections of the divine reality into creation. The transcendent purpose of such 'sendings' is that finite reality might come to exist in God in a new way. In this sense, Son and Spirit are sent for the sake of enfolding all in God, in the one realm of Being-in-Love. Though God exists in the world in a new way, it is for the sake of the world existing in God in an ultimate way. In assuming our humanity, the Word opens the finite to the infinite mystery of the Father; in the coming of the Spirit, human liberty unfolds as a relationship to infinite Love.

Here the dominant paradigm is procession. This is to say that the Mystery gives itself out of its own self-constitution. In reality, a self-communication takes place. The divine mystery unfolds on its own terms, or as we say, in its eternal being, in terms of what God essentially is. The 'Godself' communicated to creation is the Self that God is: the divine self-constitution is not a subjectivity expanding through time, as in the human case. God does not need time to be Love. As eternal, the infinite Being-in-Love makes history, but is not made by it. God's relations with everything else come from the free self-gift of Love. God does not become Love as an afterthought or as a virtuoso improvisation. That, it seems to me, is the fundamental meaning of the Trinity. There was never a time when God is not Love, even if God takes time in expressing the truth and reality of this in human history , to allow humanity to have a true history.

To speak of God as Father, as the origin of the self-giving Love, means that there was never a time when God is not turned toward creation in this self-communicating way. He chooses us "before the foundations of the world", destining us in love to be his sons and daughters through Christ, the Beloved, looking to the full revelation of this Mystery in the glory of grace (Eph 1:3-12). God as Love is always "so loving the world" (Jn 3:16). While the Father is always himself in our regard, the Love that he is has to take time to address human history, to enter into the human conversation, into the capacities of human freedom. The Spirit is given preparing for this self-utterance of the Mystery: before the Word can be fully spoken, the alphabet of human existence has to be formed, its vocabulary has to develop and be refined, our discernment and spiritual senses develop, our freedom grow.

Then in "the fullness of time", the Word is uttered into human history: the Word was made flesh and dwelt amongst us. In Jesus, in his life, death and resurrection, the truth of what God is, and of what we are meant to be in God, is disclosed to be enacted in the Spirit. This disclosure identifies the Spirit as the Spirit of Jesus, whilst the Spirit enacts union with him, and intimacy with the Father through the mediation of the Son. As it is conformed to the way of the Son, history is opened to the culminating communication of the Father. God with us, God within us, looks to the point when God will be "everything to everyone" (I Cor 15:28).

This kind of approach lives from one simple principle. Self-communication is made possible by self-possession. Love is only possible when lovers enjoy their own identity as loving and loveable. Love may arise out of the 'moral necessity' to be true to oneself; but that is not need. One is often struck how theology speaks of God's Love in terms which, in any human case, would sound like such neurotic need, the 'needing others to need us' syndrome. As counsellors have pointed out to the lovelorn for so long, self-giving is not self-destruction; loving is not dissipating one's selfhood in the other, but finding the mystery of that selfhood accepted, affirmed, and promoted. In the analogical probing of theological language, it does no harm to keep these common human instances in mind. God's eternal self-possession as Love makes possible the communication of that Love in its fullness. All lovers have to live in 'eternity', in a radical self-possession, if their loving is not to destroy them, but to be the communication of their best selves. One must wonder if process thought has appreciated this side of human experience....

More to the point, if the paradigmatic reality is understood in terms of 'process' instead of the 'processions' of Being-in-Love, severe problems result for Christian theology—to say nothing of Christian sensibility. For example, if God is subject to the process like all else, is the process or the force of development really the divine reality since God is contained within it?[22] Given the contingent

---

[22] See W. Hill, *op. cit.*, pgs. 185ff.

quality of all interactions within the dynamics of process, in what do we place our hope? What assurance do we have that the process will endure?.... Or that God, conditioned by the process, will survive it?.... That Love will keep on being love, grace keep on being grace, that resurrection, not death, will be the outcome? I suspect that these questions can only be answered if Process Thinking draws more from 'Procession' theology.[23]

Any discussion on the use of process categories in Christian theology might do well to attend to two types of radical data. The first is the essentially Christian datum of the incarnation of the Word: "the Word was made flesh", or in the terms of Chalcedon, one and the same subject, the Son, is truly God and truly man, without division, separation, confusion, or change. The most intimate self-expression of the divine is existentially uttered into the world. The divine person of the Word assumes a human nature into his personal identity, thus to experience human "being in the world". Because Christologies 'from below' have dominated the recent theological scene, one may well ask whether or not process thought is a kind of compensatory category somehow intending the reality of this essential Christian doctrine.

The second radical datum is that disclosed through the self-appropriation of the dynamics or 'process' of human consciousness. Now, Process thinkers take their stand on 'experience'. But do they, one may ask, sufficiently attend to the experience they aim to elucidate, namely, the consciousness of the self-in-action? For this is not just a flow of atomistic experiences, a series of discrete happenings. Rather, as consciousness expands through all its levels in activities of sensing, understanding, reflecting, deliberating, loving and adoring, it discloses the subject as a fundamental 'given', the conscious 'I' who is the agent. The same identity occurs in all these operations and finds fulfillment by following them through. By attending to this utterly fundamental experience of being a self-in-action, we have the experience which makes self-knowledge possible. It is this experience of self-constitution that is the fertile ground for trinitarian analogies—not any kind of experience, least of all, mere

---

[23]See my "Trinity and Process: Relevance of the Basic Christian Confession of God", *Theological Studies* 31(1970), pgs. 393-414.

sensory awareness.[24]

It is true that freedom has to be applied analogously to God's essential self-constitution as Love, and in the communication of this Love, to creation. Theology is not unaware of the dilemma: if God is Love, how is God necessarily God, since love implies freedom? How can Love constitute the Being of God? If God is necessarily Love, how can creation and the subsequent fulfillment of creation in grace be a free self-giving? In such questions it is important not to reduce freedom to 'multiple choice'; freewill, in that sense, would be pure contingency. Again, the analogy must be the self-constitution of the human subject: the good we seek and the love we aspire to can only be denied at the peril of our existential self-destruction; yet this can be realized in a limitless number of possible ways. The contingent arises out of the free consent to limitless self-transcendence in love, in the direction of the truly good. Analogously, the divine essential self-realization of God as trinitarian Love is contingently realized in creation. To respect the divine freedom we have to say that the world could have been otherwise, or could not have been at all. But, in the historical enactment of trinitarian Love, we find the assurance that there was never a time when God was not 'in Love' with creation, and never a time when this Love was not in God. This is so, even if this creation is in time, even if God has to take time to communicate such Love within human history, with all its times of preparation and fulfillment.

In short, all trinitarian theology is a kind of original 'process theology': the divine processions are the origin of reality and its dynamism ; or as we would say here, the divine processions disclose the meaning of God as self-constituted Love. Procession gives rise to the process.

Further, in the limited, current sense, 'process' is a valuable new model for theological thought. Problems arise when the 'process model' is erected into a system which seems to exclude basic trinitarian data. Once it is admitted that the divine processions are the ground and goal of all human and cosmic process, then the 'process model' can be elaborated with most positive results. The divine

---

[24]For an impressive analysis of these issues, see Michael Vertin, "Is God in Process", in *Religion and Culture. Essays in honor of Bernard Lonergan,* eds. Timothy Fallon and Phillip Bo Riley (Albany: State University Press, 1987) pgs. 45-62.

processions of Word and Spirit can then be grasped as the source, structure, dynamism and goal of the universal process.

7. The Divine Compassion

One reason for the attractiveness of the process model in contemporary theological thinking is that it concurs with so much of our experience and understanding of the universe. Today, as was pointed out in the first chapter, the accent is rightly on the dynamic inter-relatedness of reality. This inspires the "Grand Field Theory" in physics, solidarity in politics, ecological responsibility in the environment, global responsibility in economics, the transpersonal sense in psychology and mysticism.

More to the point, Process Thought aims to express how God is compassionately involved in the emerging processive cosmos, both conditioned by it, and in a sense, vulnerable to it, suffering our history. Such thinking seems to mitigate the scandal of the problem of evil, given the global dimensions of the world's sufferings. This awareness of the world's anguish is surely one of the major determinants of modern consciousness.

Admittedly, the traditional resources of Christian theology have not been so obviously available. Trinitarian thought was very abstract; Christology was largely exploring a formulation 'from below', with a consequent downplaying of the incarnation and cosmic aspects of God's presence in Christ. Yet, in terms of the great Christological statements of Nicaea and Chalcedon, the crucifixion of the incarnate Son means an awesome act of divine self-involvement, which cannot be appreciated by any theology restricted to Adoptionist, Arian, Nestorian, or Monophysite positions.

For the moment, however, let us pursue a retrieval of the classic tradition in terms of the mystery of trinitarian Love as we have been presenting it.

A promising starting point is found in the meaning of the divine missions. In the Thomistic tradition, the Word and the Spirit, as sent, begin to exist in the world in a new way.[25] In the crucified

---

[25]"novus modus essendi" (*S. Theol.* 1,43,1).

Jesus, the Word assumes our humanity in Jesus. The Spirit is the manifestation and power of God's Love in history. The Father, though not sent, is given as original Love intimated in the Word and Spirit, and as ultimately to be glorified by all creation.

This means, that as Love, the three are conscious of themselves in a new way. For the divine mystery exists in a new way in the human world, affected as that world is by human intelligence, human decision, and human evil. God's Love is not unconscious of the finite world as it suffers from all the effects of separation from God and exhibits its power to reject Love and the humanity it inspires. God is kenotically related to the world (Phil 2:7), not by becoming something else in the world, but by being nothing but Love in history, by refusing any other mode of action or presence. Such self-emptying is not therefore a lessening of the divine reality but its proper manifestation. It is not a question of God becoming one more victim in the world, but of Love being truly itself in a world of 'false gods'. Though this Love has its own mysterious creativity in the resurrection, it does not save the Son from the cross, nor the Spirit from grief, nor the Father from offence.

Such dramatic psychological expressions have to confront that other affirmation of the tradition, namely, that God is unchanged, and that the divine relationship to the world is not a "real relation", but only a "relation of reason".[26] Though such a statement appears fateful to any sense of God's real involvement in the world, let alone suffering its evil, our notion of God as Love can show both the limitation of such expressions and their critical theological value.

The tradition says rather awkwardly that God is not changed by his involvement with the world. The point here is that Love does not depend on anything outside it to be what it is: God is not dependent on the world to be God. The divine self-communication to the world increases the being of the world, not that of God. God's gifts are given out of pure Love. Because of this unconditioned Loving, God can be himself totally in and for the other: there is no part of the divine that has to be realized on the outside, as it were. All the conditions for God self-involvement come from God; just as this

---

[26]See my, "God: How near a Relation?", *The Thomist* XXIV/2 (April 1970), pgs. 191-229. Much discussion has gone on of course since this article was written, but I think the point on the relationships still stands.

self-giving is purely to do good to the other: there is literally 'nothing in it' for God himself. This I take to be the meaning of the technically philosophical statement that God is not 'really related' to the world. Divine reality is not conditioned by the world, but, as Love, God can be pure self-gift in its regard.

But there is some relationship between God and the world. Since the world is really changed, and God is not, the Thomistic tradition feels forced to say that this relationship has to be a "relationship of reason".[27] As contrasted to a "real relationship" this sounds totally unreal, especially given the mystery of the incarnation of the Word and the cross. A helpful way of dealing with this deficiency of language is to translate the "relation of reason" as a "relationship of meaning". The full reality of the human world is constituted by meanings. Meanings mediate our consciousness of reality, especially when such meanings are most personal. For example, in the ancient terminology, a poem is really related to the poet only as it is a physical or intellectual production: the physical sounds, the mental acts. But that would leave the human reality of the poem unexpressed: its meaning as constituting the poet's vision and sense of the universe in which he or she might live. It is an expression of a universe re-meant, revalued. This does nothing to the physical reality. But it is immeasurably significant in the meaningful life of the artist. The world is related to poets, and they to the world in a new way. Can this be an analogy for what we are saying here? God is meaningfully, lovingly, consciously related to the world in everything he is as Love. In the eternal freedom of what God is, in the universe of meaning, the divine is intrinsically related to the suffering and alienated word.

As Creator, God is the Love "infusing and creating goodness in things" (Aquinas): creative Love is the origin, sustenance, and goal of the universe. The Be-ing of God is more intimately involved with creation, as the transcendent cause of be-ing in everything and everyone, than any finite agent could be.

Through the incarnation, Divine Love's eternal decision to communicate itself fully to creation is expressed. God assumes this self-transcending universe into a personal identity with himself in order

---

[27]For an accessible and very fair discussion of these deep issues, see *God and Change* (Special Edition), *The New Blackfriars* (May 1987), especially Michael J. Dodds, "St. Thomas Aquinas and the Motion of the Motionless God", pgs. 233-242.

to 'amorize', trinify, divinize it, by transforming it. To that degree, God does not just have a good feeling about the universe. He is more than the "fellow sufferer who understands". He is unimaginably within creation as the giver of its self-transcending being, its *esse*. Then, through the incarnation, he owns it 'from within', as personally a part of it, and possesses it through the indwelling Spirit. The crucified Christ manifests the irrevocable act of God's being involved with this universe. This is a different order of being-related to the world compared to what might be imagined in emotional or organic terms. To say that the trinitarian Love is compassionate, is not a statement of ineffectual feeling, but a statement of total self-involvement.[28] That is why Liberation theology represents such a gain in Christian sensibility: it represents God as overcoming human suffering. It does not glorify suffering as somehow divine, or divinely willed. There is no need to isolate pain as the sign of divine sincerity, even though in the cross there is real pain and real vulnerability in the Word Incarnate. For the Word expresses all that God is as Love, the self-expression within the divine consciousness. This includes in the divine consciousness of the Word a consciousness of himself in the world, even in the world as separated from God. Further, in assuming human nature, the Word enters the world of feeling and human intersubjectivity. In such a world, God may seem absent; and death, evil, lovelessness seem to be the enduring realities. Thus, the divine and human consciousness of the Word incarnate in the context of God's self-giving Love is the foundation of the great metaphors of divine Compassion.[29]

This approach to divine compassion takes us further than saying that the only divine feeling is that of being displeased with our sins: we are looking for a new mode of speaking of the divine affectivity. Love relates God to the world in a divine passion. Narrowly moralistic sensitivities need to be replaced by a more comprehensive sense of religious affectivity.[30]

---

[28] See the excellent article of Herbert McCabe, "The Involvement of God", *The New Blackfriars* (Nov 1985) pgs. 464-476.

[29] For a different view, see Moltman, *op. cit.*, pgs. 81f and *passim*. There is no denying the emotional grandeur of such theology, something akin to the genre of grand opera.

[30] For wise comments on this topic, see Jacques Maritain, "Quelque réflexions sur le savoir théologique", *Revue Thomiste* 69 (1969) pgs. 5-27.

However I see no point in re-issuing a modern version of Patripassianism: the whole Trinity is not incarnate, even if the whole Trinity is a self-communicating Love. The self-expression of this Love occurs in Jesus, who, in trinitarian language, is the incarnation of the Word.[31] In Jesus, the Word is the divine subject who is hypostatically related to human existence by assuming humanity into identity with himself. This is God's self-expression in human history. As a divine subject within human history, he is the subject of human self-transcendence. He feels; it is he who is scourged, who is crucified, who rises from the dead. Only the Word/Son is thus organically, 'emotionally', corporeally, involved in the human world. Only the Son suffers the human condition in this way. The Father and the Spirit do not suffer in this way. Certainly the Spirit undergoes the *kenosis* of emptying himself into the world of the heart of stone, into the world of resistant human liberty, where the demonic seems so often more powerful than the Spirit of Love. Certainly, the Father empties himself into being God only in the self-expression of the Son, in a world that is anti-Love, enclosed in its own idols. But, as I said before, this emptying has more to say about the illusions of human history, rather than any change in the identity of God. The meaning of this emptying is the divine refusal to appear or be present in any way other than that of Love.

This founds the Christian rhetoric of grieving the Spirit and offending God. The Father is not corporeally or emotionally involved. The theology of the cross is not about the glorification of pain or suffering for its own sake. It is about the glorification of Love as compassionately involved with the human condition, as transformative of human freedom, as protologically and eschatologically ultimate in regard to the universe. The essential theological notion is Love, not suffering, and not any kind of suffering love, but Love truly transformative of human existence: "If the Spirit of him who raised Jesus from the dead dwells in you, he who raised Jesus from the dead will give life to your mortal bodies also through the Spirit who dwells in you" (Rom 8:11).

In short, God is not 'un-godded' by evil, but turns evil into an

---

[31] For an outstanding treatment of the deeper metaphysical issues involved in a strong theology of the incarnation, see Thomas G. Weinandy, *Does God Change? The Word's becoming in the Incarnation* (Still River, Mass.: St. Bede's Press, 1985).

occasion for a greater manifestation of Love: God is not part of the problem of evil, but its solution. This is quite consonant with transcendentally victorious Love as it is explicitly or implicitly expressed in Genesis, in Deutero-Isaiah, in Job, in the resurrection accounts, in the final vision of Revelation. The history of evil occasions the revelation of God's Love in its transcendent, unconditional reality. For it is neither defeated by evil nor subject to any finite conditions.

This leads one to say that the cross is 'in God' in the same sense that the resurrection is: Original Love is, of its nature, an unconditional Word of Love's self-giving, in God and for the world. It keeps on being true to itself in the creativity of the Spirit.

How then does God suffer? The answer has to be: God suffers because God is Love. It is Love that gives being, that unites itself with the other, and transforms what is other through the gift that it is. Is the Father conscious of being rejected? Is the Father conscious of his Word being denied and of his beloved Son being crucified? Of his Spirit being resisted? Of the world organizing itself as anti-Love, and of the momentous self-destructiveness of this resistance? The answer to all such questions has to be affirmative.

Yet, God does not suffer our evils the way we do. As McCabe puts it, "It is not the nature of God to be involved in the suffering of the world as spectator, sympathizer or victim, but it is in the nature of God nonetheless to be involved with his creatures more intimately than any creature could be involved with another."[32] The humanity of Christ is the organ of the Mystery of Love expressive of the being of God as it refuses to be anything else but Love. The total mystery of Christ is that of Love keeping on being Love despite the most intense evil of the world, as Jesus abandons himself to the mercy and creativity of Love. But the result is the resurrection of the Crucified, the beginning of a new creation in which Love, not evil, is the ultimate force.

Still, the passion of the Crucified points to a deeper level of Love's mystery. God is not transcendentally removed from our existence, but transcendentally involved in it. Love is the giver of our existence, not just a promised future fulfillment in an almost extrinsic manner.

---

[32]McCabe, *op. cit.*, pg. 464.

To this degree, as the origin, form, and dynamism of our being, God suffers our evils more than we do ourselves. For God is more involved in our destiny than we are ourselves, individually and historically. One thinks of the pain of parents watching over a sick child, of prophets suffering the evil of their times, of Jesus weeping over Jerusalem....

I am appealing to a realistic notion of suffering: the greater the love, the greater the suffering awareness of the other. Indeed, the greater the love, the more suffering it occasions, since it is calling forth in the other a painful dispossession. It dramatically confronts self-centeredness in the other, as it provokes the tension between a self-transcending love and the self-to-be-transcended. As any actual love eventually is experienced as 'harsh and dreadful' in its demands, so divine Love occasions all kinds of projections onto God as indifferent and heartless in regard to a world locked in its self-sufficiency.

In short, the Trinity is not a consolation as miraculously abolishing all suffering. Rather it comes into human experience as the space in which all suffering can be transformed. The Father, as the Loving origin of the universe, the Word Incarnate as the Loving assumption of the human, the Spirit as the Loving enabler of a new humanity, work to transform the problem of evil into the further radiance of Love. This alone illumines the darkness of human suffering with hope, meaning, and energy. Whatever the appalling power of evil to create its own vicious circle of hatred and despair, there is always a new beginning. Love keeps on being Love as the beginning and end of existence: Love keeps on being mysteriously given. Whatever the absurdity and meaninglessness, Love keeps expressing itself in the divinely human Word, contesting purely mundane, dehumanizing versions of human life. However paralysed in moral impotence a human situation is, Love keeps on being true to itself in the unspent creativity of the Spirit taking us where we do not dare to go. It is possible to read such statements as 'lightly made', as though theology were thinking of toothache as the paradigm of our agonies. But they are more than that....:in "tribulation, or distress, or persecution, or famine or nakedness or peril or the sword..we are more than conquerors through him who loved us." (Rom 8:35-37)

Today there are many names for the cosmic threats and forces that seem more real than the reality of God as Love. Paul's language dealt with "the principalities and powers", "things present and the things to come", the dimensions of a preternatural "height and depth" menacingly encompassing human existence. The modern version of these pervasive threats are present in the technological and political and cultural forces oppressing our humanity on a global scale. But only the love that draws its life from the heart of God, "bears all things, believes all things, hopes all things, endures all things", remains (I Cor 13:7f). In this sense, the ultimate reality is trinitarian Love: "... nothing in all creation will be able to separate us from the love of God in Christ Jesus our Lord." (Rom 8:39)

8
MODELS

In this chapter we want to develop further how the mystery of the Trinity is an agenda for human living, whether we interpret such living in psychological, political, or religious categories. Because the reality of God is trinitarian Love, it makes a difference. This difference is felt, I hope to show, in the deeper registers of the individual or collective psyche, and in the outer reaches of political and social belonging in the one human history. At that intense point of the intersection of our journeys inward and outward, the Trinity also makes a difference. Further, it inspires a new hopeful apprehension of the religious history of our race. In each of these contexts, a trinitarian faith, hope and love functions as a principle of conversion. For it demands that we leave behind inauthentic forms of existence for the sake of an ever renewed and hopeful openness to what is not yet. In other words, the Trinity occurs to Christian faith as grounding, structuring and fulfilling the way of self-transcendence.

1. The Therapeutic Significance of Trinitarian Faith

First of all, trinitarian faith functions as a redemptive critique of religious ideology and its related pathology. What such a pathology is, has, of course, been powerfully analyzed in the Freudian tradition of psychotherapy. To state it with utmost brevity, religion is the ultimate refuge of the immature,—those who refuse the painful growth to adult freedom, who seek to escape its sufferings and demands, by hiding in an infantile psyche which displaces human responsibility onto an all-indulgent, all-powerful divine 'Father'.[1] How does trinitarian faith counter such neurotic religious propensities to promote an authentically Christian creativity? How does it structure a passage from infantile illusion to genuine self-appropriation? How does it challenge self-absorption with the summons to self-transcendence? Or, in more specifically religious terms, how does one's faith in the Trinity function as exorcism of the familiar demons of religious imagination?

In this brief note, we will try to indicate how the symbols of Father, Son, and Spirit function in human affectivity. For such powerful images can inspire or block psychological development. In accord with previous remarks, we will suggest that if these three symbols are allowed to function in their proper interplay, they will keep our affects or development open and healthy. God, apprehended as Father, Son, and Spirit, keeps occurring as a radical challenge to the infantile self-projection, so prone to narcissism and self-protective strategies of denial and escape. If mere religious fantasy takes over with the result that any one of these three key symbols is wrenched from its trinitarian interplay in the social life of the church, problems will result. With the mutilation of religious imagination, psychic affectivity is stunted.

The most critical symbol is that of God as "Father". The "father image" requires a close evaluation in its affective function.[2] The risks are obvious, and the great 'masters of suspicion' have pointed them out: Is it merely a fixation of psychic development at a primitive stage, merely a projection of an unhealthy infantilism protecting the believer from the pain of development and the responsibilities of freedom, as Feuerbach and Freud have claimed? Or is it a social manipulation of reality apt to secure one's acceptance of, or resignation to, an unjust economic structuring of society as Marx has asserted? If it functioned in either or both of these ways, the image of God the Father would hardly be guiding psychic development into the genuine self-transcendence of faith and service.

The questions are sharp, but they are healthy: when I confess God as Father, am I indulging in an elaborate projection? For is not this

---

[1]In this section I am greatly influenced by the brilliant little book, Christian Duquoc, *Dieu différent. Essai sur la symbolique trinitaire* (Paris: Editions du Cerf, 1977).

[2]Duquoc, *op. cit.*, pgs. 99-105.

image of the all-wise, all-powerful, all-loving paternal being nothing but an instinctive compensation for the pain and dread of being human? Religious pathology has its own odd creativity in fabricating fantasy at the expense of reality. God, uncritically confessed as 'Father', can say more about our unacknowledged infantile need with its fear of relating to the world of others in an objective universe of reality.

Contrasted to this kind of psychic fixation, is the true but painful development of personhood. Human growth has to respect a certain dramatic structure. To emerge as an autonomous individual capable of some form of self-giving, the ego has to suffer. The traumas of development, separation, and adaptation are experienced as a kind of death. For instance, the child has to emerge from the womb of symbiotic dependence on the mother. It has to enter, through all the subtle negotiations of the Oedipus complex, the world of the father, where objectivity, individual existence and responsibility begin to be felt. Such a bloody entry makes the developing individual ready for the real but conflict-ridden world of brothers and sisters and all the demands of social relationships.

In this drama of development, the "father image" does of course have a positive function: it minimizes the pain involved in emerging as an autonomous human being. The seemingly all-wise, all-competent, accepting and demanding 'other' legitimates the development of individual autonomy in a threatening world of many others. Yet, at some stage the child has to renounce the father-image. Development leads to an encounter with the real and disconcertingly limited father. This in turn leads to a more conditioned dependence, just as it implies the acceptance of limitations in the father and oneself.

Trouble results when this development does not occur. The real father is still apprehended in terms of "father image"; and there begins the elementary neuroses associated with self-acceptance, the fear of the other, dread of the world, intolerance of the new, and horror at the evidence of mortality.

How can one's religious confession of God as "Father" not further compound the problems of development connected with the image of the 'father'? Does it merely evidence the triumph of neurotic projection, with religion appearing as the ultimate pathology, as the infantile psyche perversely fabricates an enduring "father image" in the domain of untouchable transcendence? After all, the image of a divine Father is far more subtle and powerful: the psyche effects a displacement of its security out of the real world, where ordinary human fathers are finally revealed as limited human beings, into an unchallengeable religious realm.

The risk seems so great that silence on the subject of "God the Father" might appear as a step in the right direction. But a moment's thought will suggest that silence cannot be the answer. Human development is still going on; and the "father-image" still powerfully structures the dynamics of human growth. To ignore the issue would only mean to increase the range of possible pathology. It is at this point that we can raise the matter of the trinitarian significance of God the Father.

The important point to notice is that God is invoked as "Father" in Christian faith in the context of an other-directed social way of life. It is never the fabrication of private fantasy, a private psychomythology. Rather, it is a social, publicly-recognized symbol directing our relationships to others, and calling forth a life of self-sacrificing love.[3] As a socially-celebrated symbol, such a God is not 'my God' but 'our Father'. He is the Father of Jesus, the adult Son, not the 'Infant Jesus'!. This Father does not spare this Son suffering and death. The unique and exclusive relationship of Jesus to the God he invoked as 'Father' is not an escape from 'the harsh and dreadful' demands of love. In no sense does such a social symbol evidence a manipulation of reality to serve one's archaic fears or infantile projections: the "Our Father" is invoked as one who is hallowed in the works of the kingdom: there is indeed surrender to love and mercy, but the existential condition of this is collaboration with the divine Love, being as merciful as our Father in heaven is merciful (Lk 6:36): "Forgive us our sins as we forgive those who sin against us." (Lk 11:4) The Father is invoked as drawing us into a new realm of self-giving Love, not as a fantasy legitimating a flight from reality.

This Father is portrayed in the Gospels as the One whom Jesus invokes in the context of his solidarity with the powerless and the oppressed. In the name of this Father, he involves himself with the socially unacceptable: such praxis contests the false gods of ordered

---

[3]Duquoc, *op. cit.*, pgs. 95ff. This author employs the useful distinction between 'l'imaginaire' (an individual psychomythology) and 'la symbolique' (a publicly accessible and socially responsible image).

religious security and the oppression it sanctions. Far from being a manipulation of reality, Jesus' devotion to the Kingdom of the Father leads to the cross with all its sense of abandonment and defeat. The "beloved Son" enjoys no privileged position in the face of suffering and vulnerability to evil (Hb 5:7ff). The Father does not send the "twelve legions of angels", nor does Jesus ask for them!(Mt 26:53). The event of the cross purifies the notion of God from any association with a 'father image'. It lets God appear in the originality of self-giving Love, giving what is most intimately 'his own' into the drama of the world; God keeps on being Love in and through such involvement in the mystery of the resurrection. There is no denying the complexity of the 'father image': an uncritical use of the Gospels can reduce the Father to 'the good daddy' who spares his children pain, and keeps Jesus always in the state of being 'the infant Jesus'; on the other hand, it can turn God into the 'wicked father' capriciously demanding the death of the Son, well-pleased in blood sacrifice. The only way out of these monstrous images is a continued critical sense of the social impact of the symbols that the Gospel employs.

Crucial to this social interplay of symbols of Father and Son in interpreting divine mystery is the symbol of the Spirit. The Spirit is sent by the Father in the name of the Son, to indwell human consciousness as a witness to the truth, as enabling a new range of relationships, as transforming human freedom. As a symbol, the Spirit breaks the symmetry of any image depicting the reality of God as an enclosed, self-absorbed relatedness purely in terms of Father and Son. In contrast to this, the Spirit-symbol evokes a kind of space within the Godhead, a dimension of divine freedom whereby the Father and Son are united in self-surrender rather than in an undifferentiated, quasi-symbiotic manner. As the inspirer of such a unity-in-difference, the Spirit is given as the liberation and transformation of human liberty. Again, it is worth noting that the Spirit is not a more or less demonic manifestation of self-indulging fantasy. It is no pathological construct enclosing the psyche in the delusion of infantile omnipotence but a divine energy opening the believer to the kind of Love existing between the Father and the Son.

This can be further elaborated. There are at least four ways in which the symbol of the Spirit functions in Christian experience.[4]

---

[4] *op. cit.*, pgs. 105-111.

First, and most obviously, the Spirit functions as overcoming the inertia of the past, or better, the inertia of a present trying to establish its security by privileging the past as the paradigmatic golden age. It works against a version of ultimate reality in terms of repetition of what has been. As breaking the binding power of the past, the Spirit impels the believer into the possibilities of the future. It does not permit any return to an untroubled existence. It guides Peter to the house of the pagan Cornelius (Ac 10); it surprises the early community with the unsettling gift of the former persecutor, Paul (Ac 9:13ff). It is the advantage that comes upon the departure of the earthly Jesus (Jn 16:7). It leads to a knowledge of things that could not be borne before (Jn 16:12f). The symbol of the Spirit functions in opening the religious imagination to the radically, the imaginably, new.

Secondly, the symbol of the Spirit counters both the pathologies of legalism and irresponsibility. The Spirit inspires genuine liberty (2 Cor 3:17). Whilst it gives a joyous expansion of the human spirit, this is far from licentious self-indulgence. Genuine liberty is marked by the exigence of self-giving and self-sacrifice (Gal 5:16-25). It leads to a liberty which both breaks the perverse security of legalism and accepts the social necessity of law and structure for a responsible social existence (I Cor 8:8ff; 10:23ff;14:26-33). It lets God be God, beyond the idolatry of legalism or the demonic excesses of licentiousness. Once more the symbol of the Spirit creates a space for Christian liberty between the alternatives of idolization of law and the demonization of liberty.

Thirdly, whilst the Spirit is associated with unity, it is not the unity of some form of undifferentiated infantile symbiosis. In the same vein, the "unity of the Holy Spirit" is not uniformity. The Spirit stands for an inspired unity-in-difference, a community of distinct persons (I Cor 12:12-30). He allows communication in the different languages of Pentecost (Ac 2:5-12). He inspires a unity which both manifests and depends on a variety of gifts for the achievement of the common good (I Cor 12:7). The Spirit forms the Body of Christ with its different members. He abolishes differences in race, religion, social status and sex insofar as such differences may cause unredeemed isolation and aggression, not insofar as they may be gifts in the one body of believers. In short, the Spirit is the symbol of gift, of the gift to be found in the genuinely other. As such it is far from being an oppressive uniformity. Here the Spirit-symbol stands for the space in which true unity-in-difference can be achieved.

Fourthly, the symbol of the Spirit counters the pathology of a false transcendence. To a disincarnate spiritual realm of religious individualism it opposes the reality of history and its challenging tradition. Above all, it links genuine faith to the "dangerous memory" of the crucified Jesus: genuine spirituality is not a socially irresponsible religiosity, but a matter of being conformed to the self-sacrificing love of Christ Jesus. It demands a solidarity with Christ and his members: without a discerning responsibility to the Christian tradition of meaning and to the word and example of Jesus it transmits, the symbol of the Spirit is vitiated (Rom 8:11; Jn 14:26; I Jn 2:22-25). Here the Spirit-symbol stands for the space in which history can occur with its fidelity to the past and openness to the future.

The interplay of these symbols Father, Son, and Spirit occurs in a social context. As such it is designed to produce a way of being and acting in the human community. Far from legitimating an infantile or alienated religious fantasy life in which God is the all-indulgent supreme 'father', where Christ is ever the 'sweet infant Jesus', where the Holy Spirit is at best an affective afterglow or the rationalization of irresponsible enthusiasm, the dynamics of trinitarian symbolism arise out of and lead into the praxis of self-sacrificing liberating love. The symbol of the Father is correlated to the liberating activity of Jesus, as is the gift of the Spirit.

In other words, the essential trinitarian symbolism of Christian faith functions as inspiring and supporting a more authentic conversion. It does not legitimate infantile self-absorption. It is entirely directed to self-transcendence.

By introducing this kind of psychological reflection into trinitarian theology, I hoped to indicate how the intellectual conversion of theology must subsume the requisite psychic dimension of conversion if it is to affirm the reality of the revealed God in the most effective terms. Such an approach, largely dependent on the Freudian tradition of psychotherapy, can be further complemented by a more Jungian type of reflection.

2. The Trinity and Psychological Development

In the writings of Carl Jung, the doctrine of the Trinity is accorded considerable importance. The great Swiss psychologist evaluates this

Christian doctrine in its capacity to guide and structure the development of the psyche into a fuller realization of the collective self. Jung both presents and criticizes the Trinity in this light.[5] Indeed, the meaning of this central Christian article of faith seems to have intrigued this great analyst from his earliest years.

The general context of Jung's presentation of the Trinity is his sense of the degree in which Western culture has become alienated from the great archetypal images which guide and inspire our collective psychic development.[6] His overall concern is with modern man's spiritual bankruptcy. Indeed, in his aim to provide a therapy of culture, he is not addressing religious believers, let alone trying to reduce their faith to a purely psychological meaning.[7] It is true that he does examine the Trinity in its relationship to a kind of trinitarian structure of the psychic process. But there is nothing to stop this from being understood as penetrating to the very ground of the universe.[8] Still, his aim is to revitalize our appreciation of the fundamental symbols guiding humankind's collective development. If they are to be gainfully appropriated, they must be criticized, and in some sense reconstructed. For that reason, any reflective Christian believer concerned to communicate with the emerging culture has much to learn from his analysis.

Within this larger concern for cultural development, Jung treats a number of classic Christian doctrines. Here he finds fixed, clear and formalized articulations of faith. They have achieved such a sturdy form because they bring to expression mysterious, irreversible developments in the human psyche. As such, they nurture and protect what has been achieved. Such doctrines are the "repository of the secrets of the soul"[9]

In his specific reflection on the Trinity, Jung indicates a general

---

[5]Jung treats of the Trinity especially in *Psychology and Religion: East and West* (New York: Pantheon Books, 1958). For a concise and illuminating treatment of these and related issues, see Clifford A. Brown, *Jung's Hermeneutic of Doctrine,* AAR Dissertation Series 32 (Ann Arbor: The Scholars Press, 1981). Here I am especially indebted to this work. For the general background in mythology and history see, Erich Neumann, *The Origins and History of Consciousness* (Bollingen Series XLII: Princeton University Press, 1973).

[6]Brown, *op. cit.,* pg. 101.

[7]*Op. cit.,* pgs. 119; 192 n.16.

[8]*Op. cit.,* pg. 194 n.58.

[9]Quoted in Brown, *op. cit.,* pg. 103.

historical context in which trinitarian symbolism can be placed. He is not saying that these antecedent patterns somehow caused the Christian doctrine of the Trinity. Rather both the historical antecedents and the trinitarian doctrine emerge out of an archetypal pattern. This is a universal symbolic structure preforming the psyche to develop in the direction of true selfhood.

Typical of these historical antecedents of the Trinity are, for example, the Egyptian and Babylonian triadic deities, the Pythagorean theory of numbers, and certain positions of Plato, especially as we find these latter in the *Timaeus*. In this material, Jung is mainly concerned with the inter-relationship of the three divine figures. He takes note of the monotheistic direction of such symbolism. For there is an essential correlation of the numinous 'father' and 'son' figures, with the third being a relational force binding them more intensely together. In Pythagorean speculation on the significance of numbers we find the question explored: how can there be unity in diversity? The tension between the first and the second is resolved in the third. In this way the lost unity is restored. Reality is recognized in this 'coincidence of opposites', at least in a provisional manner. Nonetheless, Jung seems to have been intrigued by the incompleteness of this symbolic solution. With Plato in the *Timaeus* he asks, 'One, two, three ... but where, my dear Timaeus, is the missing fourth?' It is in his effort to answer this question that Jung's trinitarian reflections become somewhat disconcerting for classical Christian theology. In his judgment, the "missing fourth" in abstract, ideal, airy Platonic philosophy is the concrete element of experience, with all its conflict, darkness, actuality. He sees this concrete element also missing in the trinitarian symbol. How does Jung explain this?

He certainly understands Father, Son, and Spirit as representing each a stage of development in humanity's collective psyche. The figure of the Father is expressive of an undifferentiated child-like consciousness in which the psyche enjoyed a kind of original oneness with nature. The figure of the Son stands for a development in consciousness in which the tensions of otherness, doubt, isolation, conflict begin to occur. This is the moment when the problem of suffering and evil begins to raise questions about existence. The Spirit represents a more integrated consciousness: as a symbol it stands for an overcoming of this existential distance and tension. "Common to the Father and the Son, he puts an end to the duality, to the 'doubt' in the Son..."¹⁰ The third figure is the healing, reconciling force. Through the Spirit, the lost unity is restored.

It is not Jung's intention, as we have said, to reduce the truth of Christian faith to its archetypal significance as though the three divine persons were merely personifications of psychic structures. Nevertheless he is certainly transposing Christian doctrine into a realm of psychic interiority. This unfamiliar displacement of doctrinal meaning is, naturally, not without ambiguity. On the one hand, the doctrine of the Trinity is understood as articulating the 'life-process' of the deity; on the other the significance of this is extended into the human psyche. Admittedly, this is not an unfamiliar thought in Christian theology: for "man is made in the image of God". Nonetheless, Jung is certainly emphasizing the psychic significance, without going so far as to say that God is made in the image of man. Though only an expert analysis of his writings can clarify his precise intentions at every point, it does seem clear that, for him, the doctrine of the Trinity is the revelation of both the divine and human essence. In this way, the Trinitarian doctrine articulates the development of the human self.¹¹

In this sense, the Trinity has functioned as a symbol guiding human development. Its value lies in compactly articulating a third stage in the evolution of human consciousness. It expresses a unified and differentiated self-consciousness, along with a sense of the transcendent realm of the good. Evil is definitively excluded from ultimate reality. The three divine persons in the completeness of their reality shut out, as it were, all darkness, evil, tension, and incompleteness.

In an effort to attune such a doctrine to the demands of ongoing psychic development, Jung's position is that the very success of trinitarian doctrine is now its limitation. It must now be extended to allow for a fuller integration of human experience into the development of the collective self. For instance, he notes the exclusion of the feminine and of the darker, demonic side of experience, "the dark side of God".¹² To assure the continuing psychic creativity of this

---

¹⁰*Op. cit.*, pg. 118.
¹¹*Op. cit.*, pg. 121.
¹²*Op. cit.*, pgs. 126f.

doctrine in human development, we need now to introduce "the fourth" for the sake of a more complete integration of experience. Quaternity is the necessary symbol of holistic development: in this regard, the traditional Trinity is too abstract and immaterial.

This fourth element is worldly materiality and concreteness. It represents the maternal, the feminine, and even the demonic: "The dark weight of the earth must enter into the picture of the whole"[13].

The fourth element is introduced, not so much as an addition, but as a split occurring within the representation of the second person, the Son. This representative space must now include the warring opposites, Son and the Devil. The divine quaternity is thus: Father, Son-Devil, and Spirit: the archetypal three must function within the context of a more fundamental four.

To say the least, such a reconstruction certainly seems rather startling to Christian tradition. On the other hand, I think most Christians might begin to suspect what Jung is getting at when they examine their own sense of the utter abstractness of trinitarian faith and its irrelevance to human life. Today, the emergence of a critical feminist consciousness has produced an immense literature lamenting the one-sidedly masculine manner of imaging God in a patriarchal culture. And even more urgently, along with one's experience of oppressive patriarchy or other forms of sexual ideology, the pain and suffering of the peoples of the earth under all the weight of poverty, starvation, racial, political and economic violence have raised the question of how God is involved with suffering humanity, and what place such suffering has in the heart of God.

Needless to say, I would hope that the leading themes of this book, God as self-involving Love, inviting and inspiring our collaboration in the transformation of the world, would not be irrelevant in overcoming the stultifying abstractness of so much trinitarian thought. This present effort, and most illuminating modern works on this theme, do in fact envisage a 'fourth' in the Trinity: God is known and experienced in his self-involvement with the suffering world. Concretely, it is within our experience of this 'fourth' that God is known, it is in our experience of the dark side of existence, in our interpersonal and sexual relationships that God is revealed as

---

[13] *Op. cit.*, pg. 195 n.83.

Love. Whether one wants to say this in terms of the identity of the immanent and economic Trinity, or in a deeper reflection of how God suffers our struggle for existence and fulfillment does not much matter. The point is that implicitly we have taken Jung's point. The question for Jung would have been: Has he realized the experiential locus of our affirmation of the Trinity, above all in the incarnation, passion, death and resurrection of the Son? The Son is revealed precisely in his conflict with the demonic, as he confronts the human problem of evil.

Looking at the problematic that Jung has so dramatically expressed, one acute philosopher has noted,

> So far as the Christian symbol of the Trinity is concerned, it does in fact seem to invite a fourth member. Christian tradition holds out the missing place to be filled by each one who is adopted into sonship. Jung appreciates the symbol of the Assumption of Mary in precisely these terms.... And since Mary is the exemplar of all who respond to revelation, the Assumption announces that each believer forms a quaternity with God[14]

There is no need to deny that quaternity, as a symbol of psychic development, is superior to trinity. There is no need to be involved in some naive, psychological "numbers game" at this point. Indeed, the psychological deficiency of trinitarian symbolism is precisely a way of indicating why the Trinity of Christian revelation is not a mere doctrinal statement, but the profound structure of the rhetoric of Love: it is Love speaking its Word and communicating its Spirit to invite the other to respond and to surrender. God is openness to the other, to the community of others. Trinitarian Love looks to "the fullness of him who fills the whole creation" (Eph 1:23).[15] Trinitarian language is the language of Love: it is divine self-giving into the depths of our human struggle for self-realization, "unto death, even death upon a cross" (Phil 2:8). Far from shutting out in its completeness the dark drama of human existence, the revealed Trinity is

---

[14]David Burrell, *Exercises in Religious Understanding* (University of Notre Dame Press: 1974), pgs. 229ff.

[15]Cf. Burrell, *op. cit.*, pg. 230.

continually engaging and including "the fourth": it is communicated to our human selves with our demonic propensities and idolatrous projections. God's Love works that we might be truly "trinified" in openness to the ultimate mystery of belonging in "our Father", in union with the Son, crucified and risen, as the expression of our ultimate humanity; as transformed by the Good Spirit, the power of Loving that alone can exorcise the demonic self-destructiveness with which the contemporary world is horrifyingly familiar.

Jung's concern was to re-immerse the classic trinitarian doctrine of Christian faith in the "warm red blood of experience pulsating through it"[16]. I believe that developments in trinitarian theology have in large measure done this. One must of course wonder whether equating the feminine with the diabolical is apt to communicate anything positive in the present context. Whilst Jung's remarks on the Assumption of Mary are intriguing, I think we have to look at the large question of the "femininity of God" more comprehensively. I will reserve my own remarks on this basic issue to later.

3. The Political Meaning of the Trinity

We now come to ask, what is the political meaning of the Trinity? The previous section looked more to the journey inward with its concern for a more integrated interiority. The political meaning looks to the journey outward, toward a more responsible co-humanity. This is not to imply that there is some kind of antithesis between the two: in both the psychological applications we indicated, the Trinity functioned as a self-appropriation for the journey outward—in the one case in the direction of a more adult freedom released from a repressive religiosity (Freud), in the other, toward a more integrated cultural development, more inclusively related to the dramatic concrete character of our historical development (Jung). In short, the journey inward has social consequences. In a related manner, the journey outward demands profound psychological transformations. So far we have examined trinitarian symbolism as the form of grace-inspiring development from the inside-out, we now

---

[16]Quoted in Brown, *op. cit.*, pg. 197 n.2.

turn to reflection on the political meaning of the Trinity as affecting us from the outside-in.

At every stage of this exposition of the meaning of the Trinity, we have implied that this mystery, so central and fundamental to Christian existence, necessarily affected the way we, as Christians, should act, think, and feel in the political context of human co-existence. It is not a-political to proclaim the Kingdom of God the Father as a realm of ultimate justice and love. Nor is our understanding of the Word Incarnate as crucified in his solidarity with the poor a politically disinterested point of view. Nor, finally, is the gift of the Spirit of the Father and the Son, pervading all creation and forming the eschatological Body of Christ out of all peoples and races and nations, a politically neutral force. The God of self-giving Love is healing and transforming grace for the whole of our relational existence. The traces of the Trinity (*vestigia trinitatis*) are eminently detected in communities of loving concern and involvement: for there the Spirit of God is breathed, the meaning of God as Love is understood, and the mystery of that Love is adored. Such communities, whatever the political situation of the society, make a difference.

They make a difference because one's conception of God makes a difference. If the paradigm of the ultimately and radically real is self-giving Love, if the ultimate form of life is that of Being-in-Love in a communion of self-giving persons, if personhood is understood as loving relationality, what does such a vision do to other versions of "the real"?[17] The individualism that has reigned in psychology, the narcissism that is lamented in modern culture, the capitalism that has ruthlessly dominated the economy, the autocracy manifested in governments, owe little to the trinitarian confession of God. If there is any religious legitimation for such inhumanities, it is to be found in a kind of deism which intellectually allows for a remote self-sufficient deity unconcerned in human affairs. Such a projection thrives since it makes no difference to established self-serving economic, political, social and cultural arrangements. If, however, the real God is the inspiration and fulfillment of other-directed love, widespread political consequences must follow.

---

[17]For an excellent, succinct little essay, see Michael J. Himes and Kenneth R. Himes, "Rights, Economics and the Trinity", *Commonweal* (March 1986), pgs. 137-141.

By making such remarks, I am not imagining, of course, that the Trinity is merely a new insight in the history of ideas, as though we have, in such a doctrine, just a nice construction put on reality, hence with some cultural consequences. Christian faith bases its conviction on the fact that the trinitarian God is first of all an event in human history: the Father sends the Son and the Spirit into human history. God's self-involvement is an historic turning point in the formation of our co-humanity. The divine intention is "to make a difference".

At the present axial stage of world-history, in which all the separate histories of the earth's different peoples are being brought together into a global development or destruction, the doctrine of the Trinity comes into its own. The world-stage is, as it were, big enough to allow the political meaning that has too often been dormant in Christian faith to awaken to new and certainly challenging proportions.

As significant studies have shown,[18] it is not as though the early church was unaware of the political consequences of its trinitarian faith. It confessed this faith in the face of a widespread philosophical and political presupposition that the ideal of unity was achieved through one principle, namely, "a plurality of leaders is not a good thing. Let there be one."[19] Monotheism and monarchy were often tied together by the early Christian apologists and theologians (especially Eusebius), concerned as they were to overcome polytheism and to gain political acceptance.[20] The unity of Trinity, as the ultimate expression of love and community, was implicitly subversive of the monarchian or imperial ideal of One God, one Logos, one Emperor, one world-order, one faith, one church. The Trinity continued to be the paradigm reality for the unity of the churches in a *communio* of unity-in-difference—even though, with the dogmatic exigence of defining such a faith against error, the expression of faith came to be increasingly abstract, and finally abstruse. The growing centralism in the church, and insistent imperialism in politics militated against a full expansion of trinitarian meaning in an ecclesi-

---

[18]Cf. the seminal work of Erick Peterson, e.g., "Der Monotheismus als politisches Problem", *Theologische Traktate* (Muenchen:Koesel-Verlag, 1951), pgs. 49-147.

[19]The closing lines of Aristotle's *Metaphysics XI*. The philosopher is quoting the *Iliad*.

[20]Thomas D. Parker, "The Political Meaning of the Doctrine of the Trinity", *Journal of Religion* 60(1980), pgs. 169f.

astical and political form. Monarchy in church and state came to be the prevalent style, extending itself in a hierarchical unfolding into the whole.

How far the ecumenism of today will see the model of authentic trinitarian *communio* re-emerge, with a consequent transformation of the structure and style of authority, remains to be seen. Similarly, the degree in which Christian faith and hope, living from its trinitarian foundation, will contribute to a new discourse on global politics, to replace the mutually antagonistic philosophies of the superpowers is also an urgent concern.

While it is of greatest importance to commend the Trinity as the paradigm for Christian political imagination, it is even more important to locate it in the foundations of a globally concerned social theory. Here we will try to sketch how a trinitarian faith underpins and expands such thinking, even as it contributes the dynamic of eschatological hope. The critical social theory we refer to [21], radically contests the totalitarian content and style of political ideology. Basically, these writings, despite their different emphases, try to make room for the truly human agenda of political history. Such agenda are understood as the emancipated reality that has to be implemented through the potential collaboration of all human beings as irreplaceable subjects in the one human history. The emphasis is on a radically different perception of human reality. Here we are dealing neither with a notion of 'human nature' applicable to all, nor with the production of 'the common good' in merely technical terms. It is the good that is the outcome of a shared conduct of ideally all human agents. To that degree it is not a matter of technical expertise instrumentally dominating the human world, nor of a totalitarian ideology, but the genuine human truth which, in biblical terms, can be spoken only in love (Eph 4:15), or at least in the open conversation of a human history. Here the subjects of history are not sold out to technical expertise as instruments, or as disposable material significant only as contributing to an ideological utopia. It is a matter of

---

[21] Here I have in mind the writings of J. Habermas, M. Horkheimer, W. Benjamin, and the theologians who have appropriated them, such as J.B. Metz, E. Schillebeeckx, H. Peukert, M. Lamb, D. Lane, to name but a few. For a transcultural critical application of Social Theory, see Dennis P. McCann and Charles R. Strain, *Polity and Praxis. A Program for American Practical Theology* (Chicago: Winston Press, 1985).

mutually enabled and shared self-determination. For the aim is not control but consensus. Potentially, all human beings must be accepted as agents of a co-humanity, if we are to resist oppression, and not rest content with anything less than the fulness of life for all.

It seems to me that there are two basic analogies for understanding how this new notion of 'human truth' is discovered in its socially transforming effects. Each of them opens up dimensions of trinitarian reflection.

The first, perhaps surprisingly, is the praxis of the psychotherapist.[22] The therapist is certainly intent on elucidating the genesis of the modes of behaviour that oppress the patient. The concern of therapy is to provide a context in which insight into crippling patterns of behaviour can emerge in ways leading to the possibilities of a fresh self-determining freedom. The experience of suffering intimates, in a negative manner, what might be hoped for. By entering painfully into such therapy, suffering is already being productive of a new freedom. The sufferer is hoping for change. He freely enters into the risk of a conversation about what might be. The therapist as partner in this conversation enables the truth of the patient's past to be discovered and, eventually, named. In such naming the problem is clarified and begins to become manageable. The possibility of real choices emerges along with new capacities for a free and freeing self-determination.

In the therapeutical context, the skill and scientific training of the therapist does not put him or her in possession of the truth about the sufferer: that can only emerge in the praxis of conversation concerned for the freedom of this other. The truth begins to be spoken, begins even to be lived, when the patient is accepted and respected as a free subject, and when he is met in empathetic imagination. Such empathy implies that the therapist himself is not appearing as the absolute master of his own existence, invulnerable to the suffering the patient is bearing. To repress his own history of suffering would be to remain aloof in a spurious transcendence above the human condition and outside of any genuine communication with the patient. At best, the sufferer would be regarded as an object of therapeutical concern.

---

[22]Helmut Peukert, *Science, Action and Fundamental Theology. Toward a Theology of Communicative Action,* trans. J. Bohman (Cambridge, Mass: MIT Press, 1984), pg. 13f.

On the other hand, to the degree the therapist appropriates his own suffering existence, he has the resource to be bound to this patient in a disciplined compassion: out of this authentic human relationship, life-transforming truth can emerge. In this dialogical relationship, the patient can reappropriate his history, no longer locked into the repressive fixation of fear and failure, no longer displaced into a threatening future. The whole truth of the patient's history is thus 're-membered'. The whole truth is the healing truth. It lives with creative possibilities. The thrust to self-transcendence is once more released. The truth is recognized by its power to transform. Though the affirming presence of the therapist is part of the patient's celebration of his rejoining the human race, his re-entry into hopeful human history, it would all end in failure if the result were either a new form of dependence or a mere adjustment to an uncriticized social milieu. The aim of therapy is release from the relationship of dependency into open, hence healthy, social interaction. In turn, this means release for a creative criticism of the (at least, partially) diseased, oppressive social milieu of family, school, culture, etc. which adversely affected the patient in the past, and still affects others. Thus, facing the past means a more self-determined approach to the future. Full recovery is conditioned by what the sufferer is freed for: self-giving creativity as parent, spouse, or child, as teacher, artist, worker or mystic....

Thus, the truth discovered in therapy is a truth discovered in a deep kind of conversation. It is revealed as truth in its transforming power: to give freedom where before crippling anxiety was the prevailing condition. I might mention in passing, without pushing the point too far, that the therapeutical context has a trinitarian form—a point hardly irrelevant to Christian therapists and those engaged in the deeper healing of the human spirit. It would seem that the field of communication in which sufferer and therapist converse presupposes a shared beholdedness to a gracious Mystery of the Future, the unspeakable Silence in which we relate. The words and gestures of hope live within such an horizon. It ensures that human conversation is never finished, and that none of us, alone or together, can remain barricaded against the possibilities of further development. The self-transcendence at stake can be truly affirmed only if human existence is accepted as transcendence into an ineffable, welcoming Other, attracting us to itself—the Father, "God whom no one has ever seen". Further, the therapeutic dialogue is not dealing in terms of sheer otherworldly transcendence beyond death: its concern is this present in human history where sense has to be made out of human suffering. Meaning cannot be found outside the realm of human meaning; human existence must be valued in itself. The incarnate Logos, crucified and risen, is God's "affirmative action" on behalf of human sufferers. Through Christ, "God with us", the way of the cross and resurrection are the liberating structure of human existence now, in the present. The patient is not being defined as one who is imprisoned in pain and guilt, but as one who is being offered a transformed humanity: the Word of self-giving Love has entered the human conversation. Owning the suffering reality of oneself in the light of such a Word (explicitly or implicitly heard) releases the Spirit of self-transcendence, in the recovery of a hopeful and loving self. The Spirit that comes to such sufferers out of the Silence drawing them into conversation, is now given in what is commonly experienced as 'beyond measure' after the hearing of the redemptive Word.

Admittedly, such passing remarks indicate the direction of a more ambitious theology of psychotherapy, and that is beyond our present scope. Still, it is worth making the connection.

The second analogy for understanding the human truth sought in global social praxis is that of friendship.[23] The communication of friendship is not that of an interview or a case study. It is ruined by a prior controlling theory of the other. Rather, friendship also occurs in the interplay of a conversation which is in principle not confined to any subject, nor limited to any particular purpose: it deals with The Whole Thing, "what it's all about". Fundamentally, friendship is an experiment in freedom, an experience of reaching beyond and even refusing the roles, masks, controls, laws, scripts, pragmatic concerns of every day life. As such, it is a release into a radical order of co-existence, shared humanity, convivially celebrated as a gift, as asserting its right to be present in any future that might happen. It discloses the human truth that can only be discovered by participation. It can neither be planned nor be complete. Its human worth

---

[23] See Fred R. Dallmayr, *Polis and Praxis, Exercises in Contemporary Political Theory* (Cambridge, Mass: The MIT Press, 1984), pgs 217-221.

is not primarily that of a theory, nor information, nor skill. For truth appears in friendship at the mysterious point of breakthrough, or of continuously 'getting through' to the human reality of the other: beyond the structures and even barriers of society and culture, even beyond age and sex, it keeps on occurring as another version of the humanity we live. One denies or refuses it at the peril of losing what is best in oneself and others, and of renouncing the promise of a more human world.

Friendship nourishes and, perhaps, most realizes elementary human justice. The uniqueness of the other, with the gifts and limitations entailed, is affirmed, appreciated, accepted in what approximates to an unconditional degree. It creates the space where the great human hopes and sufferings can be expressed. It enables the self to be spoken, to be heard, to be enjoyed. The kind of transforming truth friendship enables is not marked with the abstract completeness of a theory, the impersonal effectiveness of a technique, the distanced style of research, the professional disciplines of therapy, the pragmatic disinterestedness of an exchange of information, nor even, for that matter, the passionate exclusiveness of lovers. Yet it does have its own unconditional acceptance of the other. This enables communication and the human truth to appear. The interpersonal solidarity that marks friendship is the space where the deepest human truth is, as it were, 'conducted' as an ongoing interaction. This unity-in-difference is, in a sense, the event of conversation: it lets life be an unfinished mystery where no one of the friends possesses the answer: the other is not a unit to be administered nor a commodity to be exploited nor a case to be studied. Whatever its limitations in the larger world of experience and responsibility, friendship is a striking paradigm of the praxis of the human. Its horizon lives from the gift of an often surprising further, hopeful version of human existence. Its conversation expresses a liberating Word of the meaning and worth of the individual persons. It lives in the 'friendly Spirit' of something experienced as an impulse to a fuller, freer, richer humanity. However implicitly and obscurely, it manifests a trinitarian dimension.

In both these cases, the context of therapy and the relationship of friendship, the profound human truth occurs as a 'conduct'; and the conduct is in the communication. These two instances of the meaning of praxis are paradigmatic for the emerging political meaning of praxis: the political truth is in the transformation that occurs in the moment of liberation. It is understood in its power to enable suffering humanity to come to a new liberative moment of self-determination. It occurs as a revelation when, through unrepressed communication, human beings find themselves united in the solidarity of a common destiny.

Despite the intrinsically limited interpersonal context in which they usually occur, these two instances of transformative truth are very suggestive for any appreciation of the wider concerns and sophisticated analyses of Social Theory, emerging as it has in the wake of Marxist revolutionary praxis, and in the context of a generally more pragmatic turn in philosophy.[24]

To avoid being one more ideology of power, one more way of ignoring the human, any critical social theory must presuppose a universal solidarity: such unconditional, open solidarity is the condition of genuinely human history. Just as no one, no group can be sacrificed to the interests of the other, none can be, in principle, excluded from the human conversation: the witness and worth of everyone must potentially, at least, fall within the concern of all, unless liberating praxis is going to be oppressive from the start. All must be accepted into the unfolding of the one human history. Each one has a right to be part of the conversation: hence, a disciplined, open-minded, concerned interest in human liberation means a solidarity with all.

This contrasts with a purely instrumental knowledge which gives the expert the right to solve our problems, and to distract us from those which have no human solution. The aim of critical social philosophy is not technical domination but to build consensus. This is an informed 'conspiracy' to subvert what is unjust and oppressive. Its only foundation must be seemingly defenseless exchanges of rational and concerned conversation. It looks not to an exercise of power but to a shared spirit of self-determination. As such, it relativizes technological control just as it contests any totalitarian 'solution'. For that purpose, political philosophy goes back to more traditional meanings of reason as *Logos*[25]. It is open to the whole

---

[24]See Peukert, *op. cit.*, pgs. 128-210.
[25]Cf. Dallmayr, *Polis and Praxis...*, pgs. 225f.

communicative potential of human speech, for it has no intention of being limited either to purely technical discourse—for that would ignore true communication—or restrict it to purely subjective discourse unable to articulate its vision of reality in a shareable way.

Typically, too, those who are most voiceless, most silent in determining the meaning of human development are given the hermeneutically privileged place. For these are the least affected by the blandishments of the reigning ideology, least bolstered by the establishment justifying a privileged position, most nakedly exposed to the essence of our humanity, most open to a hope for a better human history.[26]

What is the significance of this sense of solidarity, this space of communication open to everyone, and privileging the witness of those most inarticulate and oppressed? The intention to communicate and belong in these proportions, in some implicit way, anticipates an ultimate stage of human belonging. To aim at such a consensus anticipates the hope of a shared fullness of life. So, it seems to me, Christian theology has a valuable opportunity to articulate within such an horizon what Christian hope extends to; namely, the Reign of God, the final revelation of the one already invoked as 'Our Father', the God whose final meaning is to be "everything to everyone". For in him we are called home to find a welcome in a house of many rooms (Jn 14:2).

This kind of open-minded solidarity to all potential participants in the human conversation raises a piercing question. Given the temporal character of our existence, how open can such a conversation be? In an obvious sense all solidarity is limited to those who are now alive on this planet. The inclusiveness of conversation stops at the limits of death. But do the defeated and the dead of past generations have a voice in what it means to act humanly? Is amnesia the condition of human happiness? Are those on whose past sufferings the present is built, to be dispassionately assigned to oblivion, after having served their purpose as raw material for our development and emancipation? Do those who have died to give us this hopeful present belong only to the past, entombed in failure? Can they in any

---

[26]This point is movingly made in John S. Dunne, *The Church of the Poor Devil. A Riverboat Voyage and a Spiritual Journey* (London: SCM, 1982).

sense belong with us in the present to the real future? In short, have they died out of history, or into it?

Not to wonder about the answer to such questions is to leave the present all too naively immune to challenge: did they really die for *this*?. To possess the past merely as the residue of defeat and death, despairingly circumscribes the reality of our one human history. The eschatological question has in fact been courageously accepted and sharply denied by leading social theorists.[27]. At stake is the meaning of the human as a truly historical solidarity: is our violent and dismembered present the only privileged place? Or may we have hope for the whole of human history where no one is left out, where those who struggled for freedom are not finally swallowed up in an ultimately impersonal universe, but, however mysteriously, find their place in the new creation to whose transformation they have contributed?[28]

Here the Word incarnate in the human conversation, as Jesus Christ, crucified and risen, is the utterance of God's irreversible self-involvement in human history. The Body of Christ, the formation of the new humanity, are familiar Christian notions awaiting their full extension into the concept of solidarity.[29] In the resurrection, the Crucified still bears the stigmata of his worldly being for others. Jesus is glorified precisely in his other-directed life, in his solidarity with the poor, the hopeless, the historical failures, and with the martyrs and prophets who gave their lives to serve them. This Word of victorious Love resists any foreclosure on the human conversation. In the present context, the paschal mystery of Christ stands for the liberation of our humanity to be unlimited in its hopeful solidarity. The life, death and resurrection of Jesus is the parable, the basic language of the social hope expressed in so much of contemporary reflection. In the light of the resurrection of Christ, the martyrs are understood to die into the real future of the world. And more generally, all whom time and death have gathered out of

---

[27]Peukert, *op. cit.*, pgs. 208ff.

[28]Peukert, pg. 235. Besides, what does Vatican II mean when it says, "For after we have obeyed the Lord, and in his Spirit nurtured on earth the values of human dignity, brotherhood and freedom, and indeed all the good fruits of our nature and enterprise, we shall find them again, but freed of stain, burnished and transfigured...." (*Gaudium et Spes*, #39)?

[29]See Peukert, *Op. cit.*, pgs. 202-245.

this world, still live in the region of hope: "I am the resurrection and the life; he who believes in me, though he die, yet shall he live" (Jn 11:25). The grain of wheat is isolated if it does not die into the earth of human history, "but if it dies, it bears much fruit . . . he who hates his life in this world will keep it for eternal life" (Jn 12:24f).[30]

If the consciousness of emerging human solidarity lives from the all-welcoming mystery of the Father, if the deepest human conversation lives both from this Silence of what can not yet be spoken, and the Word that has been uttered as a blessing in the limits of our history, there remains that other dimension. It is disclosed in the question arising out of boundless hope for a humanity so owned by God: what is the ground of this humanity's freedom to work for a more human future? Confronted with the defeat of the best and the power of evil to crush human dignity and imprison its capacities for self-determination, what is the guarantee of freedom's ongoing energy and inspiration? Every praxis of social solidarity summoning human beings to collaboration risks defeat, both from the outside through the brute power of evil, and from within through despair, disillusionment, capitulation to mere technical control. This limit of experience invites a fresh appreciation of the role of the Spirit, the presence of God as surprise and novelty in human history. It inspires dreams for the old and visions for the young (Ac 2:17). On the one hand, this Spirit is not the "spirit of slavery to fall back into fear" (Rom 8:15) but that of joyous acceptance of God as our ultimate future in Christ: ". . . if children, then heirs, heirs of God and fellow heirs with Christ. . . ."(v.17). On the other hand, the Spirit is the energy of self-giving love in the following of Christ. Hope is built not on optimistic theory, but on an universal Loving indwelling the courageous praxis of hope (Rom 5:5).

The words of a theologian expert in social theory sum up the burden of what we have been suggesting here: "A theory of intersubjective interaction in history becomes a hermeneutical basis for a

---

[30]Note the words of J.B. Metz on the significance of the resurrection of the Crucified: "(it is) a word of justice, a word of resistance against any attempt simply to truncate the ever-renewed desire and search for the meaning of human life, and to reserve this meaning for those who are ever to come, who have already somehow managed through it all, to certain extent for those lucky ones who are the final winners and who enjoy the benefits of our history. ('Unsere Hoffnung', *Synode* 6 (1975), pg. 25f).

theology of the Trinity that, even as discourse on God himself, remains a theory of experience."[31]

I have been trying to indicate how the Trinity can be understood as a model of praxis. Specifically, the praxis is that of universal solidarity in suffering and hope: a "theory of experience". The "intersubjective interaction" implied takes place within the horizon of an unbounded, often unnamed and always incomprehensible Love for the whole of human history. It speaks out of the abiding "silence of the Father", but in a Word of hope for all who may lay down their lives for others, and in a Spirit which keeps on inspiring courageous hopeful solidarity in the face of every human reason against it. Such, indeed, is "a hermeneutical basis for a theology of the Trinity"!

---

[31] This is Peukert's concluding remark on Karl Rahner's theology. (*Op. cit.*, pg. 275).

9

Trinity and World Religions

Here we explore how the mystery of the Trinity can be understood as the form, inspiration and horizon of humanity's religious development. In this context, religious development is not being understood as a confrontation of religious 'superpowers'. It is rather a movement toward dialogue, an exchange based on unity-in-difference in which conversation can take place. Here the commanding issue is the reality of ultimate mystery and the manner it draws men and women of good will and genuine faith into a more reconciled, hopeful sense of human destiny.

1. The Trinity and Religious Dialogue

There can be no question of re-issuing a new form of Christian imperialism, now more subtly annexing the religious territory of others. Once more, it must be a matter of adoring the Trinity as Mystery of Love. Just as adoration cannot mean possessing God, Love cannot mean dispossessing others in God's name. What is at stake is the degree to which Christian theology can let God be original Love at work in all lives and traditions, uttering itself as an unconditional affirmation of the worth of all humanity and communicating itself as ever creative Lovingness to the desire and aspiration of the human heart. For what is exclusive to Christian faith is its understanding of how the divine mystery is inclusive of all (1 Tim 2:4; Eph 4:6). If all humanity, indeed, all creation, has its goal and origin in the Love manifest in Christ, we Christians cannot summarily impose on others the particularity of Christian history, as though all history is reducible to what has been lived as our history in the Christian churches for two thousand years. We baptize in the trinitarian name, not in our own. It is a delicate point of faith, to let God be free, to be the divine self in regard to all;[1] this is more demanding than letting others be free in regard to God. But, especially today, that is the challenge of Christian catholicity: to adore the God revealed in our history, but not to idolize the past forms of that history in a recalcitrant orthodoxy. It is an exigence of current ecclesial experience of mission to reach, in dialogue, beyond the categories of European culture into the depths of other cultures, to associate spiritually with all men and women who search for, and are found by, the Mystery (Ac 17:22-31). Such is the grace of our times.[2]

If the church is present to the world as the People of God, the practical adoration of such a God provokes the concerns of reconciliation, dialogue and unity amongst all peoples:

> For all peoples comprise a single community and have a single origin, since God made the whole human race to dwell over the whole face of the earth (Ac 17:26). One also is their final goal: God. His providence, his goodness, his saving designs extend to all (Ws 8:1; Ac 14:17; Rom 2:6f; I Tim 2:4), against the day when the elect will be gathered in that holy city ablaze with the glory of God where the nations will walk in his light (Rev 21,23f).[3]

It falls within our aim to reflect on how this horizon of dialogue is enlarged and enriched by a trinitarian theology. In principle, no one theology can pretend to a finished statement in this matter since, with the Spirit blowing where it will, dialogue is in progress on so many levels. The current literature is quite vast.[4] One must begin

---

[1] See the brief but illuminating reflections of Ch. Duquoc, *Dieu différent*, pgs. 125-145.

[2] Vatican II, *Nostra Aetate*, #1; See too *Lumen Gentium*, #16; *Gaudium et Spes* #22; *Ad Gentes* #7.

[3] *Ibid.*

[4] I have been especially helped by the following: Raimundo Panikkar, *The Trinity and the Religious Experience of Man* London: DLT, 1973); Ewert Cousins, "The Trinity and World Religions", *Journal of Ecumenical Studies* 7 (1970), pgs. 476-498; William Johnston, *The Inner Eye of Love. Mysticism and Religion* (New York: Harper and Row, 1978); William Hill,

from where one is—a starting point which, for a Christian theologian, includes adoration of the Trinity of self-giving Love at work in all human lives.[5] It also includes as a consequence a reverence for such lives and the traditions that nourish them: the fruits of love, wisdom, and holiness abound. As one reflective writer stated,

> The great mission of our times is to create the global human tradition for the first time. Until this generation, mankind has lived in distinctive traditions, even though they influenced each other to a certain extent. But from here on each of us must accept the totality of the human tradition as our own *personal* tradition.'[6]

As might be expected, simplifications are not unknown; indeed, they might be necessary if anything resembling dialogue or learning together is going to be possible. Necessarily, there is a risk of uncritical and impatient syncretism. This evidences more an impatience with the ways of God in history than true trinitarian faith. The eagerness to bring everything and everyone together at all costs must end in self-defeat: since the ways and reality of God have ceased to be the main issue. But if the reality of God and the ways of God with us human beings remain central, those who share this concern are already united in a 'Holy Spirit' of shared adoration and mutual reverencing. In such an atmosphere, the spiritual meeting, theological dialogue, and social alliances can begin to bear fruit. Admittedly, we are only at the beginning of this new way of theology. It is obviously the right time to contribute as best we can to any event of spiritual belonging and interchange, with all its promise on the level of global peace and care for the world's poor. Given that this is the first time in history that the peoples of the great religions are able to experience their differences and similarities in the emerg-

---

The Three-Personed God... pgs. 307-314; John T. Marcus, "East and West: Phenomenologies of Self and the Existential Bases of Knowledge", *International Philosophical Quarterly* (March 1971), pgs. 5-47.

[5]This wider trinitarian perspective is very well expressed in Frederick E. Crowe, *Son of God, Holy Spirit, and World Religions: The Contribution of Bernard Lonergan to the Wider Ecumenism* (Toronto: Regis College Press, 1984).

[6]Thomas Berry, "The Word inspires us: Interreligious Dialogue", *Cross Currents* 24/2 (1974), pg. 248.

ing global context of world history, the choice is between making this new thing an occasion of grace or letting it be a further intensification of isolation and even the dismemberment of the one human race.

On the other hand, the right time is never the right time: apart from a few extraordinary scholars, few are in the position to be aware of all the dimensions of what is happening, and to meet their brothers and sisters of other faiths with an informed, appreciative knowledge. But, I suppose, every time, in theology or prayer, we reach out to these hidden spiritual worlds in which so many of our fellow human beings live, the promise of something new is expressed. So, this sense of the 'right time' has to confront a sense of being ill-prepared in so many ways. Obviously, on the Christian side, no one can be confident of a secure discernment of the Spirit's movement, of a complete comprehension of the liberating meaning of Christ, nor of the number of the "many rooms" in the Father's house. Even theologically speaking, who can pretend to a complete grasp of the content and applicability of the Christian message in the emerging world? Certainly, very few can pretend to a thorough knowledge or even a priority-concern for all the religions and cultures involved; few have had the time or training for even a superficial reading of all the key documents of the various religious traditions and a first hand experience of the actual corporate life of the various believers.[7] More humbly, one is forced to admit that one's personal conversion to the mystery of self-giving Love leaves much to be hoped for: without the evidence of purified faith will one see the reality of God in the other, even though it be staring us in the face? The solidarity of the heart's deepest experiences is the only field where this inter-religious communication will make redemptive sense. Still, we must do what we can.

For the reasons just mentioned, I think the best way to present my own comment on the inter-religious significance of the Trinitarian doctrine is to say: from the standpoint of Christian faith, the Trinity gives an heuristic orientation toward the meaning and experience of

---

[7]However distant, the goal remains a "global trinitarian patristics"; see Daniel P. Sheridan, "Grounded in the Trinity: Suggestions for a Theology of Relationship to other Religions" *Thomist* 50/2 (1986), pgs. 260-278.

other faiths. By this I mean, it opens one's Christian faith out to experiences of God other than those realized in historical Christianity, allowing the Christian both to hear his or her own belief in new terms and to express the meaning of Christ Jesus more clearly and redemptively to others.

2. The Trinity as Orientation to Mission

In this context, let us recapitulate some of the positions that have structured our whole reflection up to this point:

First, trinitarian faith is inherently open to further experience of God's presence. As the central meaning in the life of the church, the meaning of the Trinity performs not only a communicative function in giving the church a way of expressing the kind of community it is. It is also an effective meaning: it orientates the People of God to be an open circle, ever beyond itself in its concern for universal salvation. Adoring the universal Word of Love in Christ, it must be aware of its imperfect realization of the full meaning of its faith. In its adoration of the Spirit poured out on all the world, it has to confess its limitations on the level of love, communication and discernment of this Spirit's presence in the world. In its adoration of the ultimate mystery of the Father who welcomes all to the home of many rooms, the church is aware of how relative it is in showing the real face of God to the whole of human history, of how insensitive it can be to other spiritual traditions where the ultimate is present, reverenced, known and invoked in other languages and in other silences.

Secondly, as the normative structure of Christian faith, the Trinity inspires a more genuine conversion. Conversion to the trinitarian mystery is conversion to the ultimate meaning of Love, the Word; conversion to the supreme Value of "Being-in-Love", the Spirit; conversion to the Infinite Source and Fulfillment of such Love, the Father, in the one universe of grace. In demanding such listening, such self-giving and such self-surrender, it structures and inspires an ever greater self-transcendence in the service of self-communicating Love. Nonetheless, human ways collide and conflict. In examining the causes of such scandal, especially religious scandal, we have to ask what in our horizons is closing us against the full 'enworlding' of the Self-giving Love we adore. To what extent is religious imperialism replacing other-directed mission? To what degree has cultural totalitarianism worked against the discernment of God's universal presence? To what extent have hard-won formulae of orthodoxy made us insensitive to the silences in the hearts of others which cannot be spoken? In other words, has the trinitarian mystery really structured a conversion to the every greater reality of God at work in the world? Or, has it kept the 'Gospel of God' in the attic of classic beliefs as a somewhat puzzling doctrinal heirloom of no significance to us or others?

Thirdly, trinitarian conversion is inherently redemptive. For it implies not only a surrender to the transcendent reality of God, but to God as Lovingly self-involved in the human world of struggling and conflicting co-humanity. Conversion to Love's Word requires that listening be the condition of speaking if the Gospel is to affect the human conversation. Conversion to the Spirit beyond the present realization of unity to a greater unity-in-difference opens to greater possibilities of human consensus. Conversion to the Father relativizes everything against the horizon of unlimited hope for everything and everyone.

Fourthly, the Trinity expresses an eschatological hope for all creation. The ultimate mystery is essentially one of self-giving Love. Despite our different ways, the fragmentations and conflicts involved in the human condition, the Word keeps on being spoken. Despite the diversity of our inspirations and spiritual concerns, even despite the demonic self-destructiveness of our world, the Spirit keeps on being given. Despite our different experiences of darkness, emptiness and fear, the one mystery of Love keeps on being Love for all: "one God and Father of all, who is above all, and through all and in all" (Eph 4:6). The mystery of the Trinity is our most intense expression of hope, that the fullness of life is stronger than any futility, divisiveness or despair.

Fifthly, trinitarian meaning must allow for an empirical crossing of the ways. Here we take for granted that any Christian belief in the universal self-communication of God demands a proportionate catholicity of openness to the presence and activity of God in all ages and cultures. The particular point in this context is that our words, even Christian words about the Word, limited as they are to historical contexts, can only be a genuine human meaning when they are part of the global conversation. As we converse, commending, defending, certainly enriching our understanding of the Word, we participate in an ever fuller incarnation of the divine Word. Further, the unity in the Spirit can only be credible when it is a unifying and reconciling unity, opening out beyond itself to appreciate the other manifestations of the Spirit disclosed in the presence of the Spirit's fruits (Gal 5:22). Provisional Christian unity is thus impelled to reach out to other communities, cultures, religious traditions. The incarnation of the Word and the enheartening of the Spirit demand that we be attentive to the experience and the expression of all those who, through the conditions of Christian history, have been excluded from communion or conversation with us, especially believers in the tradition of other faiths which, for the first time, are being encountered in the global context of the one humanity.[8]

To sum up, in trying to cooperate with the grace of our time—the hitherto impossible global interfaith dialogue—the Trinity is both an "expressive" and "experiential" model for the theology of dialogue.[9] It is expressive in that it is the normative articulation of the three interrelated personal modes of expressing the ultimacy of Love as origin, meaning and presence: what kind of ultimate sense of reality do we have? What is the ultimate language for its expression? To what action does it invite us?

It is an experiential model that invites us to see the limits of our actual experience of God's self-gift. Who has come to an ultimate familiarity with the original Mystery? To an experience of ultimate dialogue with and in the Word? To an experience of being completely possessed and transformed by the Spirit? Such questions posed in the light of the mystery of the Trinity invite us to an ever fuller experience of the God of our faith in the global context of the present.

3. The Trinitarian Model of Inter-Faith Dialogue

We must now examine how a trinitarian global awareness can, in many ways, extend and surpass the traditional Logos universalism

---

[8]Panikkar, *The Trinity...*, pg.42.

[9]This distinction is borrowed from E. Cousins, "Models and the Future of Theology", *Continuum* 7/1 (1969), pgs. 79-92.

of the Catholic tradition. From Justin's claim "that all who lived according to the Logos are Christians, even though Socrates and Heraclitus among the Greeks were considered atheists" (Apologia, 1, 46), to Teilhard's vision of Christ-Omega and the Christogenesis of the universe,[10] a christological universalism has been operative.

It has its advantages. For it enabled theology to locate itself in the mainstream of Greek philosophical reflection, while relating itself to Judaism in terms of expectation and fulfillment. Further, by stressing the incarnation of the Word, it could differentiate itself from Islam. Then, as it accented the Word of divine truth, it achieved its own doctrinal articulation against heresies and became adapted to the great medieval intellectual adventure and to the subsequent history of European intelligence. As a word of final revelation, it energized with its clarity the great missionary efforts as a truth communicable to others with all the authority of the imperial cultures in which it has taken root. In our time, through Teilhard's mystical and imaginative scientific expansion of incarnational faith, it finds itself advantageously located as a faith within an evolutionary world-view.

Still, however much progress we can appreciate and maintain in this line of tradition, we are now confronted with new elements in the global situation of inter-faith encounter. For now Christianity is seriously faced with the great 'non-Logos' religions, principally Buddhism and Advaitan (non-dualist) Hinduism. The Word seems to have no ultimate place in the Buddhist religious experience. For Buddhism looks to an absolute fulfillment for human existence in a realm of enlightenment where word and image and even question and answer, must be reduced to silence. The religious word is surpassed. Similarly, the Word issuing from God, let alone the Word incarnate in Jesus, runs counter to the religious concentration of Advaitan Hinduism we referred to. The Hindu tradition emphasizes, not so much the silence of the Word, as an absolute unity in the realization of existence: through progressive purification, the empirical, historical ego is dissolved into the true self. Here there is not a question of dialogue with the divine but of dissolution into it. The finite contextualized ego is a deceptive covering hiding the real self. This inner-worldly apparent self must yield to the Divine Self if the

---

[10]Still a most useful book is Christopher F. Mooney, *Teilhard de Chardin and the Mystery of Christ* (New York: Image Books, 1966).

goal is to be reached. Any religion of the Word, let alone the Incarnate Word, belongs to the world of deceptive appearances: the real cannot be expressed in any word for the Buddhist; and any historical expression of the divine is at best provisional in the light of the non-dualist True Self of ultimate realization for the Hindu experience.[11]

Now this new element in inter-faith encounter makes the Christological Logos approach at best irrelevant, at worst intrusive, with all the appearance of alien imperialism ignoring the particular experience of the two great 'non-Logos' religious traditions. With such concerns, theology has begun to re-appreciate the Trinity as model of convergence in the differing worlds of religious experience. It is too early to speak of a new trinitarian synthesis of theology. The best we can aim at, is a new model structuring an openness to the God-experience of other faiths, out of which a great new theology may eventually emerge.[12]

4. Different Spiritualities in East and West

Informed and sensitive scholarship has made some suggestions.[13] Three great religious traditions, namely Buddhism, Hinduism, and Christianity (with its historical connections with Judaism and Islam) tend to be formed around a basic type of spiritual experience particular to each. Buddhism accents silence, darkness, the negation of all religious expressions. Hinduism stresses the divine immanence and the non-duality of the self and God. Christianity and the other religions of the Word are formed around the notion of revelation. Some will see this summary as a lamentable simplification. But it is a starting point. For example, contemporary Christian theology can positively appreciate the fundamental Buddhist spirituality in terms related to our Christian experience of God as 'Father', whom no one

---

[11]See Marcus, "East and West...", pgs. 19-30.

[12]As a small step in this direction see my, "The Gifts of the Spirit: Aquinas and the Modern Context", *The Thomist* 38 (1974), pgs. 193-231.

[13]For example, R. Panikkar, *The Trinity and the Religious Experience of Man.* E. Cousins extends his remarks in the article, "The Trinity and World Religions", *Journal of Ecumenical Studies* 7/1 (1970), pgs. 223-254.

has ever seen, the God who dwells in inaccessible light, who is known only in the other.[14] In a related manner, the Hindu experience can be brought home to the Christian more in terms of the Spirit indwelling the depths of our being. Finally, the historical experience of Christianity in its concrete relationships to Israel and its conflict with Islam, is formed by our experience of God as Word and Son.[15]

But has not Christianity always been essentially characterized by trinitarian faith? From one point of view, yes. Still, one can make a distinction between Christian faith and the actual forms of historical Christianity, between Christianity as a global religiously reconciling community and its present largely European form. For it has had to defend the incarnation of the Word as its distinctive truth; it does have its doctrine of the inspired Scriptural Word; it has articulated its classic dogmas; and, very obviously, it has constructed an extraordinarily refined and complex superstructure of theological understanding. For such reasons, it certainly is a 'Word religion', a faith intent on a final revelation, and it celebrates such faith now in word and sacrament.

Let me insert the reminder that theology is not dialogue in the desired personal sense merely because it studies the classic texts of the various traditions. Whilst this is quite necessary, and only at its beginning for most of us, we have to keep reminding ourselves that religions do not exist save in people; and unless such people are present as living participants in any meeting, the reality of dialogue is not yet! Nonetheless, we can begin to develop a theological model preparatory to such dialogue and spiritual conversation, when ,as Christians, we understand the openness to which the Trinitarian mystery invites us, and even more deeply, appreciate the trinitarian depths of all dialogue—solidarity in the mystery of ultimate belonging, a common search for express human meaning, self-transcending love for the other, indeed for all.

We go on now to say a little more about each of these fundamental types of spirituality with its trinitarian correlation. First of all, let us look a little more closely at the typically Buddhist experience of the

---

[14]For more material on the Buddhist experience, see R. Panikkar, "Nirvana and the Awareness of the Absolute", *The God Experience,* ed. J. Whelan (New York: Newman Press, 1971), pgs. 68-88.

[15]See Cousins, "The Trinity and World Religions", pgs. 478-480.

absolute. In this context, the 'absolute' does not necessarily connote anything more than an ultimacy of liberation and enlightenment. How to speak of it is the problem, if not for the Buddhist, at least from the standpoint of believers of other faiths. For the Buddhist anticipates a state of enlightenment beyond words, thoughts, answers, questions, and even prayers. Such a state is characterised by detachment, stillness, emptiness, darkness, silence. This apparently extremely apophatic emphasis provokes inevitable questions: is negation the ultimate Buddhist statement of reality? Is it necessarily atheistic? Is it a final flight from reality into nothingness? The Buddhist way of compassion would tend to suggest, in practice, a deeply religious sense of the universe, despite the unwillingness or inability of the tradition to give precise expression to this.[16] The praxis of this kind of compassionate self-transcendence must be a profound affirmation of something! For Buddhist experience turns on an enlightenment deriving from an ultimate fulness, even if finite expressions are renounced. It cultivates an openness to the absolute which is necessarily beyond human expressiveness. Only in that way can the human spirit be free from futile desires to express and possess: this is quite opposite to nihilistic extinction. 'No-thing-ness' does not mean nothing at all. The smile on the face of the Buddha must mean something![17]

Now the Christian correlation to this fundamental Buddhist spiritual experience of the ultimate is notably found in our experience of God as 'Father'. When God is adored precisely as transcending everything that the world is and can express, as the original silence from which the Word issues, and to which it returns, when the Father is adored as primordial and ultimate even in the context of the Trinity, then this "theologia negativa" can be aligned to the apophaticism of the Buddhist experience. For the Christian, the transcendent mystery can only be known in a "cloud of unknowing": the way of negation follows the way of affirmation as a moment in

---

[16]See Johnston, *The Inner Eye...* in his treatment of Oriental and Christian 'Nothingness', pgs, 106-125.

[17]In the context of Zen Buddhism, an excellent article is Peter Kreeft's 'Zen Buddhism and Christianity: an Experiment in Comparative Religion', *Journal of Ecumenical Studies* 8 (1971) pgs, 513-538.

the silent adoration of God "whom no one has ever seen", to the one who lives in the inexpressible realm of "inaccessible light". Though this is no new matter in mystical and theological tradition, spiritual empathy with the Buddhist experience makes the Christians appreciate in a fresh manner that the Father is known only in the sending of the Son and in the gift of the Spirit. Faith has no access to the ultimate mystery save through 'the missions': "No one has ever seen God: the only Son who is in the bosom of the Father, has made him known." (Jn 1:18; Jn 6:46) God remains unknown save in the praxis of Love: "No one has ever seen God; if we love one another, God abides in us and his love is perfected in us" (I Jn 4:12). What we mean by revelation contains its own paradox: the Father is revealed as the incomprehensible One, beyond any human access or powers of expression, except by means of what has originated in himself: "No one can come to me unless the Father who sent me, draws him." (Jn 6:44)

This apophatic knowledge of the Father must be set in the whole biblical tradition. God comes to us in his own reality, not through the forbidden graven images "or any likeness of anything" (Ex 20:4f) The divine name is revealed but in a way that evades religious or theological capture: "I am who I am" (Ex 3:14). God calls to Moses out of the midst of the cloud (Ex 24:16f). Indeed, God's communication with Moses contains the limitation: "Thou canst not see my face, for man shall not see me and live."(33:20) Despite the divine origin of all grace and mercy, God remains "truly a hidden God" (Is 45:15).

If an apophatic tradition preceded the revelation of the Father, if it continues even with the coming of the Son, with the Son alone being the one in whom the Father is seen and heard, the mystical tradition of the church is also marked by this deep sense of darkness and silence before the mystery of God. This received classic expression in the fifth-century *Theologia Mystica* of Pseudo-Dionysius, and was a deep and pervasive dimension of Thomas Aquinas's theology. Perhaps this is best summed up in the saint's remark to Brother Reginald on Dec.6,1273: "Reginald, I can do no more. Such things have been revealed to me that everything I have written now seems to be straw..I must await the end of my life."

Then, there is of course John of the Cross (d.1591) who has left us classic expressions of the darkness of our knowledge of God: "O guiding night, night more lovely than the dawn!"[18] He repeats his famous, "Nada," in the context of our utter incapacity to express or possess the divine reality:

> Nothing, nothing, nothing,
> nothing, nothing, nothing
> and even on the mountain, nothing.[19]

Yet it remains that the most obvious dimension of Christianity today is that of the Word. Not only do modern communications emphasize this aspect, but the special conditions of our historical and cultural mentality make it inevitable. There is of course something quite intrinsic to our Christian hearing of the Word. This amounts to a special intensity in contrast to the faith of Israel and Islam, for the simple reason that Christians believe that the Word is God, and that this Word became flesh in the man Jesus Christ to "dwell among us". Christians witness to this culmination of the experience of the Word through the logic of God's self-communication to human history: "He who has seen me has seen the Father." (Jn 14:9). This does not imply a comprehensive possession of information about God, but an experience of being established in the ultimate truth by following the way of self-giving Love: "I am the way, the truth and the life. No one comes to the Father but by me." (Jn 14:6) Thus, the Word is incarnate in the Son, redemptive in the unconditional Love of the cross, victorious in the resurrection, sacramental in the life of the church, inspired in the sacred writings and preaching, narrated in the Gospel story, defined in church dogma, systematic in the creativity of theology through history, social in Christ's identification with our neighbor, cosmic as the coherence of all reality, eschatological as the irreversible and unsurpassable revelation of God as Love. All in all, a very 'wordy' experience!

The rich and manifold experience of the divine as Word in historical Christianity is now blossoming into a further manifestation

---

[18]*Ascent of Mount Carmel,* stanza 5, translated and edited by E. Allison Peers (New York: Image Books, Boubleday, 1958) pg. 12.

[19]These words are a translation of a versicle of St. John of the Cross found in his sketch of the 'Monte de Perfeccion'. It is reproduced in *Vida y Obras de San Juan de la Cruz,* edited by Crisogono de Jesus, Lucino del SS. Sacramento and Matian del Nino Jesus, 3rd ed. (Madrid: Biblioteca de Autores Cristianos, 1955) pg. 492.

of that Word. This is the religious reality of dialogue, especially with the other great religions of the Word. For the Word is now heard only in the acoustics of the "Father's home of many rooms". The very culmination of the Word in Christ provokes a special kind of dialogue with Jewish faith. This is made obvious in any trinitarian theology as it turns to Israel's scriptures for data essential to a Christian understanding of God. For in the light of Jewish hearing of the Word, Christianity possesses its own original meaning. Christians have to make their own the whole faithful "listening experience" of Israel in order to appreciate the fullness of their own faith. For Christian faith, Israel is a sacrament of God's presence in history. It manifests the historicity of the Word as promise and summons, calling forth an ever greater hope. In this historical consciousness of continuity and promise, Christians are always challenged to appropriate the authentic faith of Israel as a condition of their own affirmation of God. In this sense, Abraham is recognized as "our father in faith".[20]

Christian-Islamic dialogue is inherently more complicated. The striking religiousness of Islam, the most religious of all religions, invites us to a challenging world of the cultural and social significance of religious values. The fact that Jesus is revered as a prophet in Islam assures the promise of dialogue once the wounds of history have been healed.[21]

In short, Christian faith in the Word made flesh leads us progressively to the realization that the 'flesh' is essentially a 'conversation'. Continuing revelation in history demands its times of listening as well as speaking, in an expanding world of mutual presence. The Word is not incarnate in an imperialistic shout drowning out other voices, but as an ever-original and healing address in the conditions of human speech. If the Word is God, the whole truth has not been heard. It is this whole truth that is the healing truth, at least to assure all who meet as hearers of the Word that our humanity, however finite and fragmented, is not yet finished.

---

[20]Vatican II, *Nostra Aetate* #4. Also P. Lapide and J. Moltmann, *Jewish Monotheism and Christian Trinitarian Doctrine* (Philadelphia: Fortress Press, 1981)

[21]For a provocative article from the Muslim point of view, Isma'il A. al Faruqi, "Islam and Christianity: Diatribe or Dialogue", *Journal of Ecumenical Studies* 5/1 (1968) pgs. 45-77.

In the dimension of the Spirit, Christians can come to a positive appreciation of the Hindu experience of the immanence of God. In the language of the upanishads, the self (atman) and the 'I' (ahman) and the God (Brahman) are one: as one Indian scholar expresses it,

> In this infinite and true self there is no difference, no diversity, no *meum* and *teum*. It is like an ocean in which all our phenomenal existence will dissolve like salt in water ... The true self manifests itself in the processes of our phenomenal existences, but ultimately when it retires back into itself, it can no longer be found in them. It is a state of absolute infinitude of pure intelligence, pure being, and pure blessedness.[22]

In our theology of the Spirit we are well used to thinking of the presence of the Spirit indwelling human persons, individually and corporately, in the conspiracy of Love. There, the Spirit is understood, as it were, as the fulfillment of the divine selfhood: God in the distinction of Father and Son are one in the joint creativity of breathing the Spirit. In breathing this one common Spirit, the Father and the Son dissipate their identity or communion, but achieve their selfhood in pure self-giving, in the communion and mission of Love.[23]

This Spirit of Love is communicated within the struggling history of our co-humanity: the one Spirit in two divine subjects becomes the one Spirit in a myriad of human subjects. God's Spirit is "intimior intimo meo", more within us than we are within ourselves. The gift of the Spirit manifests itself in the experience of our truest selves as "being-in-Love". It is this identity that must be realized as true life. By being drawn out of themselves in the experience of the Spirit, human persons realize the consciousness of their ultimate selfhood. God, in this perspective of the mystery of the Spirit, is not so much the supreme other, but the deepest self. Compared to this experience of the divine self in our selves, all our other dimensions of selfhood

---

[22]Surendranath Dasgupta, *A History of Indian Philosophy,* vol. I, (Cambridge: University Press, 1957) pg. 61.

[23]For further comment on Panikkar's approach, Nalini Devdas "Theandrism of Raimundo Panikkar and Trinitarian Parallels in Modern Hindu Thought", *Journal of Ecumenical Studies* 17/4 (1980) pgs. 606-620.

are recognized as provisional and illusory. This deeply interior experience of the Spirit is something that the classic Hindu experience of self-realization can teach us.[24] Thus, the Loving Self of the Spirit makes audible the Word of self-identity in Christ, and the original Love that gives ultimate selfhood to our finite selves, the Father.

Because the church is living from the mystery of the Trinity it can never settle into a monodimensional style of cultural spirituality, it must be ever more converted to the mystery of God. In the converging global context, Christians are being drawn into encounter with the other great religions of the world. This is to experience in a provocative way the transcendence of the living God over the partial realizations of our faith and its religious forms. Nonetheless, because the ultimate mystery is clarified in our faith as Father, Son, and Holy Spirit, we are able to enter into dialogue with a liberating confidence, able to learn from the experience of an ever-greater God, and able to commend the dimensions of ultimate Love without doing violence to any authentic religious experience. What seems to be opening out before us is a way of adoring the eschatological mystery of God, and to find in that adoration a sense of unity in diversity. Thus we pursue the grace of our times, recalling the trinitarian doctrine to its experiential roots. We are being caught up in that conversion of all religions to be truly concerned with what can save us in an imperiled human history.

5. *The Resources of Tradition*

To ensure a fair hearing for the above type of reflection, let me briefly refer to other more acceptable "universalizing" tendencies and practices in trinitarian theology.[25] It is a matter of transposing the elements of theological tradition that recognized different Christian ways of referring to God into the current context of dialogue in a world of religious differences.

Augustine's "vestige" and image doctrine, with its underpinnings in Greek exemplarism, is a good instance.[26] In Catholic tradition, it

---

[24] Panikkar, *The Trinity . . .*; pgs. 64-66.
[25] Cousins, "The Trinity and World Religions", 483-492.
[26] *De Trinitate* VI; VIII-XV.

developed into a typically Franciscan cosmic sense of all reality sacramentally manifesting God. Richard of St.Victor in his existential reflection on human love—the lover, the beloved, their mutual love—suggests a deep communitarian and contemplative way of approaching trinitarian theology.[27] Robert Grosseteste, as he contemplated the speck of dust, saw in its existence, form and goodness a manifestation of the three divine persons.[28] Bonaventure contemplated "the creation of the world as a book in which the creative Trinity shines forth. It is read according to the three levels of expression, the ways of vestige, image and likeness. By these, as up a ladder's steps, the human intellect has the power to climb by stages to the supreme principle which is God."[29]

For his part, St. Thomas sums up the themes of the great Greek theologians, especially Athanasius and Gregory of Nyssa, when he treats of the presence of the Trinity in the act of creation:

> ...the divine persons are causes of the creation of things in the order of their procession, since God acts from his knowledge and will as a craftsman acts in regard to what he produces. The craftsman acts through a word conceived in his mind and through love in his will in reference to what is to be made. Hence the Father creates through his Word which is the Son, and through his love which is the Spirit....[30]

Hence the trinitarian mystery is involved in the very mystery of what it means to be a creature. This insight promotes the disclosure of the three divine persons through the common attributes, by way of 'appropriation'. Typical examples, in reference to the Father, Son, and Spirit respectively, are power, wisdom and goodness; unity, equality and harmony; eternity, beauty and form; omnipotence, omniscience and will; efficient, exemplary and final causality (not unlike *sat, chit, ananda*—being, consciousness and bliss—in reference to the Brahman in Hindu thinking).

---

[27] *De Trinitate*, III.

[28] Servus Gieben, "Traces of God in Nature according to Robert Grosseteste", *Franciscan Studies* XXIV (1964) pgs. 154-156.

[29] *Itinerarium Mentis in Deum*, c.3, n.5.

[30] *S. Theol.* 1, 45, 5 ad 2.

It seems, then, to be a reasonable step within the context of trinitarian universalism to consider the whole of our known human reality, including the realities disclosed in interfaith dialogue, as a vestige or image of the Trinity. Thus with some profit, we can enrich the tentative explorations of theology with new types of appropriation and so "manifest the divine persons" while appreciating the spiritual depths of other traditions. It is not just a play on the word 'appropriation' to suggest that its classic meaning, manifesting the divine persons by attributing essential divine attributes to them in different ways, must now lead to a new Christian self-appropriation in the present global context. Where before trinitarian faith was a way of excluding other faiths as imperfect, it is now a way of including them in its evidence.

6. Different Phenomenologies of Self in East and West

One of the radical determinants of the diversity of the forms of religious experience is the differing phenomenologies of self in East and West.[31] Different senses of the reality of the self necessarily lead to different concerns for the realization of what is regarded as the true self. An approach like this qualifies the hurried generalizations that bedevil so much discussion of religious diversity: for example, the East is mystical and the West is rational. Rather, any dialogue that promotes the reality of unity-in-difference of the great religious cultures of the world must be aware of the different ways humanity is experienced and understood. There are at least three classic experiences of authentic selfhood. Significantly, each of them is experiencing its own crisis in modern times.

In the West, the true self is always the concrete, historical acting ego.[32] Even in the vision of God this will not be absorbed, dissolved, or annihilated. Westerners typically sought the salvation of the 'soul', a full personal liberation in the resurrection of the dead. It is this self, in history, guided by conscience, that seeks salvation from sin, guilt, death. This type of experience of self envisages a perfection

---

[31] J.T. Marcus, "East and West..." is a key article.
[32] Marcus, pgs. 18-20.

beyond time achieved in time through ethical action, especially on behalf of others. Its ideal is to affirm the human dignity of all individuals in a community of loving relationships where justice can be implemented and human rights secured. Even the mystical strain in this history never contemplates the disappearance of the self, but a perfect communion and union in which the concrete ego is united to God, in the communion of saints and in a transfigured world.

But in the contemporary world, this kind of ego-consciousness is not without its problems. Darwin has inserted this self into the processes of biological evolution; Marx has dramatically sketched its social structure and conditioning; Freud has pointed to the demons of the "unconscious", just as Jung summoned forth the angels of the "archetypes". Further, there is the insistent demand to understand our humanity in a more ecologically attuned way and as responsive to nature. In short, the naively understood ego is now appreciated as deeply immersed in a manifold of social, economic, psychological, biological and ecological systems.

Chinese culture, out of its millennial traditions, has experienced the reality of the self more in terms of the inherent 'right connectedness' of relationships.[33] The true self results from a harmonious integration into the family, the people, all the social and living structures of the cosmic order. Such is the sacred order of the *Tao* and the pure form of *Li*, in the equilibrium of *Yin* and *Yang*. The self is realized in harmony with all else. Genuine selfhood cannot be understood as possible outside this realm of 'philharmonic' relatedness and organic connection with all things. Thus, personal consciousness is realized in sympathetic harmony with the rhythms of the all-encompassing and all-pervading "right Way".

With the historical ruptures of Communism, 'The Long March' has entered Chinese history. The traditional experience of self has suffered the rigours of Marxist critique and the traumas of social revolution. The drama of history has entered as a dissonance into the cosmic harmony. A new and threatening element has entered into the classical Sinic sense of the self.

In Indian culture, the true self has never been the historical or cosmic self in either the Western or Sinic sense. Rather it is a self

---

[33]Marcus, pgs. 21-26.

realized above and beyond the *maya* of deceptive appearances of the acting or cosmic self.[34] It is a transcendent, 'eschatological' self, necessarily devoid of historical particulars and personal characteristics. The illusory self of history and the world must be shed if the true self is to be attained through dissolution into the ultimate. The attainment of unity is the "supreme goal of every responsible life."[35] The West cannot but see in this a radical depersonalising of history and a negation of world and destiny. And of course, modern India, has begun in its own national and social developments to allow for the social imperatives of political democracy and self-determining history, with all the implications of individual and social rights. The self has returned to history to be contextualized in a social, cultural and national form.

If these comments approximate in some way to the complex realities involved, an opportunity must be opening up for global dialogue on the deepest issues of human existence. From a Western point of view, now critically aware of its own limitations, it would seem that the ingredients for an understanding of the human self in global terms are present: the Western sense of the dignity of the individual and its historical unfolding; the Sinic sense of cosmic relationship and harmony; the Indian sense of a trans-historical, 'eschatological' unity. Each of the traditional patterns of self-awareness is threatened, just as each can be helped by what is distinctive in the others. Might one express a hope that the open global history of the present might produce, out of the wealth of its great though particular traditions, a sense of the human self at once individual, relational and looking to future fulfillment?

If this is the case, the mystery of the trinitarian selfhood of God as self-giving Love, can have redemptive meaning for those who contemplate the current situation from a Christian point of view. Understanding the three divine persons as Father, Son, and Spirit is not unrelated to the three classic senses of 'self' we have been describing. The Father, the vision of whom consummates the divine self-communication, is, in this context, more assimilable to the Indian ex-

---

[34]Marcus, pgs. 26-30.

[35]Mircea Eliade, *Yoga: Immortality and Freedom,* trans. W.R. Task (New York: Pantheon Books, 1958) pg. 124.

perience of the eschatological self. The self-expression of the Word, incarnate in human history, is most easily linked and aligned to the Western experience. And the Spirit as the subsisting unifying force of Love can be evocatively linked with the Sinic experience of harmony and relationality. As self-giving Love, the Trinity is redemptively present as a model for a reconciled, global version of human selfhood. Are we not discovering one more dimension of our humanity "made in the image and likeness of God"? The least that can be said, is that this approach is possibly a suggestive complement to what I sketched above in the third section of this chapter.

It is desirable to have both the patience and expertise to survey all the data of a "global trinitarian patristics". Failing in both at this point, I feel it still worthwhile to emphasize, in the light of the one datum of God as trinitarian Love, that we are liberated to contemplate, reverently and productively, the promise and crisis of our times.

10

Conclusion

In pursuing this long reflection on the Trinity, our concern has been, through all the connections, analogies, applications, models and extensions, to present the mystery of God in terms of Love. It is up to the reader to make his or her own conclusions about how appropriate or compelling this essay has been. The problem all along has been to express a trinitarian theology of Love while avoiding an ideology of love. A delicate correlation had to be achieved between the scriptural and doctrinal data of authentic Christian belief in God and the appropriation of such data in terms of the experience of love. I have tried not to sound too romantic about this; after all, love is very matter of fact even if it is the apex of human development as that which gives momentum and direction to our living. All in all, I am convinced that we are at the beginnings of a great new trinitarian theology. What I hope is that this present work has contributed some elements to such development. I freely admit that what I have written here belongs to a transitional stage. Surer formulations, more settled patterns of elaboration will be the outcome of a long process of deeper research and wider conversation. Nonetheless, the basic thesis seems to stand. God occurs in human experience as the mystery of Love: an original self-giving Love establishing its own truth and meaning in the Word, and endlessly creative in the abiding novelty of the Spirit. Because we have been dealing with the Trinity of Love, I have been careful not to over-emphasize the distinction between the immanent and economic Trinity. Once "being in love" is accepted as the focal analogy in trinitarian theology, that distinction is not entirely relevant: Love is really love or it is not: the realism of self-giving Love presupposes a self in the giver, a self in the gift, a self in the giving. God 'in se', the divine mystery 'in itself', is engaged and involved. At this point, a question surfaces: does not the distinction between the immanent and economic Trinity belong more to a stage of theology not yet confident of its own experiential basis? If God is thought of primarily in terms of undifferentiated Be-ing, the Love that is shown forth in the economy is somehow secondary. When the context is ontological, and not phenomenologically based in Christian life, distinctions like the one I just mentioned have to be made. But once the transposition has been made into the terms of Love, such distinctions do not have the importance that a more theoretical theology accorded them. At least, I am inclined to think this is the case.

On the other hand, if even our most familiar human loves have their own incomprehensibility, even their own eternity, I want to emphasize the necessity of respecting the incomprehensibility of the divine mystery of Love and its eternal character. Love keeps on being Love. It leads to a consummation which will not contradict the divine self-involvement in human history. Rather, that history, finally transformed by the Love at work, will be drawn into a universe of Love as its fulfilment. The mystery of the Trinity is the eschatological revelation of Love's source, Love's meaning, Love's transforming power.

Though this Trinity is an eschatology of Love, it makes a difference now, and as we have stressed, inspires its own trinitarian praxis. In this concluding section, let me make a brief remark on two contentious matters.

1. The Trinity and the Feminine

The first deals with the feminist turn, more correctly perhaps, the conversion ot the feminine, which is so deeply affecting current theology.[1] Obviously, I have made no special effort to replace the

---

[1] See my "Christian Coversion and the Feminine" in *The Force of the Feminine*, ed. Margaret Franklin (Sydney: Allen & Unwin, 1986), pgs. 175-187; and "Liberation from the Half-Human: the Feminine Side of God" in *Seasons of Hope. Christian Faith and Social Issues* (Melbourne: Dove Communications, 1984), pgs. 92-98.

biblical and historically given symbols of Father, Son, and Spirit. They are part of the historical consciouness of Christian faith, and, in their origins, were never intended to legitimate, as far as I can find out, an oppressive patriarchalism or androcentrism in any form, even though they may have often been pressed into such a un-Christian service. But times change and cultures change; and with the emergence of contemporary emanicipation movements, our history and the cultures that nourished it, have to be more critically examined in the light of the oppression such as history either caused or permitted. Hence the sensitivity of modern theology to hear the voice of the various liberation movements, and to imbibe their spirit in the struggle against racism, capitalism, imperialism, militarism and, in what concerns us here, sexism.

There seems to be no doubt that at least in the cultures that affected Christian theological understanding, a onesided and defective anthropology has held sway. Though theology, tutored by its classic sources in scripture, church doctrine and mysticism, knew that God was incomprehensible, was not subject to gender classification, was imaged forth in both male and female, that "in Christ there was neither male nor female", an at least implicit philosophy seems to have been the most powerful element in forming our notion of God: the masculine principle was identified with what is active, powerful, formative and rational, and the feminine with what is passive, malleable, receptive to form, emotional and so forth.[2] This philosophical myth was nourished by an ignorance of reproductive biology, just as it was promoted by the general patriarchal bias of the culture. Modern biology has destroyed the physical basis for such a myth, just as contemporary psychologies and anthropologies endlessly point out the truncated humanity of androcentrism and its patriarchal excesses. The matter is taken out of the realm of tranquil scientific theory by the dramatic witness of modern women in every domain of contemporary culture, including that of the church.

A responsive theology knows that the only issue is not that of our notion of God conceived of in predominantly male terms. The rights

---

[2]The researches of Franz Mayr are seminal in this context, e.g., "Patriarchalisches Gottesverstandniss?", *Theologische Quartalschrift* 152(1972), pgs. 224-255; "Trinitätstheologie und theologische Anthropologie", *Zeitschrift fur Theologie und Kirche* 68 (1971), pgs. 427-477.

of the women in the church, their role in Christian ministry, the value of their experience, and so forth, can be discussed as distinct issues. But such discussions are harldy separable from the notion of God which is meant to be the space where the human community finds a redemptive point of belonging and shared hope. After the usual disclaimers of the limitations of analogical knowledge, that Jesus' "Abba" invocation is not directed to a patriarchal idol but to the liberating God of the kingdom, attempts to revise our notion of God tend to run along one of three lines, each of which has its own value.[3]

The first is a matter of emphasis. Theology will point out that all its language is analogical, and that God is incomprehensible. While it is true that masculine analogies have been favoured in a tradition so emphatically confessing the Trinity in terms of Father and Son and Spirit, various feminine analogies are not only appropriate but are well founded in scripture (e.g., Is 42:14; 66:13). Thus God is also depicted as mother, crying out in labour, giving birth, nursing and cradling the child, showing a mother's love.[4] In the contemporary context of feminist discussion, while the emphasis is welcome as indicating an historical datum, the problem is with those who do the emphasizing. The balance is always on the side of a masculine or patriarchal world-view which, while conceding the value of the feminine, still defines it, both in women and in God. To put it another way, God is still predominantly 'Father' showing some maternal traits.

The second approach is more expressly trinitarian. For it seeks to locate the feminine not only in the divine behaviour or attitude but as a distinctive property of one of the divine persons, namely the Holy Spirit. Though Father and Son are obviously defined in masculine terms, the Spirit is most expressed in feminine and maternal symbolism: the Spirit broods over creation, nurtures to life, forms the Body of Christ in head and members, leads to the Father, is an all-encompassing, life-giving gift in the way a mother's love is given.[5] This approach re-activates those neglected aspects of Catholic tradi-

---

[3] For an outstanding article, see Elizabeth A. Johnson, "The Incomprehensibility of God and the Image of God male and female", *Theological Studies* 45 (1984), pgs. 441-465.

[4] See Johnson, *art. cit.*, pgs. 445-448.

[5] Johnson, *art. cit.*, pgs. 457-460 for abundant references.

tion which tended to deliver them into modern consciousness only through devotion to the Blessed Virgin Mary. Once more, however, contemporary feminist consciousness cannot be altogether happy with this: the Holy Spirit is still the 'third divine person', usually edged out of Christian consciousness by the strong male symbolism of Father and Son who, in trinitarian theology, are the joint principle of the Spirit. When the Spirit is merely a kind of divine afterglow once the really important things about God have been said, a concerned feminist theology naturally has reservations about linking its concerns to the weakest aspect of trinitarian theology.

And so a third approach attempts a more thorough affirmation of the feminine reality of God by more radically explicitating the analogical character of our knowledge of the Trinity. It focuses on the highest analogue, that is, the human person her/himself. Most simply put, since human beings are made in the image and likeness of God, and since "male and female" God created them, both sets of symbolism are necessary if our affirmation of God is to have its strongest foundation. Indeed, even for the understanding of "generation" in God, there is no longer any absolute need to limit this to the image of male generativity, now that it is scientifically clear that the female primciple is equally active in the generative process from which the analogy arises.[6] Authors instance both biblical expressions of feminine deity such as Holy Wisdom (*Sophia*) and extra-biblical examples such as the goddess figures of Ishtar and Shakti to show how, within and outside the established tradition of masculine expression, there are invitations to a more adequate notion of the divine.[7]

Thus these three progressively valuable approaches reduce to the attitudinal, the pneumatological, and the integrally human. In the conclusions of this present work with its emphasis on the Trinity as "Being in Love", I think there are two points to be added.

The first points to Love as the most liberating context in which a sexist critique of trinitarian language can take place. It seems to me

---

[6]M.A. Farley, "New Patterns of Relationship: Beginnings of a Moral Revolution", *Theological Studies* 36 (1975), pg. 640.

[7]Johnson, *art. cit.*, pgs. 460ff; Leonardo Boff, *The Maternal Face of God The Feminine and its Religious Expressions,* trans. Robert R. Barr and John W. Dierksmeier (San Francisco: Harper and Row, 1987), pgs. 87f. Both these authors quote the words of Pope John Paul I, "God is my Father but especially my Mother".

that, to the degree that the original, expressive, and boundlessly communicative character of God as Love is not given the first and fundamental place in theology, the other absolutes creep in and establish their own self-justifying ideologies. How often the emphasis on God as Father has been linked to the affirmation of God as omnipotent, as supreme being, with the Word as God's all-rational and authoritative expression. At some later stage this established supreme, all-powerful, non-feminine One begins to show 'love'; but so often this has been merely appropriated to the rather shadowy and derivative activity of the Spirit. I don't mind risking this caricature to dramatize the 'untheological' character of so much of our ordinary theology. When explicitly or implicitly, the dominant notion of God is power and ontological supremacy, the feminist critique of theological language is marked with the discord of the battlefield rather than the consensus of a conversation in a healing space. The established patriarchy, defensive of its power, resists a feminist uprising jealous of male dominance. On the other hand, once we return to the primary notion of God as self-giving Love, with all its appearance as foolishness in the realm of our mundane conflicts, the feminist questions must be appreciated, not as an unheard-of strident subversion of the traditional faith, but in the depth of their challenge.

In earlier times not yet sensitive to the feminist issue, the integrity of the Love had to be articulated to answer other essential threats such as Modalism, Arianism, etc. The issue was largely affirming the presence of three co-equal divine persons so that the divine character of Love in the giver, in the gift, and in the giving could be secured. There was no essential critique of the received terms, 'Father, Son, and Spirit'. But if Love is to keep on being Love, and if, in those open to it or hoping for it, the Christian message is to resonate with the conviction of a "truth that will make you free", with the assurance of a "peace that the world cannot give", with the promise of "life to the full" and a "joy that no one can take from you", Love demands that languages and their concepts, and the ideologies they carry, be criticized. There is something deeply wrong if Christian women are not experiencing God as Love. The word, Love,—perhaps I have overdone it?—is more primary to Christian vocabulary than any other, including the name 'Father'.

The second point bears on the context in which God is invoked as trinitarian Love. Such a context is the dynamic state of self-transcendence which, with Lonergan and others, we have described as fulfilling the unconditional "being-in-love". When we are most turned out of ourselves in loving concern for the other, then the trinitarian mystery of Love makes most sense. The incalculable happening of love as something at once all-meaningful and creative, not only takes us to some analogical understanding of the presence of Divine Love in our world, but invites us to share in it. God's making of our humanity in the divine image as male and female as Gn 1:26f states it, implies the paradigmatic case of this self-transcendence evidenced in loving and generative relationships between men and women. It seems to me that the more this paradigmatic instance of being-in-love is understood as sublated into our relationships with God, the more sexual expressiveness of faith and its transcendent love will have far-reaching effects on our sense of God. Indeed, granting the legitimacy of the current feminist critique of androcentric or patriarchic theological expression, I find myself wondering, should this critique be refused, whether it is not women who are the losers, but men. After all, women, as dozens of great female mystics have shown, can obviously engage their passionate sexuality in the love of God: they are not necessarily loving a transcendent patriarch, but a Love. In contrast, with the stunted androcentric theological imagination, how is male sexuality engaged in loving God with all one's heart and mind and soul and strength? Unless Holy *Sophia* is somehow intimated to men with all the implications of beauty and encompassing, inspiring presence, male sexuality remains somewhat awkwardly exterior to the self-transcending thrust or fulness of union with the mystery of Love. Do men have to be spiritually homosexual? An odd way of putting the question, but it does make the point. And the point, most of all, is that the Trinity occurs as a matrix of Love enfolding the wholeness of our humanity into it. Perhaps only poets and mystics will solve the language problem in the end. In the meantime, theologians and spiritual directors have much to learn from the challenge of the feminist critique. By accenting the Mystery of Love as the foundation of trinitarian theology, we have a kind of redemptive space in which healing and inspiring exchanges can occur between the women and men who are the living image of that Love which is the meaning, energy and destiny of their existence.

2. The Filioque

Given the renewed effort to come to grips with this daunting ecumenical problem, so emblematic of the tensions between Eastern and Western traditions of Christian faith, I am well advised to limit myself to a brief remark.[8] It has to be in the form of a question: has this entire controversy sufficiently recognized the Trinitarian mystery it sought to analyse, as the mystery of Love? A review of the current or past literature on this radical controversy does not inspire any great expectation of an affirmative answer to the question. Certainly, the theological and ecclesiastical praxis has often not been notably trinitarian: one does not get the impression that either side of the debate was intent on stressing the incalculable Love of God, let alone embodying its risk and folly! To that degree, is it not all a rather incredible scandal in the past and present history of the Christian church? To the Greek theological mind, the Western trinitarian analogies seem too pat; they are too successful in explaining the mystery and deducing it from an all-to-knowable divine essence. Further, the utter originality of the Father as source of all the hypostatic reality of the Trinity is comprised by the procession of the Spirit from the Son as well as from the Father. Far from being the Breath in which the Word is spoken and the Son conceived, the Spirit becomes a vague and unimportant addendum both in the mystery of God and in the constitution of the church. The standard Latin response has always pointed to the necessity of maintaining some "relationship of opposition" between the Son and the Spirit, otherwise there would be no grounds for their distinction. And the only foundation for such oppositional relationships is origin within the divine mystery. Hence the emphasis on the Spirit's proceeding also from the Son.

Seven hundred years ago, Western theologians sought to accommodate the Greek emphasis by allowing the formula, "through the Son", *per filium*. This was an attempt to underscore the prime originality of the Father in the breathing forth of the Spirit. The Son

---

[8]For a useful digest of the current situation and a careful appraisal of different theologies, see Yves Congar, *The Word and the Spirit*, trans. David Smith (San Francisco: Harper and Row, 1986), pgs. 101-122.

could only be a source of the Spirit inasmuch as he received this property from the Father. Today, of course, Western tradition acknowledges its deficiencies in pneumatology. Vatican II mentions the Spirit two hundred and fifty eight times in its documents; theology examines its sources and history, [9] and embarks on bold new speculative efforts [10] Nonetheless, I still have the suspicion that no real breakthrough will occur until, in theory and practice, we re-locate these millennial trinitarian controversies in the mystery of Love. There seem to be at least three questions preliminary to any doctrinal discussion. [i] What is there in the consciousness of this Love that legitimates the Greek notion of the Spirit coming forth immediately from the Father? [ii] What elements of the experience of Love ground the Latin insistence on the procession of the Spirit from the Father "and Son"? [iii] What is there in our experience of Love's ultimate mystery that makes room for a higher synthesis where both positions can be respected, and even brought together? These seem to be the big questions behind the ongoing controversy, even though the notions of love and experience do not figure very prominently, to say the least.

The short answer to the first question is that the Holy Spirit is the first in human experience: Christians and all men and women of good will are united in a conspiracy of loving. They inhale a shared 'Breath' of loving energy that puts no limits or conditions on their self-sacrificing service of their neighbour, and their surrender in faith and hope to the invisible mystery at the heart of the universe which consents to and inspires this loving, self-giving existence. In this context, the Spirit of Love occurs as tied to no conditions, no prior philosophies or limits, indeed to no direct vision of Father or Son. It is the Breath of the supreme human creativity of living not for oneself but for the other. Fittingly, the first question ends with its own question: is this what the Greeks are trying to get at when they have so insistently struggled for a more liberating, less derived notion of the Holy Spirit?

The short answer to the second question lies in the demand of

---

[9] As for example, Yves Congar, *I Believe in the Holy Spirit. vols I-III* (New York: Seabury, 1983).

[10] One of the most impressive systematic efforts is David Coffey, *Grace: The Gift of the Holy Spirit* (Sydney: Faith aned Culture, 1979).

such loving to find its meaning and assurance. Loving is neither being mindless nor self-destructive nor content with anonymity. It looks for its support and explanation in the harsh and dreadful experience of the cross. Through the creative witness of the Spirit, love finds its way and truth and life in Jesus of Nazareth. In him, his being for others in the cross and resurrection, it finds the Word it is looking for, incarnate. Without him, the Spirit would have no 'incarnation'[11] in the world. Related to him, as its source, form and embodiment, the Spirit is discerned as the Spirit of truth and eternal life. Fittingly, too, this second question provokes its own question: does not the Latin insistence on the procession "from the Son", or at least, "through the Son" aim at securing the genuine meaning of the Spirit's creativity, and the form of authentic Loving, and its power to transform the human?

The short answer to the third question stresses that we are not dealing with any kind of mystery, but precisely the mystery of limitless, self-giving Love. God must be incalculably Love as giver, as gift, and as endlessly giving. Love affirms what it most intimately is in the self-gift implied in "the only Son". It keeps on being what it is in the limitless giving of the Spirit who opens hearts and the whole world to the self-gift in the Son, and the giver revealed in that gift, the Father. An ontological schematization of divine reality, be it Greek or Latin standing outside the mystery of Love, imposes an order of sequence and derivation which cannot but be experienced as alien to the living experience of such a mystery. A more historical, empirical pattern of experience will tend to highlight the meaning of the Word as formative of all our 'Spirit-ual' experience. Whereas a more interior, eschatological pattern of experience will emphasize the Spirit as the one in which both Son and Father are known. Once more, then, a question following on this third question: has the Mystery of the Father as all-initiating primordial Lover been sufficiently recognized as the horizon in which these vexing theological issues are explored? Just to pose such a question breaks away from an ontology where divine being, intelligence and will have a strict linear sequence, and draws one to the contemplation of an infinite Being-in-Love which is ever expressing its means in continuous Loving.

[11] A bold term, I know, but well justified in David Coffey's "The 'Incarnation" of the Holy Spirit in Christ", *Theological Studies* 45 (1984), pgs. 466-480.

The Christomonism that modern theology deplores[12] results from failing to advert to the fact that our experiential access to Christ and a knowledge of him in his death and resurrection, is through the faith, hope and love that the Spirit inspires. The Spirit as the vital field of Loving inspires a search for Love's meaning, Love's Word, Love's assured truth. This Spirit-inspired search finds its answer in the Word Incarnate, Jesus of Nazarethl. But without this Holy Spirit, the connection can never be made: Love will lack its language. But in the witness and enabling power of the shared Spirit of faith, hope and love, Jesus Christ is recognized as the self-declared revelation of incomprehensible Love which no one can see, or even know, save by surrendering to it and collaborating with it. Sticking close to the phenomenology of Love means adopting the flexibility and evocative power of narrative. To say that God is Father, Son, and Spirit is first of all to tell the story of the self-disclosure of eternal Love, investing itself fully in the fate of the world. Without this sense of the mystery of Love breathing a new shared Spirit into human consciousness, and enabling that human consciousness to find the native language of Love in the crucified and risen Jesus, theology is locked in a lofty ontological mode which freely names mystery what it cannot understand, but fails to remember sufficiently what that mystery fundamentally is: an incalculable Love which has given what is most intimately its own for our human transformation. It has met our usually secret hopes for ultimate freedom by breathing into us its own Spirit. It has disclosed and affirmed its liberating meaning in "the only Son", the Word.

It would be unpardonable arrogance to think that the above is all that need be said to find a solution to the *Filioque* controversy. On the other hand, I would like to suggest that a return to the experiential basis of trinitarian theology in the narrative, symbols and living consciousness of Christian love, cannot but provide a healthier context in which a healing conversation can occur.

3. Love's Excess

So we end. A Christian must believe that the excess of Love is not spent even in the immense sufferings of our present world. A practical

---

[12]See Congar, *The Word and the Spirit*, ch. 7 "The Spirit, the Spirit of Christ: Christomonism and the *Filioque*", pgs. 101-121.

adoration of the Spirit of irrepressible, limitless Loving remains the condition for a theology of the Trinity. Only through the Spirit's witness does faith discern the truth of Love's revelation in Christ, and find a release into Love's mystery as the all-inclusive realm of the one invoked as "Abba, Father".

> The questions now that had to be asked have nearly all been asked. The things that had to be said, nearly all said. Only the prayer remains, "Come, Holy Spirit!" In my hope to be one with you, in what you are doing and willing and inspiring in the world, may I claim as my own all the loves that you have brought forth, each precious participation in the mystery of your self-giving which holds the universe together: may I lose myself in the movement of true life....
>
> Spirit of Love, we praise you in the long, tender care and dreaded letting-go of parenthood; we praise you through the years in all the moments of joy, fidelity and forgiveness of lovers content to grow old together. We praise you in the simple generosity of the young, and in the tentative wonder of sweethearts. Praise to you in the great passion of our prophets, in the lonely deep searching of our teachers, in all the humble tasks of those who awaken each morning to do the world's work with care and daily faithfulness.
>
> Praise to you, too, most Holy Spirit, in the terrible bravery of those giving their lives in vast urgent human causes, for the protection of the weak, for the making of good laws, for the curing of disease, all for a better, a more hopeful human way.... And praise to you for all the unsuspected, unknown loves and the dreadful toll of those dying uncomforted and forgotten save by your Love.
>
> And praise to you in the incredible love of the countless poor who always have enough to share; and in the love of those who have treasured and defended our humanity when it was defenceless and forgotten by most of us....
>
> All these loves I reverence, and to all such loves I join my own, with the hope that the great loves may enlarge and redeem the lesser, and that the pierced heart of all the world might unite us all in the one great ecstasy of Love, so to bring us joyfully to the light....[13]

[13]From my *Love Remains. A Meditation on Christian Love* (Melbourne: Spectrum Publications, 1979), pgs., 55ff.

Questions for Discussion

Chapter 1: Perspectives

1. What is the importance of the 'starting point' in a theology of the Trinity? Are there a number of possible starting points?
2. How is the celebration of the Eucharist an act of trinitarian faith? What about the other sacraments?
3. How does our overall sense of reality affect our approach to the Trinity? What contemporary features of our sense of universal reality are likely to make the Trinity more credible today?
4. To what degree would you say the Trinity has been a neglected mystery in our understanding of Christian faith?

Chapter 2: The Scriptural Foundation

1. In what sense is 'Trinity' found in Scripture?
2. How do the Scriptures tell the story of God? What is the significance of the trinitarian way of telling God's story?
3. How is trinitarian faith grounded in the early church's experience of God?

Chapter 3: Mystery and Definition

1. Why was the doctrinal mode of expressing authentic faith necessary? What were the consequences of this?
2. What were the main steps in the formation of trinitarian doctrine?

3. Whilst the church's language became more Greek, the church's doctrine of God was becoming less Greek. How is this paradoxical situation explained?

Chapter 4: Connections

1. How is the Trinity the Mystery implied in all the other mysteries of faith? Where, ideally, should it be studied, at the beginning or the end of theology?
2. If the Church is 'The People of God' in what sense is it "The People of the Trinity"?
3. How does the death and resurrection of Christ enter into our understanding of the Trinity?

Chapter 5: Analogies

1. Why is analogical thinking necessary? What are its features?
2. In what sense does God always remain unknown?
3. How does St. Thomas Aquinas use the psychological analogy in his exposition of the Trinity? What is his aim? What is his starting point?
4. How does he understand the divine indwelling?

Chapter 6: Transpositions

1. How can the psychological analogy be re-expressed in modern terms?
2. How does the Trinity mean the same as 'God is Love'?
3. How is the meaning of the Trinity related to our understanding of the world?

Chapter 7: Applications

1. The Trinity is a community. How can we explain this?
2. To what degree is the word 'person' still applicable to the Father and the Son and the Holy Spirit as 'the three divine persons'?
3. Is the Trinity a 'process'?
4. How is the whole Trinity involved in God's compassion for the sufferings of the world?

Chapter 8: Models

1. How is trinitarian faith a healing for the religous psyche?
2. How is the mystery of the Trinity related to true self-development?
3. How is the Trinity an invitation to involvement in the global political process?

Chapter 9: Trinity and World Religions

1. How does the Trinity motivate a larger religious dialogue?
2. How might a broader knowledge of world religions extend our Christian appreciation of the Trinity?
3. What resources does traditional trinitarian theology bring to this new situation?

BIBLIOGRAPHY

al Faruqi, "Islam and Christianity: Diatribe or Dialogue". *Journal of Ecumenical Studies* 5/1 (1968) 45-77

Aquinas, Thomas, *Summa Theologiae. Commentary on the Gospel of St. John. The Aquinas Scripture Series, 4-5*, trans. F. Larcher, ed., J. Weisheipl (Albany: Magi Books, 1980—)

Athanasius, *Orationes Contra Arianos* (*PG* 26)

Augustine, *De Trinitate* (PLxxx)

Balthasar, von, H. Urs, *Le Mystere pascal (Mysterium Salutis 12)* (Paris: Cerf, 1972)

Barth, K., *Church Dogmatics I: The Doctrine of the Word of God*, trans. G. Thompson (Edinburgh, 1936)

Beeck, van, F., *Christ Proclaimed. Christology as Rhetoric* (New York: Paulist Press, 1979)

Berry, T., "The Word inspires us: Interreligious Dialogue", *Cross Currents* 24/2 (1974)

Boff, L., *The Maternal Face of God. The Feminine and its Religious Expression*, trans., R. Barr and J. Dierksmeier (San Francisco: Harper and Row, 1987)

Bonaventure, St., *Itinerarium mentis in Deum*

Bracken, J., *The Triune Symbol* (New York: The University Press, 1985) "The Holy Trinity as Community of Divine Persons", *Heythrop Journal* 2-3 (1974) 166-182; 257-270.

Brown, C., *Jung's Hermeneutic of Doctrine*, AAR Dissertation Series 32 (Ann Arbor: The Scholars Press, 1981)

Brown, D., *The Divine Trinity* (La Salle, IL: Open Court, 1985)

Brown, R., *The Anchor Bible. The Gospel according to John* (New York: Doubleday, 1966)

Burge, G., *The Annointed Community. The Holy Spirit in the Johannine Tradition* (Grand Rapids: Eerdmans, 1987)

Burrell, D., *Exercises in Religous Understanding* (Notre Dame: University of Notre Dame Press, 1974)

Capra, F., *The Turning Point. Science, Society and the Rising Culture* (London: Flamingo Fontana, 1984)

Cobb, J.B., *A Christian Natural Theology* (Philadelphia: Westminster Press, 1965)

Coffey, D., *Grace: The Gift of the Holy Spirit* (Sydney: Faith and Culture, 1979) "The 'Incarnation' of the Holy Spirit in Christ", *Theological Studies* 45 (1984) 466-480

Cooke, B., *Beyond Trinity* (Marquette: University Press, 1969)

Congar, Y., *I Believe in the Holy Spirit I-III* (New York: Seabury, 1983) *The Word and the Spirit*, trans., D. Smith (San Francisco: Harper and Row, 1986)

Conn, W., "Affective Conversion: the Transformation of Desire" in *Religion and Culture. Essays in Honor of Bernard Lonergan, SJ*, eds., T. Fallon and P. Boo Riley (Albany: University Press, 1987)

Cousins, E., "Models and the Future of Theology", *Continuum* 7/1 (1969) 79-92 "The Trinity and World Religions", *Journal of Ecumenical Studies* 7 (1970) 476-498

Crowe, F., "Complacency and Concern in the Thought of St. Thomas", *Theological Studies* 20 (1959) 1-39; 198-230; 343-395 *Son of God, Holy Spirit and World Religions: The contribution of Bernard Lonergan to the wider Ecumenism* (Toronto: Regis College Press, 1984)

Dallmayr, F., *Polity and Praxis. Exercises in Contemporary Political Theory* (Cambridge, Mass.: MIT Press, 1984)

D'Arcy, M., *The Mind and Heart of Love* (New York: Meridian, 1956)

Dasgupta, S., *A History of Indian Philosophy*, vol. I (Cambridge: University Press, 1957)

Devdas, N., "Theandrism of Raimundo Panikkar and Trinitarian Parallels in Modern Hindu Thought" *Journal of Ecumenical Studies* 17/4 (1980) 606-620

Dodds, M., "St. Thomas Aquinas and the Motion of the Motionless God". *New Blackfriars*, May 1987, 233-242

Dunn, J.D.G., *Jesus and the Spirit* (London: SCM, 1975)

Dunne, J.S., *The Church of the Poor Devil. A Riverboat Voyage and a Spiritual Journey* (London: SCM, 1982)

Dunne, T., "Trinity and History", *Theological Studies* 45 (1984)

Dunne, T., and Laporte, J., *Trinification of the World. A Festschrift in honour F.E. Crowe, S.J.* (Toronto: Regis College Press, 1978)

Duquoc, C., *Dieu différent. Essai sur la symbolique trinitaire* (Paris: Cerf, 1977)

Eliade, M., *Yoga: Immortality and Freedom*, trans., W. Task (New York: Pantheon Books, 1958)

Farley, M., "New Patterns in Relationship: Beginnings of a Moral Revolution", *Theological Studies* 36 (1975)

Ford, L., "Process Trinitarianism", *Journal of the American Academy of Religion*, 43 (1975)

Geertz, C., "Religion as a Cultural System", in *Anthropological Approaches to the Study of Religion*, ed., M. Banton *ASA Monographs 3*, Tavistock, 1969

Gieben, S., "Traces of God in Nature according to Robert Grosseteste", *Franciscan Studies* XXIV (1964)

Gregg, R., and Groh, D., *Early Arianism—a View of Salvation* (Philadelphia: Fortress Press, 1981)

Grillmeier, A., *Christ in the Christian Tradition I* (Oxford: Mowbrays, 1975)

Hartshorne, C., *The Divine Relativity: A Social Conception of God* (New Haven: Yale Univ. Press, 1948)

Hill, E., *The Mystery of the Trinity* (London: Geoffrey Chapman, 1985)

Hill, W., *The Three-personed God. The Trinity as a Mystery of Salvation* (Washington: Catholic Univ. Press, 1984)

Himes, M., and Himes, K., "Right, Economics and the Trinity", *Commonweal* (March 1986) 137-141

Hippolytus, *Haereses*

Irenaeus, *Adversus Haereses*

Jenson, R., *Triune Identity* (Philadelphia: Fortress Press, 1982)

Johan, R., *The Meaning of Love. An Essay towards the Metaphysics of Intersubjectivity* (New York: Paulist, 1966)

Johnson, E., "The Incomprehensibility of God and the Image of God Male and Female", *Theological Studies* 45 (1984) 441-465

Johnston, W., *The Inner Eye of Love. Mysticism and Religion* (New York: Harper and Row, 1978)

Jung, C., *Psychology and Religion: East and West* (New York: Pantheon Books, 1958)

Jüngel, E., *God as Mystery of the World. On The Foundation of the Theology of the Crucified One in the dispute between Theism and Atheism*, trans. D. Guder (Grand Rapids: Eerdmans, 1983)

Kasper, W., *The God of Jesus Christ*, trans. M.J. O'Connell (London: SCM, 1984)

Kelly, A., "The Gifts of the Spirit: Aquinas and the Modern Context", *The Thomist* 38 (1974) 193-231 "Trinity and Process: Relevance of the Basic Christian Confession of God", *Theological Studies* 31 (1970) 393-414 "God: How near a Relation?", *The Thomist* 14 (1970) 191-229 *Love Remains. A Meditation on Christian Love* (Melbourne: Spectrum, 1979) *Seasons of Hope. Christian Faith and Social Issues* (Melbourne: Dove Communications, 1984) "Christian Conversion and the Feminine" in *The Force of the Feminine*, ed. M. Franklin (Sydney: Allen and Unwin, 1986) 175-187

Kelly, J.N.D., *Early Christian Doctrines* (New York: Harper and Row, 1958)

Kreeft, P., "Zen Buddhism and Christianity: An Experiment in Comparative Religion", *Journal of Ecumenical Studies* 8 (1971) 513-538

La Cugna, C., "The Relational God: Aquinas and Beyond", *Theological Studies* 46 (1985) 647-663

Lafont, G., *Peut-on connaître Dieu en Jésus-Christ?* (Paris: Cerf, 1969)

Lapide, P. and Moltmann, J., *Jewish Monotheism and Christian Trinitarian Doctrine* (Philadelphia: Fortress Press, 1981)

Lonergan, B., *Insight. A Study of Human Understanding (London: DLT, 1957) De Deo Trino I-II* (Rome: Gregorian Press, 1959) *Verbum: Word and Idea in Aquinas* (London: DLT, 1967) *Method in Theology* (London: DLT, 1972) *A Second Collection* (London: DLT, 1974) *A Third Collection. Papers by Bernard J.F. Lonergan* ed., F. Crowe (New York: Paulist Press, 1985)

Macquarrie, J., *Principles of Christian Theology* (London: SCM, 1966)

McCabe, H., *"The Involvement of God"*, New Blackfriars, Nov. 1985, 464-476

McCann, P., and Strain, C., *Polity and Praxis. A Program for American Practical Theology* (Chicago: Winston Press, 1985)

Marcus, J., "East and West: Phenomenologies of Self and the Existential Bases of Knowledge", *International Philosophical Quarterly* (March 1971) 5-47

Margerie, de, B., *La Trinité dans l'histoire* (Paris: Beauchesne, 1975)

Maritain, J., "Quelques réflexions sur le savoir théologique", *Revue Thomiste* 69 (1969)

Mascall, E., *The Triune God. An Ecumenical Study* (Worthing: Churchman Publishing, 1986)

Mayr, F., "Patriarchalisches Gottesverständniss", *Theologische Quartalschchrift* 152 (1972) 224-255 "Trinitätstheologie und theologische Anthropologie" *Zeitschrift für Theologie und Kirche* 68 (1971) 427-477

Moltmann, J., *The Trinity and the Kingdom of God* (London: SCM, 1981)

Mondello, V., *La Chiesa del Dio Trino* (Naples: Ed. Paoline, 1978)

Mooney, C., *Teilhard de Chardin and the Mystery of Christ* (New York: Image books, 1966)

Moore, S., *The Fire and the Rose are One* (London: DLT, 1980) *The Inner Loneliness* (London: DLT, 1982) *Let this Mind be in*

You. The Quest for Identity through Oedipus to Christ (London: DLT, 1985) "The New Life", in *Lonergan Workshop, Vol. V*, ed., F. Lawrence (Chico, Ca.: Scholars Press, 1985) 145-161

Mühlen, H., *Der Heilige Geist als Person* (Paderborn: Shoningh, 1963) *Die Veränderlichkeit Gottes als Horizont einer zukünftigen Christologie* (Münster: Aschendorff, 1969)

Murray, J.C., *The Problem of God* (New Haven: Yale University Press, 1964)

Navone, J., and Cooper, T., *Tellers of the Word* (New York: le Jacq, 1981)

Neumann, E., *The Origins and History of Consciousness*, Bollingen Series XLII (Princeton: Princeton Uni. Press, 1973)

O'Carroll, M., *Trinitas. A Theological Encyclopedia of the Holy Trinity* (Wilmington, Del.: Michael Glazier, 1986)

O'Donnell, J., *Trinity and Temporality* (Oxford: Oxford Uni. Press, 1983)

O'Leary, J., *Questioning Back. The Overcoming of Metaphysics in the Christian Tradition* (New York: Seabury, 1985)

Olson, R., "Trinity and Eschatology: the Historical Being of God in Jurgen Moltmann and Wolfhart Pannenberg", *Scot. Journal of Theology* (36) 1986, 213-227

Panikkar, R., *The Trinity and the Religious Experience of Man* (London: DLT, 1973) "Nirvana and the Awareness of the Absolute", in *The God Experience*, ed. J. Whelan (New York: Newman Press, 1971)

Parker, T., "The Political Meaning of the Doctrine of the Trinity", *Journal of Religion* 60 (1980)

Pelikan, J., *The Emergence of the Catholic Tradition (100-600)* (Chicago: Chicago Uni. Press, 1971)

Peterson, E., *Der Monotheismus als politisches Problem. Theologische Traktate* (Muchen: Kosel Verlag, 1951)

Peukert, H., *Science, Action and Fundamental Theology. Toward a Theology of Communicative Action*, trans. J. Bohman (Cambridge, Mass.: MIT Press, 1986)

Porter, L., 'On Keeping "Persons" in the Trinity: a Linguistic Approach to Trinitarian Thought', *Theological Studies* 41 (1980) 530-548

Prestige, G., *God in Patristic Thought* (London: SPCK, 1952)

Rahner, K., *The Trinity*, trans. J. Donceel (London: Burns and Oates, 1970)

Ramsey, I., *Models and Mystery* (London: SCM, 1964)

Ratzinger, J., *Introduction to Christianity*, trans. J. Foster (New York: Herder and Herder, 1969)

Schillebeeckx, E., *Christ. The Christian Experience in the Modern World*, trans. J. Bowden (london: SCM, 1980)

Schilling, H., *The New Consciousness in Science and Religion* (Philadelphia: United Church Press, 1978)

Sheridan, D., "Grounded in the Trinity: Suggestions for a Theology of Relationship to other Religions", *The Thomist* 50/2 (1986) 260-278

Tavard, G., *The Vision of the Trinity* (Washington: The University Press of America, 1980) *A Way of Love* (Maryknoll: Orbis, 1977)

Tolkien, J.R., *Tree and Leaf* (London: Unwin, 1964)

Tracy, D., *The Analogical Imagination* (New York: Seabury, 1981)

Vaggagini, C., *Theological Dimensions of the Liturgy* (Collegeville: Collegeville Press, 1976)

Vertin, M., "Is God in Process?", in *Religion and Culture. Essays in Honor of Bernard Lonergan, SJ*, eds. T. Fallon and P. Boo Riley (Albany: State Univ. Press, 1987) 45-62

Wainwright, A., *The Trinity in the New Testament* (London: SPCK, 1962)

Weinandy, T., *Does God Change? The Word's Becoming in the Incarnation* (Still River, Mass: St. Bede's Press, 1985)

Wilder, A., *Early Christian Rhetoric* (New York: Harper and Row, 1964)

Wildiers, N.M., *The Theologian and his Universe. Theology and Cosmology from the Middle Ages to the Present* (New York: Seabury, 1982)

INDEX

Arianism 73-80
Athanasius, St. 77ff
Augustine, St. 24ff, 116, 119

Balthasar, H. Urs von 107
Barth, K. 101-103
Basil, St. 83f
Beeck, F.J. van 30
Beer, P. 139
Berry, T. 230
Boff, L. 253
Bracken, J. 116, 180
Brown, C. 210-215
Brown, D. 50
Brown, R. 32
Burge, G. 38, 142f
Burrell, D. 214f

Capra, F. 11-13, 97, 171
Coffey, D. 257f
Congar, Y. 256f, 259
Conn, W. 154, 160, 162
Constantinople 82f
Cooke, B. 50
Cousins, E. 229, 234, 236, 243
Crowe, F. 157, 170, 230

Dallmayr, F. 175, 221, 223
Dasgupta, S. 242
Dei Filius 19f
Devdas, N. 242
Docetism 63
Dodds, M. 197
Dunn, J. 57
Dunne, J. 224
Dunne, T. 181
Duquoc, C. 46, 204-207, 229

Farley, M. 253
Ford, L. 190

Geertz, C. 49
Gieben, S. 244
Gregory of Nazianzen, St. 81f, 83f
Gregory of Nyssa, St. 83f, 116
Grillmeier, A. 66, 80

Hartshorne, C. 190
Heidegger, M. 21, 95
Hill, E. 119
Hill, W.J. 116, 120, 192, 229
Himes, K. 216
Himes, M. 216
Hippolytus of Rome 70

Ignatius of Antioch 63f
Irenaeus 67f

Jaspers, K. 11
Jenson, R. 30
John of the Cross, St. 240
Johnson, E. 252
Johnston, W. 229, 238
Juengel, E. 107, 142, 162, 174, 176ff
Jung, C. 209-215
Justin 63, 66ff

Kasper, W. 33, 39, 55
Kelly, A. 193, 196, 236, 250, 260
Kelly, J.N.D. 79
Kreeft, P. 238

La Cugna, C. 179
Lafont, G. 187
Lapide, P. 241

Lonergan, B. 18, 73, 92f, 98, 116, 141f, 150-163

Mackey, J. 50
Macquarrie, J. 95f, 180
Marcus, J. 230, 236, 244-247
Margerie, B. de 4, 63, 66-68, 114, 116
Maritain, J. 198
Mayr, F. 251
McCabe, H. 198, 200
McCann, D. 218
Metz, J. 226
Molloy, N. 135
Moltmann, J. 107, 181, 198, 241
Mooney, C. 235
Moore, S. 18, 51-54, 152, 176
Muehlen, H. 116, 179
Murray, J.C. 31, 72, 75, 77f, 86

Nicaea 74f

O'Donnell, J. 32, 67, 87
O'Leary, J. 137, 139, 141, 144
Olson 114
Origen 72f

Panikkar, R. 229, 236f, 243
Parker, T. 217
Paul of Samosarta 70
Pelikan, J. 64, 69, 74

Peterson, E. 217
Peukert, H. 140, 218f, 223, 225, 227
Porter, L. 184
Prestige, G. 62, 73

Rahner, K. 21, 103-106
Richard of St. Victor 116
Roublev, A. 1

Schillebeeckx, E. 30, 50
Schilling, H.K. 10
Sheridan, D. 231
Sittler, J. 30
Stanley, D. 142f
Strain, C. 218

Tavard, G. 116
Teilhard de Chardin 98
Tertullian 71f
Thomas Aquinas, St. 91, 96f, 100, 116, 120-135
Tracy, D. 115

Vatican II 4, 11, 113f, 225, 229, 240
Vertin, M. 194

Wainwright, A. 34
Weinandy, T. 199
Wilder, A. 30
Wildiers, N. Max 11, 136, 140